LIFE IN THE BUS LANE

LIFE IN THE BUS LANE

Pat Lunt

Carole

*Hope you enjoy the read
and maybe even try a
ride!*

Pat Lunt
6/2010

Published by:
Roundtrip Publishing

First published in May 2010 by
Roundtrip Publishing
65 Old Fosse Road, Bath, BA2 2SP
United Kingdom

ISBN 978-0-9565312-1-6

Printed and bound by Lightning Source

CONTENTS

BEGINNINGS

The teenager's mobile sent its inappropriately cheery ringtones echoing around the bus station. He answered and spoke briefly to his friend, before adding grimly, by way of explanation, "Still waiting for the bus."

The two of us had been awaiting the arrival of the Andover bus at Winchester Bus Station for an hour already. Now, if you ever find yourself in Winchester and you have any time on your hands, take a tip from me: do not spend any more of that time than is absolutely necessary in the bus station.

Winchester is recognised as being an 'historic' city. This means, amongst other things, that it is old and being old means that it has a fine collection of interesting buildings which are not only great to look at but are also architecturally significant, have links with famous figures or associations with important events. For example, there is a fabulous cathedral, long-time seat of royal and ecclesiastical power. There are several ancient churches and any number of half-timbered inns and wood-panelled taverns. There are grandiose civic buildings and streets of quaint old houses.

Then there is Winchester Bus Station. This is a space between two other buildings. Perhaps some earlier building collapsed and, as the dust settled, someone remarked casually, "If we sweep all this rubbish out of the way, this would make a nice bus station. Lick o' paint and it'll come up lovely."

This assessment was, in the politest possible terms, wrong. It is, to be honest, fairly ghastly.

While I was stuck in this place, losing my will to live, other travellers came and went—not from or to Andover, obviously. Old and young alike they happily disembarked from buses and set off to explore Winchester, or with an air of equal expectation they boarded buses to venture off to enticing destinations as yet unseen.

The temperature increased, the little breathable air was slowly saturated with diesel fumes and family frustrations began to erupt around me. I had been stranded here for an hour and a half and that was not part of 'The Plan'.

You want to do what?

'The Plan', such as it was, had grown out of a desire to do something a bit different, a bit silly, or even a bit dangerous. These urges come upon us every now and again; it might be a mid-life thing, an 'I'm fed up with this boring job' feeling or even a 'Let's leave the washing up and go' moment of madness.

I had reached such a point. I was facing a life-change and wanted to mark it in some way. It didn't need to be grand, but significant; an event I would remember.

I decided I would like to see Britain. Deciding to see Britain when you live in Britain may not sound very exciting or significant at first. It may not sound very different or silly either and certainly not particularly dangerous. Actually, it hadn't taken me long to decide that I could leave the 'something dangerous' option out and let someone like Bear Grylls carry on in that department.

But seeing Britain would be significant for me because even though I had lived there for most of my life I felt I didn't know it very well and hadn't really seen very much of it. The key to the whole exploit, however, would lie in choosing how to actually go about 'seeing Britain'. I considered my options.

My first thought was that I could walk. Well I could, but that would take ages and I only had a month—I wouldn't get far in that time.

Next I wondered about cycling. The limitations here were as much to do with my level of fitness and stamina as they were with the time.

My next thought was a re-creation of a great motoring tour, so popular in the period when the Ford Popular was popular. Such a venture was still possible but then I recalled all the problems associated with driving. For a start, you have to keep your eyes on the road and you miss so much and you have scenarios like this:

2

Passenger: *"Oooh! Look at that! Did you see the castle through the trees?"*
You: *"No, I was watching the road."*
Passenger: *"That looked lovely, didn't it? Did you see that beautiful spot down by the river?"*
You: *"No, I was watching the road."*
Passenger: *"Wow! I think that was a red kite! Don't see many of those, do you? Did you see it?"*
You: *"No, I was watching the road."*

Then you have to think about planning a route. You must identify the elusive 'best way' to reach your destination and the 'best time' to travel to avoid all the traffic. You then find that this involves leaving at 3.30 in the morning and you find yourself outside a beautiful cottage three hours before the person with the keys shows up. And driving also means that you are subjected to the delights of road rage. Other drivers get angry and abusive because you are driving too slowly, that is, obeying a speed limit, taking too long to enter a line of traffic, taking too long to leave a line of traffic or you simply have the audacity to be on a public highway when it is plain to everybody that you have absolutely no right to be there. No, driving wouldn't do.

Perhaps I could swim. Possible I suppose, but surely you wouldn't get to see very much apart from weeds, ducks and supermarket trolleys. Actually, I don't swim very well.

Briefly, I thought I could fly. But then the moment passed and I realised that it was Superman who could fly, not me.

Weighing these options in the balance I found them all wanting. Then I had an idea. I could go on the bus! Not just one bus, obviously. Lots of buses. One bus after another. I could join up all the different bus journeys back to back until I went all the way round and got back to where I started. I hadn't heard of anyone else who had gone round the country only using service buses. That meant it would be different. And who would do such a thing anyway? That would be silly. So it was perfect; different and silly but not dangerous.

When I thought about how far round Britain I could get

in my time frame I regretfully lowered my sights slightly to concentrate on England. So I set myself an amended target. I would attempt to visit the places furthest East, West, North and South on mainland England that were served by ordinary, regular bus services. I would not be using any dedicated coach services which were meant to get you rapidly from one point to another. Rather, I would be 'hijacking' existing services to achieve the same ends, ignoring the word 'rapidly'.

And that, pretty much, was 'The Plan'. Not much of one in some ways, perhaps. But I didn't want to pore endlessly over timetables and work out detailed itineraries. Rather, I fancied heading off in the general direction of one of my cardinal compass points and finding out how the buses would contrive to get me there. I hoped this would lead to circuitous meanderings through many and varied places; places I would never have heard of let alone visited. This, I felt, would be a pleasurable way in which to fulfil my objective of 'seeing Britain'. I would surely see much more of it this way, bumbling in and out of tucked-away villages and so on, than I would by simply charging from A to B.

I picked up a map of bus routes for my local area and chose a bus service. A bit of packing and I was off.

Part 1

Day 1

Go east, young man

6th August

Having completed my almost non-existent research into the venture, which consisted of noticing that there was a bus to Salisbury leaving Bath several times a day, I surveyed my belongings for the trip:

1) A ridiculously large rucksack, crammed with what I thought were simply essential items.
2) A ridiculously small tent.

I was wearing some of my most sensible 'hiking' clothes and good walking boots. I had even packed sunglasses and sun cream so I felt supremely well prepared.

It didn't start well. As I stood at the bus stop, with the slight but persistent August drizzle dribbling off my sun-creamed nose, I was forced to consider my daughter's words about waiting. Added to this, a temporary temperature inversion or some similarly awkward and unusual phenomenon caused my sunglasses to steam up. I shivered slightly, wondering if I had just missed a bus, and for a brief moment pictured how easily the whole enterprise could collapse. I even had time to think about being sensible and finding out the times when buses were due. Then I finally caught sight of my bus meandering towards me. The bus that would start it all. With a slight grumble the vehicle stopped and the doors hissed themselves apart. I climbed the shallow step and uttered the phrase that would signal the real beginning of my Great Bus Journey: "A single to the centre, please."

The journey into Bath went smoothly enough and I'd clocked up an impressive two and a quarter miles by the time I disembarked at the bus station. It had been comparatively expensive at £1.10. This worked out at about 49p per mile. If you fly to Rome from Cardiff it is 948 miles. At the bus rate it would cost you £464.52. Which is why, apart from any other considerations involving such things as the English Channel, nobody goes to Rome on the bus. However, according to the Friends of Conservation charity (*www.friendsofconservation.org.uk*), flying is the most carbon intensive way of travelling. To compensate for the carbon generated by flying to Rome from Cardiff I would need to plant 0.76 acres of rainforest. We didn't have room in the garden for 0.76 acres of rainforest. This train of thought seemed to be yet more confirmation that the bus was the ideal mode of transport.

However, if all my journeys were going to be as costly as my first, getting all the way round England would prove to be very expensive. It does seem that short distance journeys like mine into town are ridiculously expensive and that they are always going up. However, my research had alerted me to the existence of a 'Day Ticket' in one form or another, available from many bus operators. Invariably these were reasonably priced, were valid 'all day' (usually meaning from 9.30 to midnight) and allowed the purchaser to travel as far as the company operated within a certain region. That sounded a pretty good cash-for-carriage exchange.

As I've said, my meagre research into this expedition had involved looking at the map of local bus routes and spotting one route snaking off the map with the enticing words 'To Salisbury' and an arrow. This was to be my way out of the area—to Salisbury and beyond. I searched the bus station for the bay for the X6 and purchased an 'Adult Getaway' which, you have to admit, has a pretty exciting ring to it.

The bus was clean and quiet and the seats were comfortable. I mention this because many people who don't use buses suppose them to be dirty, smelly, noisy and anything but comfortable. We left—punctually I might add—and made our way through town, across the shop-lined eighteenth century wonder that is Pulteney Bridge and along the wide and elegant Great Pulteney Street. We had a fine view of the Holbourne Museum and of the full-leafed trees, billowing as we skirted the edge of Sydney Gardens. As we picked up speed along the A36, the hills rose to the right and the vale opened out to the left revealing distant, wooded slopes and open green fields. All set off by the beautiful Batheaston bypass. Oh well. We hugged the foothills below Claverton as the valley narrowed and we approached Dundas. Here a wonderful stone aqueduct from 1805 carries the Kennet and Avon Canal above the railway and the River Avon. It was also here that we turned sharp left and quit the main road, heading for Winsley and Bradford-on-Avon.

If you were driving to Salisbury yourself, you would not do this. You would stay on the main roads because these, in theory at least, give you the fastest journey time. Bus travel is not about fast journey times. If you take a bus with the concept of fast journey times in mind you will be disappointed at the very least and extremely irate at worst. No, bus travel is civilised and unhurried. It gives you the opportunity to meander into little nooks and crannies that you would never otherwise bother to visit. You must embrace the meandering slowness, or suffer.

And so we left the busy A36 behind us, briefly skirted the railway then ducked underneath it. As we climbed toward the tiny village of Winsley the steep sides of the Limpley Stoke valley were gradually revealed behind us in all their tree-covered glory. Then they were suddenly hidden from view as we crested the hill and took our little excursion through Winsley where buildings in the old section displayed the qualities of the stone no doubt dug from the local quarries. We pressed on for Bradford-on-Avon.

The northern approach to Bradford-on-Avon is high above the town and the descent is steep and lined with quaint weavers' cottages. Some of the cottages are still there but the weavers have long gone following the demise of the textile industry that helped shape the town. The road dropped down towards the river and the bus squeezed itself between the ancient buildings. We crossed the river by the Town Bridge, with its rudimentary 'lock-up' half-way across. In times past this provided overnight accommodation for those deemed to be drunk or troublesome or both. Here is the beginning of a letter I started as we made our way through the town:

Dear Home Secretary,

I know you have been struggling with possible solutions for the troublesome individuals who bedevil so many of our city centres and are currently referred to as "binge drinkers." I wonder if you have ever visited the picturesque Wiltshire town of Bradford-on-Avon...

We were all set for a pleasant, straightforward onward journey when, just on the far side of town, we met some road 'works'. A group of men were standing near a mechanical digger and looking at paving slabs. Half the road was closed and there was a long line of cones.

"Looks a bit serious," I half-joked to the driver.

"Bloody ridiculous, more like!" he replied. "Half the road blocked off and they're not even working on the road—they're working on the pavement! If you call standing around looking at paving slabs, 'working'. It adds fifteen minutes to the journey. There'll be people waiting all the way through on the other side and they'll think it's my fault we're late," he moaned.

He went on to explain about rest times and turn around times and the difficulties created by highways departments not consulting with bus operators. I suddenly understood why there was a sign warning: 'Do not speak to the driver'.

To be fair, I could understand why he might value the opportunity to say something—anything—if the only communication he had all day was "Return to the centre, please," or "Single to Hampton Row."

Once through the road works, we drove on towards Warminster, with Wiltshire's landscape of burgeoning fields and bulging hedgerows continuing to unfold around us. The great landmark of the Westbury White Horse cantered in and out of view. It may not be all that old but it is certainly very refined, unlike the Cerne Abbas Giant. The White Horse group at Westbury obviously discussed their proposed hill-carving project over a cup of tea and a few cucumber sandwiches.

Chairperson: We want to produce something that will reflect the beauty and openness of our countryside... an animal perhaps.
Maud: What about a cat?
Chair: Thank you for the suggestion, Maud, and we all know how much you love cats, but something a little more majestic.
Frank: Like a lion, you mean?
Chair: I'm sorry, Frank, but I feel a lion would be a little out of place on a Wiltshire hillside. What we need is something more local, an animal that can be seen hereabouts everyday, enjoying the freedom of our wide open spaces.
Maud: A lion's like a cat, isn't it, Frank?
Chair: Maud! We are not going to carve a 140ft cat on the hillside. No, this is a long-term project and will hopefully last for many, many years. We want our carving to reflect the character and poise of ourselves and our community in years to come and I believe I have thought of the ideal creature for our purposes: a horse! They are proud. They are majestic. Yes, a 140ft White Horse will do nicely.

So very different from the drunken decisions obviously made by the rabble down at Cerne Abbas:

Zak: I know, lets draw a big picture of a man with his willy out.
All: (Amid uproarious laughter) Yeah, great idea.

We called in at Warminster. This boasts an attractive Market Square enclosed by a number of impressive buildings which reflect its past as a busy trading and coaching centre. There also seemed to be a large military presence which is perhaps not surprising. If you want to have a large military presence somewhere, I suppose a place called Warminster is an obvious choice.

Not long after this we again left the main road and wandered in for a brief glimpse at the attractive but demure collection of dwellings that constitutes Heytesbury. A quiet village that appeared not to want to shout about itself too much, although it could legitimately brag about the stocky church of St Peter and St Paul, not to mention a cosy looking pub or two. And what an intriguing name. I was prompted to consult a book given to me by a friend for the journey—*A Dictionary of English Place-Names* (A D Mills, 2003, Oxford University Press). I knew the derivation of place names couldn't always be as obvious as Warminster. So, according to the book: *'-bury' is a common ending to place names across the country.*

It would be foolish to think that it had anything to do with burying people—English doesn't seem to work that way. I looked in the Glossary of some common elements in English place names and found: "***bury** ME (from dative byrig of OE burh) manor, manor house*" and "***Burh** (dative **byrig**) OE fortified place, stronghold, variously applied to Iron Age hill forts, Roman and Anglo-Saxon fortifications, and fortified houses, later to manors and manor houses and to towns and boroughs.*"

Wow! This was once someone's stronghold, hill-fort, fortification, fortified house, manor, manor house, town or borough.

I found it in the dictionary: *Heytesbury Wilts Hestrebe (sic) 1086 (DB) Hehtredaberia c.1115. Stronghold of a woman called Heahthryth. OE pers. name + burh*

Good old Heahthryth. Who says all these strong career women are a new phenomenon? Here's a woman from almost nine hundred years ago who has her own stronghold, for goodness' sake! Stand proud, people of Heytesbury!

When you scratch below the surface, you find that Heytesbury has, in fact, a fair deal to shout about, although that is plainly not in its nature, it being a 'quiet' village and all. For example, the fine church, although much restored, has elements from the thirteenth century onwards; and the stately home of Heytesbury House was the home of war poet Siegfried Sassoon in his later years. The settlement was a sheep-rearing powerhouse by the fourteenth century and also had a busy period in the eighteenth century when a series of cloth mills were constructed along the River Wylye's banks. So this apparently inconsequential spot is actually brimming with fascinating history, as well as simply offering plenty of aesthetic pleasures. This visit taught me early on in my travels to beware of the deceptions sometimes contrived by the appearance of a place. If you look, there's almost always something of interest.

On leaving Heahthryth's stronghold we meandered through Codford, which is not a shallow river crossing where you can catch a species of sea fish but a settlement built around a ford that once belonged to a man named Cod(d)a. I really felt I was beginning to get the hang of this name game and was confident that after a while it would become quite easy.

We pressed on through Wilton, once a farmstead on the River Wylye, home of Wilton carpets and now the Wilton carpet museum. A large number of people seemed to be getting off here and it was very gratifying to see so many individuals interested in the ancient crafts involved in the traditional manufacture of carpeting. Mind you, a lot of them seemed to be making a detour to something called 'Wilton Shopping Village' which was nearby.

We continued on our way into the stronghold at Sorvoi, better known as Salisbury. The magnificent spire of the Cathedral was visible from the bus on the approach into town and, having alighted in the bus station, I sought it out for closer inspection. I don't know much about ecclesiastical architecture—I can think of words like 'steeple', 'Gothic' and 'flying buttress' but that's about my lot. Shameful, I know. But as I stretched out on the soft grass of the Cathedral Close and gazed up at the tallest spire in Britain, ecclesiastic architectural jargon seemed very unimportant. Even though the building was partly shrouded in scaffolding and wrapped in a green gauze, it still possessed a certain majesty, an intense presence and, for a truly massive building, a degree of grace and lightness. And it was in such a wonderful setting.

I ate a lunch of bread and cheese on the soft grass, surrounded by a few other Salisburians or whatever people from Salisbury are called. A world away on the nearby city streets people rushed to and fro, queued in banks and shops and endured the hassle, hustle and fuss. Not for us upon the green where we enjoyed a serene interlude of peace and tranquillity. Sadly, I couldn't idly loaf about for too long since I needed to organise possible sleeping arrangements.

I found the local Youth Hostel Association premises and joined. The UK YHA is a worthy organisation with its origins in 1930, while youth hostelling itself was an earlier brainchild of a German teacher, Richard Shirrman. He wanted to give the young people living in cities a chance to get out of their surroundings, to breathe some fresh air and to explore the countryside. These were also the founding aims of the YHA in England and Wales and in the early days the budget accommodation was combined with a requirement to help with some menial tasks in the hostel as part of your stay. Times have changed. The hostels have adapted to suit the needs of the modern traveller, primarily by upgrading the facilities. The notion that guests might be willing to sweep up after breakfast or do a bit of washing up had pretty much disappeared. What's happened there, then? I suppose we live in times where we expect that there will always be someone else to do that sort of thing for us.

I joined the YHA because I was after budget accommodation if, and more probably when, there were times and places where camping would be impossible or undesirable. The manager at Salisbury was courteous, helpful and concerned. This last response was due to my indicating that I planned to reach Winchester and stop there. He pointed out that there were not that many beds in the small Winchester hostel and it might be full. The option of ringing ahead was not available but he said that if I had trouble, I could always come back and put my tent up in his grounds if his establishment also happened to be full. It was a very kind thought and I couldn't bring myself to explain that if I managed to get as far as Winchester *my way*, there was no chance of me attempting to come back just because the youth hostel was full. I'd have to camp in a park.

Ambling back to the bus station I considered my options. My ticket would allow me some sightseeing excursions to Stonehenge, for example, or Avebury. I decided to press on for Winchester instead—via Romsey, which would take me into Hampshire, my third county for the day.

The journey gave me more opportunity to engage in the serious business of bus travel—staring happily out of the window. I was presented with occasional panoramas across open countryside, interspersed with glimpses through trees or over hedges and walls into the more intimate workings of people's everyday lives. Agricultural workers busy in the fields, a woman hanging out washing, an older couple tending their garden, a greengrocer heaving a box of large field mushrooms to the front of his display. In one village a car was raised on an inspection ramp in an old garage which was somehow redolent of times gone by; times when a pump attendant would serve you your petrol and the pump's indicators would click over or give delicate chimes as the fuel flowed through.

I loved all these wonderful snap-shot images of people's lives. Putting them together would allow me to create an overall sense of the country through which I passed. For the moment it was rural, peaceful and largely charming, and it pretty much stayed like that all the way to Romsey.

Romsey's bus station is conveniently placed for the town centre and its attractions, amongst which we cannot truthfully number the bus station itself. This is really just a circular hard-standing area with a few shelters around its circumference. Thankfully the bus station architecture is not typical of the rest of the town. It was necessary, as I would discover in so many places, to ignore the impression of a town created by the area in which you arrive by bus. I am not sure why this should be but bus stations seem invariably to have been accorded less worth than, say, railway stations. A railway station did not have to be the vast terminus of a prestigious main line in order to be designed and built with thought and care. There are plenty of small country stations that are now recognised as buildings of architectural merit, even to the point of being listed. Very few bus stations would attract this kind of honour and in the odd instances in which they do, a developer will want to knock them down because they are 'underused'.

Romsey itself is the sort of place to have tourist signs proclaiming it to be an 'historic market town' and it has most of the things you would want to see in such a place; a space where there is or was a market, small shops, old buildings. It also has some of the things you would rather not have if you are a visitor but which you perhaps welcome if you are resident. For example, there is a supermarket but at least it has been sensitively put out near the bus station where it can't do much aesthetic damage. Generally speaking, it seems that Romsey has done a good job of balancing the old, attractive and touristy with the modern and 'essential'. Many of the shops in the centre are small and independent and there isn't a sense of the bland branding of the ubiquitous chain store overwhelming the town.

Romsey's heritage is well displayed in the centre around The Hundred and Market Place, a short walk from the bus station. This is a charming little area with cobbled streets which feel cosy but not cramped, lined with a collection of well-proportioned old buildings simply doing what they have done for a couple of hundred years.

The high street chains are here but they don't dominate or smother the character of the place. I couldn't see an intrusive, overbearing building of steel and glass, with eccentric cantilevered overhangs that are only there to show how clever we can be with our engineering and our modern materials. There was a distinct lack of 'clean, efficient lines' and nothing even remotely resembling a gherkin.

The present settlement has Saxon beginnings and the town's heritage includes at least one sacking by the Vikings, followed by a recovery and subsequent growth. It became an important religious centre, caring for lost sheep, and a wool town caring for shorn sheep. The wool industry produced mills, dyeing and fulling works. Save for Sadler's Mill on the western edge of town, the mills are largely gone. The religious foundation had an Abbey at its centre and this remains.

I found the Abbey by walking beside the Town Hall, passing through an archway and finally down a street, cleverly called 'The Abbey'.

The Abbey is, in fact, according to a helpful leaflet, a large parish church—the largest in the county—and is dedicated to St Mary and St Ethelfraeda. It traces its history back to 907AD, the year in which King Edward the Elder, son of the Saxon king

Alfred the Great, first settled some nuns there. I wonder, how do you go about settling nuns? Perhaps a simple, "Calm down, sister, please," would do it.

St Ethelfraeda was the second abbess and she is reputed to have spent much of her time singing Psalms naked in the nearby River Test.

Imagine what the papers would make of that kind of behaviour today:

PSALM LIKE IT HOT! The Sun
SYNOD SPLIT ON ROLE OF NUDE NUNS
   The Daily Telegraph
TEST RIVERSIDE HOUSE PRICES SOAR The Daily Mail

The present Abbey is a massively impressive and impressively massive Norman building, raised on the foundations of the Anglo-Saxon replacement for the original that was burnt by the visiting Vikings, led by Sweyn Forkbeard, fork-bearded swine that he was. It may lack the spectacular heights achieved by the spire at Salisbury but it certainly doesn't lack presence. Inside, all is calm and, despite the towering columns and high ceiling of the nave, there is a simplicity which conveys demureness rather than austerity. As well as the stone memorial to Earl Mountbatten of Burma there are other earlier and more ornate carved memorials to admire as well as stained glass windows of great scale, grandeur and craftsmanship. I could only fall into silent wonder in front of them.

Moving on from the Abbey, I noticed the street changed its name and became 'The Meads'. This led to some 'meads'. The people who dreamt up these street names really knew their stuff. The 'meads' offered green open spaces for sitting or even lounging, which is almost as good as 'loafing'. There were opportunities for a gentle stroll in the ordered War Memorial Park and along the footpath to the River Test. No nude nuns there that day.

The river would have been the town's powerhouse during the time of the woollen industry and today is regarded as one of the finest chalk streams in the world. It makes for a lovely feature for the town.

I checked out the Romsey Heritage and Visitor Centre which is based in the medieval building known as King John's House. This building is so named because Mr Walter Andrews, who 'discovered' it in 1927, thought he had found King John's Hunting Lodge. It is now thought that the house dates from the mid-thirteenth century but it's still called King John's House. Well, who'd go and see 'Nobody Special's House'? Even though it may not have a royal pedigree, the buildings are full of interesting features including medieval graffiti and a floor made of bones!

'Mmmmm, I like what you've done here, Hannibal. Very contemporary."

I could have lingered longer in Romsey but I remembered the tip that the Winchester Youth Hostel was small and I began to wonder about a bed for the night. So I made my way back to the bus station and boarded the 66. A very pleasant ride through the countryside, though not especially exciting. This was a bit of a disappointment as I was always led to believe that 'kicks' were available on Route 66. That being said, the journey did mean that I had reached my intended destination for the day quite painlessly, in a fairly straightforward manner and for a few pounds in bus fares.

The completely nondescript nature of the bus station in Winchester was emphasised and almost mocked by the extravagant Victorian pile that is the Guildhall, sited across the road. An imposing flight of stone steps leads to the building's main entrance which is surrounded by columns and arches. Above here, three rows of arched windows of varying size gaze from the wide front of the building and to top it all in the central section is a tower with a steeply-pitched roof, surrounded by decorations that do a reasonable impression of surface-to-air heat-seeking missiles. Perhaps they *are* surface-to-air heat-seeking missiles, who knows?

Turning left from the bus station and across a roundabout, I found (eventually, after walking past it and over another roundabout and up a hill and asking in a pub) Water Lane. This taught me to read the directions given in the YHA guide and it made me promise myself to do that very carefully in future because my backpack was heavy enough without having to wander pointlessly around a town. Anyway, enough self-chastisement. I found Water Lane and just as quickly, the door for the YHA.

The hostel in Winchester was housed in a National Trust property, the old City Mill, which spans the River Itchen. The rooms had been cleverly planned to fit into the roof spaces and the beds and bunks equally cleverly positioned in the nooks and crannies in the rooms. It was a very warm August evening and a fan was circulating cold air around Room 4 as I entered. I traversed a bridge which had been built to allow access from the door, over a huge beam, to the far side of the room. Here, one of the two available beds lay. I dumped my backpack gratefully by the bed, sorted out a few things, and headed off to explore a little bit of Winchester and the possibility of sustenance.

Like Salisbury, Winchester is a town whose long history is in evidence through its architecture. Attractive buildings flank wide streets, cosy streets and narrow alleyways in equal measure. The alleys would not be built these days because they would contravene some EU Health and Safety directive on 'Lateral space requirements for safe and efficacious conduits for human perambulation in an urban environment' or some such thing. Thankfully, these old alleys have been left and even more fortunately one of them houses The Baker's Arms, hidden away between the High Street and Market Lane. Although you couldn't really describe Winchester as a heaving metropolis, it is still nice to find secret little corners that offer a bit of peace and quiet, away from the melee. Or what passes for a melee in Winchester at least. What better than to sit in the small courtyard of a friendly little pub sipping a pint of beer?

I enjoyed an unhurried walk around the town, which, like Romsey, is doing a reasonable job of suppressing the onslaught of high street uniformity. You can easily escape down a little alleyway or old street or wander the cathedral precinct.

After a simple supper I set off to return to the hostel through the warm night. I had a brief conversation with a rather inebriated man who explained his plight while clutching his can of Special Brew. It transpired that he needed some money for a fare home to his wife whom he had left in a bit of a state after an unfortunate argument about... well... his drinking. He wanted to go back and put things right with her which was very commendable. I wasn't sure how successful the strategy of getting completely bombed on strong lager before going back to do this would be, but there you go.

Back in the hostel I negotiated the beam and the bridge that led to my bed and settled down while the fan still purred away, wafting cool air in my direction. A few other hostellers appeared and took to their beds. I hoped the fan would not be wafting anything other than air in my direction during the night.

Day 2

London—over or under?

7th August

If anything else was wafted about, I didn't notice. I slept soundly
and woke at about seven to the gentle sound of someone pol-
ishing his shoes! The other members of the dormitory began
to slowly regain consciousness and to make use of the washing
facilities. As befits a shared bedroom experience everyone tried
to fill basins, scrape off beard bristles and brush away plaque
and dog-breath as quietly as possible.

Before breakfast I wandered around the mill. The National
Trust is almost certain that a Saxon mill stood here more than
a thousand years ago. This was owned by the Benedictine nunnery in Wherwell. The mill, and Winchester, experienced
mixed fortunes depending on harvests and it was taken into
crown ownership by Henry VIII in 1439. He gave it to his
daughter who gave it to the city. Today's mill is a new one—
new in the sense that it was built in 1743. I strolled round the
small island garden, enjoying the summer flowers and the rush
of water, before returning to eat.

The quiet atmosphere of breakfast had none of the frantic
behaviour which must have filled this place through most of its
life. It was a time for people to chat and exchange stories about
their routes and holidays and plans for the day. At the table
were a girl from Germany, who was touring by car, and a family
who were cycling. The man with the highly polished shoes was
on his way to a job interview in the area. He was in fire protection and retardation.

"Smoke alarms work because of the tiny particles in smoke," he
told us. "And a lot of problems happen in summer because tiny

19

thunder bugs can get into them and set them off." We were also informed about the activation of sprinkler systems by liquids in bubbles of glass expanding due to a rise in temperature before exploding. An education as well as a good breakfast! I mean, you don't get that sort of information on the side of a cereal packet! And who says English people can only talk about the weather?

We enjoyed a joke with the manager about his desire to see the good old days back again and his guests helping out by sweeping the floors and cleaning the toilets. At least, I think he was joking.

I wandered into town via Abbey House, an attractive building of red brick, dating from around 1700. Now the official residence of the Mayor of Winchester, it stands on the site of a monastery and a later Abbey. Apparently, this was once used by Benedictine nuns fleeing the troubles of the French Revolution. The owner was obviously operating in the spirit Edward the Elder had shown in Romsey. Surely, if any nuns needed settling, it would have been these poor souls.

The gardens nearby were of a fairly typical 'municipal' style with formal beds and wide areas of grass. A stream which once provided the power for a mill burbled quietly by as I sat on a bench and consulted a bus timetable. I decided to catch the 11.10 to Andover. I made up my mind to head for my eastern destination by attempting an arc to the west and north of London, through Berkshire, Oxfordshire and beyond.

So, I didn't have much time left for Winchester Cathedral. This was a pity because it had plenty to admire. High vaulted ceilings in the nave, intricate carving, tombs and monuments and all the remnants from the twelfth century as well as the bits that have been added on by subsequent generations. Not to mention Jane Austen's grave. After a brief tour I headed to the bus station to catch a bus since this was, after all, a pretty major element of this whole jolly escapade.

The decision to go for the 11.10 to Andover was not a good one. In fact it was a completely rubbish one. It would be on a par with the impetuous purchase and consumption of a late night Kebab after a few bevies in Bristol many moons ago. That produced unpleasant results and so did this, although of a different nature. Far from being trapped beneath London, which is what had made me choose this route, I found myself trapped in Winchester bus station. I say 'trapped' because I was caught by the fear that if I left the bus station to buy a paper or a sandwich or retain my sanity, then *that* would be when the bus would arrive. After an hour and a half of this faltering and fuming about the lovely, relaxing and absorbing time I could have enjoyed in the cathedral, I decided to enquire of a person in the operational nerve centre about the 11.10 to Andover and its apparent failure to materialise.

"Sometimes it's a small blue mini-bus," he explained.

"I see."

"I think it was in earlier."

"Not since 10.50," I said. "Not in the bay for 'Buses to Andover' at any rate."

"He may have pulled into a different bay, of course. Problem is, *he's not one of ours*, so I can't really help you."

I could not be bothered to ask why the bus to Andover needed to be in the form of a small blue mini bus which the driver would sneak into a bay for 'Buses to Basingstoke' where he would quietly sit for ten minutes instead of climbing onto his roof and hollering to all of us poor wretches in the 'Buses for Andover' bay something like:

"Anyone for Andover, I'm over here! Sorry, I've had to pull into the bay for Basingstoke buses but you know how it is. Anyway, here I am so if you want to get a bus to Andover, this is the one!"

When I rejoined the teenager who was waiting with me he was engaged in another unhappy conversation with his friend on the mobile. There were obviously some time constraints on the activities planned for that day.

"There's no way I can get to Andover by then," he continued. Then: "Well, I guess you'll just have to go without me. No. You go. See ya."

He ended his call dejectedly, referred to the public bus service in a less than complimentary manner, rose slowly and shuffled off. His day had been ruined and mine was slowly ebbing away.

My daughter had tried to point out that this was precisely the sort of catastrophe that would ensue if I insisted on going by bus.

"*Buses?*" she had exclaimed when I announced my intentions to her. "I *hate* buses." I decided this was due to too many years of taking buses containing other young people on their way to or from school. Such buses are jolly places of ribald banter and humorous exchanges. True, the air is sometimes thick with expletives, individuals are referred to as parts of the human body not normally mentioned in polite conversation and you can sometimes inadvertently receive too much information about who is doing what to whom in terms of their voyages of sexual discovery. But surely this exuberance is only a reflection of the high levels of excitement and anticipation felt by these young people as they make their way in to their educational establishments in the morning and by the adrenaline buzz they are still feeling at the end of a stimulating day as they make their way home? Such high spirits are often misconstrued by other members of the public as rudeness, arrogance and a lack of consideration. Much misery could be overcome by simply adopting the right frame of mind, filling your head with kind thoughts towards these future leaders of the country's industries, services and government.

My daughter had plainly not managed to see things this way during her school years and such encounters had contributed to her dislike of bus travel. This, and the notion she had that you had to spend an inordinate amount of time *waiting* for buses. "No..." I had confidently asserted, wishing to defend this environmentally sound means of transportation, "...there are timetables. Buses run to timetables. As far as possible buses run to timetables." She was looking at me blankly. "In order to function as a business, the companies will have to endeavour to make sure that their buses run according to the timetable," I insisted.

"Yeah, right!" she said.

The arrival of the 13.10 bus for Andover should have been a cause for celebration but I was not in the mood.

The journey there cheered me up slightly, even if we were in a small blue mini bus, as we wound our way in and out of the pleasant villages dotted around the northern reaches of the Test Valley.

If you need an advert which lets people know how beautiful this country is, you could do a lot worse than the Test Valley. This is not beauty on a grand scale. It may not be described as breathtaking, but then much of England's beauty is not. It is calm and quiet. It is secluded. We like our big open spaces, but we also seem to enjoy enclosed manageable spaces as well.

Here the sunlight was playing through broad-leafed trees. The sky was revealed and then hidden again by the leafy canopy. It was all so very... well... pleasant. We passed through village after village of thatched cottages, half-hidden from view by the profusion of flowering plants in the gardens. Places like Chilbolton, or Ceolboldingtun as you would have known it if you passed through in 909, and Wherwell, with its well-hidden water source, and all the while criss-crossing the River Test. In this manner we continued our meanderings to Andover.

Despite the pleasant journey I was still a bit jaded after the wait at Winchester. This negativity was at least in part a response to me having to learn a lesson the hard way. None of us particularly enjoys this and in my case I knew that it was costing me quite dearly in terms of the distance I would be able to cover that day. Andover was going to have to pull out all the stops if it was going to have any chance of lifting my spirits. It was a tough call and Andover really wasn't up to the challenge, at least not the part where the bus deposited me.

I was in a modern shopping area and needed an escape. Consulting a mounted tourist map I worked out a route to St. Mary's Church, which benefits from being sited on a hill a little above the town. I shared the peace and tranquillity of the pleasant grounds with the many others who seemed to choose this as the spot for a relaxing break from the day's schedule. As a backdrop for a lunch break, the church would be hard to beat; an impressive stone exterior together with a strong, tall tower.

My day's schedule had been completely stuffed, thanks to the apparent policy of disguising the 11.10 Winchester–Andover bus and sneaking it into a misleading bus bay. It was already well into the afternoon so I sought out the Tourist Information

Centre and asked for information on camping near Newbury. It may seem a bit perverse to go into an information centre in Andover and ask about camping in Newbury, but the staff members were unperturbed. They simply informed me, quite reasonably, that such information would have to come from the Tourist Information Centre in Newbury and they gave me the phone number. The pleasant voice at the other end of the line informed me that there were two sites on their lists on the south side of Newbury, one on the Basingstoke road, one on the Andover road. Given my present location I didn't have to weigh the options for too long. On ringing Oakhill Farm, I was told that they had plenty of places and received brief instructions on how to find the site from the bus stop. I was resigned to the fact that I wasn't going to get very far that day and was just glad to have sorted somewhere to sleep.

The No.20 bus whisked me out of Andover along a wide dual carriageway whose historical significance was evidenced by it being named 'Saxon Way'. I could picture all the Saxon traffic hurtling up and down as people made the rush hour commute to Newbury before joining the 8.13 ox-drawn wagon to Lundenwic.

I was grateful when we left the urban environment behind us and engaged in another pleasant meander through wooded lanes and cosy villages, including the intriguingly named Enham Alamein. A quick look in *A Dictionary of English Place Names* confirmed that the 'Alamein' was affixed from 1945, commemorating the battle of El Alamein. You could easily spend several days hopping on and off the bus at these places, perhaps walking between one or two, or taking a stroll further up the Test Way onto the North Wessex Downs. You would have to take care not to get lost in Tangley and beware in the dangerous-sounding Wildhern. Or you could simply dismiss the whole idea, as presumably do the residents of Faccombe.

I alighted, as instructed, at the bus stop by The Woodpecker public house in the village of Washwater. As far as I could make out, The Woodpecker public house *was* the village of Washwater. The camp site was a right turn and a short walk, then another turn off and down a lane away from the main road.

There were several camper vans and caravans about. The site owner pointed out the field where I could pitch my tent. He also pointed out the toilet block, a nearby drinking water tap, showers and sinks and a van that contained a baby. "I should pitch somewhere away from there 'cos the baby wakes in the night."

I paid my three pound coins and turned my attention to choosing where to pitch my tent.

The ridiculously brief preparatory reading I had managed before departure had included some wisdom about where to pitch a tent and where not to. Apparently under trees is not a good idea for the following reasons:

- Creatures fall on you
- Creatures' droppings fall on you
- Sticky secretions from certain species of insect fall on you
- Sticky secretions from certain species of tree fall on you
- Rain, which you go under trees to avoid, continues dripping on you long after it has finished out in the open.

Having chosen a spot away from the trees, not too close to the ablutions block and well clear of the potential midnight wailing baby, I turned my attention to the tent. It was a glorious evening and even at six o'clock turning my back to the sun was like warming it beside a fire. I was looking forward to using the new tent I had purchased for the journey. I opened the tent bag for the first time and spilled the contents onto the ground. I read the instructions.

'Always check the contents before going on your trip.'

I had a moment of panic. The picture of a distracted tent packer flashed into my mind. Just at the moment when the all-important pole should have been inserted into my bag someone called out to them and they inadvertently missed my bag and placed it in the next one. I would be pole-less and miserable beneath the stars in Washwater, while someone, somewhere in a distant part of the globe, would be speculating feverishly about where they should be inserting the extra pole. If I, the tent pole, and the distracted tent packer were ever in close proximity I knew where I would be inserting it. But I need not have worried. The wonderful, diligent, hard-working people in the tent-packing department had done a wonderful job and everything I could possibly have needed was there. I read on:

'Always practice erecting the tent before going on your trip.'

Again, that's very good advice, I'm sure. But I wasn't up a mountain at the moment. The weather could not have been more benevolent, and the tent was said to be of a 'simple robust design' that 'erects in minutes'. So, I reasoned, it couldn't possibly take more than 59 minutes because only one more than that and they'd have to say 'erects in just one hour'. Nonetheless, I didn't want to be kneeling here in an hour with the light fading and a crowd gathering. Again, my fears were unfounded and I managed to produce a reasonably tent-like structure in about twenty minutes. As I shovelled all my belongings into the tent a young woman arrived in the field on a bicycle. She made for the fence under the trees. Either she was unaware of the problems of camping under trees or she was from Faccombe. The reason for her choice of location became apparent as I walked over to say hello. She had no tent.

Nina was making a shelter from some plastic tubing, lengths of cord, a sheet of tarpaulin and some pegs. With the help of a fence post she made a cosy place to sleep into which she placed her sleeping mat. I was impressed and said so. She confessed that the reason for doing things this way had partly come from indecision about buying a tent and partly through a desire to minimise weight. We talked about our respective journeys. Nina was a long way from home, hers being in Townsville in the Northern Territories of Australia. She was *cycling* from London to Snowdonia where she was going to join a group of volunteers repairing pathways and such in the National Park. She wondered about me. I felt rather embarrassed about what, in comparison, seemed a rather tame excursion.

"I'm going round England on buses," I offered.

"That's cool," she said, kindly. "Why?"

Here was a question I had not really answered for myself.

"I think I need a change. I need to get out and do something a bit different. Maybe it's a mid-life crisis thing."

"Cool. Most guys would go out and buy a Harley or a Porsche or something."

I was momentarily taken aback. Was this my mid-life splurge? Had I wasted the opportunity of a Harley Davidson on a few bus rides?

"Sounds a bit sad, doesn't it?" I ventured.

"No, it sounds like fun."

The Winchester experience had left me feeling rather deflated and I needed to be reminded of that aspect of my quest.

We talked for a while longer before I returned to my tent and left her under the tarpaulin under the trees. Sufficient light for reading lasted till about 9.30 and I continued briefly by torchlight before settling down. I woke in the night to the sound of gentle rain on the tent and a strange chattering sound. It was my teeth. I was freezing. I squirmed into some more clothes. I drifted off into sleep, and dreamt of being in a large tent surrounded by people sleeping contentedly on comfortable air beds, wrapped in thick sleeping bags.

Day 3

BOGOF on great seats of learning

8th August

When I woke and poked my head out of the tent, the morning sky was gloriously blue and the air was beginning to warm up. The rain in the night had not amounted to anything and now, although it was ridiculously early, I got up and made my way to the shower block. Suitably revived, I returned to my tent for breakfast.

At 8.30 I took the tent down (in 10 minutes!) and went over to bid farewell to Nina. She was a bit of an inspiration in many ways, being young, happy, capable and confident. She was an antidote to both the negative image presented of 'the young' and also to the pervading sense of doom and danger that was spreading across the country. She didn't seem worried about being thousands of miles from home, alone in a country where you could be forgiven for thinking that a sex attacker or paedophile lurked in every bush. I was pleased to have met her. She had a positive 'go-getting' attitude, a little of which had rubbed off on me.

At the bus stop a woman, smartly dressed in a white trouser suit, joined me to wait for the 9.27 into Newbury. After the usual greetings she asked if I was the man in the tiny tent at the camp site. I confirmed that I was.

"That looks so good," she said. "Just carrying a little home around with you. What are you doing, just travelling?"

I explained my quest.

"That's great," she continued.

"And you?" I queried. "You're a long way from home, I think." I was referring to her antipodean accent.

"Yes, we're from New Zealand," she explained as the bus

28

arrived. "We decided we needed to do something different with our lives. I mean, you just don't know what's ahead of you, do you? So many of our friends back home have got cancer or something just as bad; or they've already died. We wanted to get out and do something before anything like that came our way. So we sold the house and came over here. We bought the camper van second-hand and we're just touring and working. My husband drives diggers and excavators so he can get contract work quite easily and I'll do anything to earn a bit of money. I'll clean toilets if that's all there is—it doesn't bother me. And then, when we've worked for a while we decide to move on and explore somewhere different. Lots of our friends back home think we're mad, but just as many are really jealous. They'd do it too but I guess it's too frightening for them."

"Is that what it is, do you think, fear?"

"Oh yeah, I'm sure it is. People are frightened of losing face, frightened of losing their jobs, frightened of being in debt. But you can't live your life in fear, not really."

The two people from the other side of the world I had met in the last twelve hours were doing anything but that. It was a real tonic.

We said our farewells at Newbury bus station. I turned my attention once again to the exploration of cheap bus travel. I had enquired on the bus into town whether there was a 'through ticket' available and had been told that there was not. Newbury and its immediate surroundings to the North are covered by Newbury Bus Services. I would need a Newbury Bus Services ticket to get out of town. I looked at timetables to choose a suitable destination for the next leg of the journey, scanning places on the furthest reaches of the Newbury Bus Services territory. I had vague childhood memories of Didcot being a kind of transport hub on the rail system and there being routes to Oxford. So, Didcot would be my next choice, even if it was based on foggy memories related to an entirely different and unconnected transport system.

I didn't let the dubious grounds for my decision-making worry me and instead took the opportunity to explore the town of Newbury which, at some stage, presumably replaced an 'old bury' or maybe just a 'bury'. A date of *c*.1080 is given for the earliest known reference to the new name. Newbury was still waking up as I wandered by the Clock House and watched the sun on the river. It seemed a nice enough, neat little town but I was really just interested in getting a move on. Yesterday's frustration made me determined to clock up some miles today. If my hopes regarding Didcot were fulfilled, I reasoned I could journey from there to Oxford and perhaps even beyond.

The journey through West Berkshire proved to be a revelation. It was precisely the kind of thing I wanted and needed from the expedition; a new insight into 'familiar' territory. I had travelled through this part of the country before but was used to being channelled through it on the M4 hurtling towards London. The journeys along the 'M4 corridor' with its commerce, busyness, speed, and the rush, rush, rush of modern times had given no clue to the fact that I was tearing along on tarmac that was laid through the middle of an Area of Outstanding Natural Beauty. As we meandered through the open upland that forms the heart of the North Wessex Downs I saw it all in a new light. The gentle swaying motion of the bus was mimicked by the grain billowing in the fields, glowing golden under the August sun.

We made our way through the chalk landscape of the Chiltern Hills, passing through settlements such as Beedon (the place in the tub shaped valley) and East and West Ilsey (the woodland clearings belonging to a man named Hild). All of these were charming and we all owe a great deal to Hild and people like him for taking the time to clear all that woodland all those many years ago.

As we journeyed into Oxfordshire we paid a brief visit to the Harwell International Business Centre and passed a very long fence behind which the United Kingdom Atomic Energy Authority (UKAEA) was up to something. It was impossible to see what was going on but I can't imagine that it was anything alarming or dangerous or secretive. 'Alarming', 'dangerous' and 'secretive' just aren't words you would ever associate with the UKAEA. I think it was actually some environmental restoration, part of the process of decommissioning the site and making it available for other things, such as the annual outing for the Amateur Geiger Counter-Users Association (AGCUA).

We pressed on into Didcot, about which I can say nothing because I simply got off one bus and waited around for another one. Some people might say that that's about as much fun as you can have in Didcot but I wouldn't know; you'd have to check it with them. While waiting for the bus a young man's mobile rang. He answered:

"'Lo."

The conversation continued, with his contributions being, "Uh?" "Bus," "Dunno," and "Bye."

It is marvellous to think that the heights of human technological advances enable such stimulating verbal exchanges to take place anytime and anywhere.

I bought a Stagecoach 'All day' ticket and settled down for the ride to Oxford. Now I was getting into my stride and beginning to feel that I was making progress. I was heading for Oxford and it wasn't even lunch time!

The origins of Oxford are not clear. Some say that it was King Mempricius who founded the city about 1400–1500BC. Unfortunately he seems to be mythic. Others contend that it was in fact the Trojans who landed in about 1100BC and set it up. There is plenty of rubbish left around by Neolithic individuals—you know, arrowheads and that kind of thing. But certainly by the Bronze Age people were starting to see the potential of the place as a property developers dream.

The Romans, in an uncharacteristically bad move, appear to have ignored the chance to develop the settlement into a town but rather used it as a kind of industrial estate providing pottery and such. The Saxons weren't so dim. They knew a good thing when they saw it and quickly developed Oxford or Ohsnafordia as they would insist on calling it, into an important town on the trading route between Mercia and Wessex. Alfred the Great, King of Wessex, is thought by some to have founded Oxford University, but whatever else he founded the idea of burhs was certainly his.

These 'burhs' were fortified towns which were going to help keep the Danes and their relentless sales of bacon safely in the

East. Oxford was among the towns earmarked as being suitable for becoming such a town and this happened in 911. From then on it just kept growing, property prices boomed and the county's estate agents cleaned up. Sadly, the city was attacked by the Danes in 1009 during the reign of Ethelred the Unready. Needless to say he wasn't prepared for this and the place was ruined. The property developers and estate agents rubbed their hands and got to work. Only four years later the place was again invaded by the Danes. But really, the Danes loved the place and not just because you could rear pigs so successfully in the surrounding countryside. Canute even decided that he wanted to be crowned there in 1018.

Oxford continued to grow and prosper into the Medieval Period with the slight hiccup of being burnt to the ground in a fire of 1138. Oxford Castle was built in 1071 by a Norman lord, Robert d'Oily, the inventor of the small ornamental mats on which to put a plate. The castle proved very handy for the self-proclaimed Queen Matilda who was involved in a messy legal wrangle with her brother, the self-proclaimed King Stephen. Matilda was under siege in the castle but escaped by being lowered out of a window. Fortunately it was the middle of winter and a thick snowfall meant that nobody saw her because she was wearing a white dress—clever Matilda!

Oxford was firmly established as a seat of learning by the thirteenth century, attracting students from across Europe. The Black Death visited from 1348–1350. The population plummeted but this was good news for estate agents and property developers in the guise of the colleges, who bought up vacant land and properties all over town.

Oxford saw its fair share of turbulence under the Tudors. Henry VIII decided to completely change the syllabuses at the colleges, banning the teaching of canon law and instituting such things as medicine, Greek, Hebrew and media studies instead. His daughter Mary enjoyed her privileges and made her own contribution to the history of the town, but not in a good way. She ordered the burning of prominent and persistent Anglicans, the Bishops Latimer and Ridley and Archbishop Thomas Cranmer, who became 'the Oxford Martyrs'.

The Civil War found a city divided. The city supported the Parliamentarians and the colleges were staunchly Royalist. The University being so powerful meant that the city became a place of refuge for King Charles. Having won his victory, Cromwell, being such a good man, of course decided to let bygones be bygones. Oh, all right, he didn't. Oxford was punished by having all its defences destroyed.

Oxford now has new defences against a new enemy. The motor car is the enemy and the defences, modelled on the iron age hill forts' circular ditches, are massive ring roads which draw the unsuspecting motorist off in huge arching sweeps away from the town... These are supplemented by signs suggesting that visitors may like to use the Park and Ride service. They say, 'For City Centre, Please Use the Park and Ride', the words often accompanied by a helpful drawing of a car, a plus sign and a bus. The signs occur quite frequently but I fear they are too polite. Start off polite, by all means, but they've got to know you mean business eventually. A suggested sequence follows:

First sign
For City Centre, Please Use the Park and
Ride (with drawings if you like).

Then
Oh go on, please use the Park and Ride—
it's jolly good you know.

About 200 meters later
Look, really, don't drive into the City
Centre, use the Park and Ride.

Then
Have you any idea what it's like in the city centre? Traffic
everywhere, fumes polluting the air, and you'll just be stuck
in a jam. Look, we've spent loads of money on the Park
and Ride and the turning is coming up soon so use it.

Then
Next left for the Park and Ride.

Then
*Well, you've missed the turning for the Park and Ride
but you do have the opportunity to turn round at the
next roundabout and make your way back there.*

Then
*You selfish bastard. You obviously don't intend to use
the Park and Ride. Oh no, not you, you're much too*

Next sign
*important and posh to use 'Public Transport'. Well,
go on then, drive your stinking, polluting car right
into the centre and make everybody's life a*

Next sign
*misery. And as you've obviously made up
your mind that that's what you're doing you'll
just have to go and use one of the*

Next sign
*car parks that are... er... conveniently
located... er... close to the... er... shops.*

We arrived with our consciences intact in the very centre
of town where I duly alighted and heaved my bag onto my
protesting shoulders. Why did I have to bring my protesting
shoulders? I should have brought the amenable, co-operative
ones.

Parts of Oxford are wonderful but they were not obvious
to me from where I stood. The impression I had was of a fast-
fading newness and a predominance of brick. Once again the
bus was not dropping me off at the prettiest part of town. Anyway, for me it was more of a stop-off point between buses and
a place to grab some food. I bought a 'Tourist Map of Great
Britain' to peruse while I munched on my 'Special Lunchtime

Offer' lunch in a restaurant, a branch of which I could have found in numerous other city centres. Again, my surroundings didn't really bother me. I was looking for a route east. I had to think of places which would be likely to be on a bus route. Having picked them on the map I would have to find them on a bus timetable or spot them on the front of a bus. Although the day was wearing on, my ticket still had plenty of life in it. I decided to go for the 'Seat of Learning Double' and make an attempt for Cambridge. It was a good distance away and achieving this would go some way towards making up for the time lost to the Winchester–Andover bus debacle. It was worth a try.

There seemed to be plenty of buses for Cambridge and the one on which I travelled was every bit as comfortable as an express coach, being modern, clean, quiet and well-upholstered. The main differences were the lack of curtains at the window, the lack of overhead video screens and the lack of toilet facilities. This last point is one to bear in mind when undertaking a long bus journey. You need to know that you can go the distance without needing to go.

I was feeling pretty pleased with the way things were going. My present journey was covered by the ticket I had purchased for £5.50 in Didcot earlier in the day. Although we were doubtless taking longer than an express coach we were travelling east fast enough for me. All in all it was ten class points and a sweet from the jar for the bus company, compensating slightly for the lunchtime detention and three hundred lines the other bus company had earned in Winchester.

As with most other rides, I had no idea of the route we would take to achieve our ultimate destination of Cambridge and was quite surprised as we approached the legendary town of Milton Keynes. I should not have been surprised to find Milton Keynes here, since this is where it has always been. No, the problem was with me again. I knew that it was sort of in this area but hadn't really logged it as being anywhere near Oxford. In some ways, of course, it's not. It's about forty miles away and even a couple of hundred years ago the chances are that if you lived in one of these places you'd never get to see the other. Forty miles would have seemed like a world away to most people.

I wasn't sure what people from the past would have made of Milton Keynes today. In fact, I wasn't sure that it had a past from which people could attempt such thinking. After all, it's a new town, isn't it? I half-heartedly glanced at my place-name dictionary, not really expecting what I took to be such a modern town to get a mention. How wrong could I be? Although 'Milton' is, apparently, a very common name meaning 'middle farmstead or estate', the 'Keynes' is a manorial affix from the de Cahaignes family who were there in the twelfth century!

Today's town has a bit of a reputation. It is not a reputation for bright lights and glamour. Nor is it famous for dimly-lit, smoky rooms where gravel-voiced veterans sing authentic blues. Nor are the benefits of the local spa waters or even the existence of a unique funicular railway what makes this such a special place. No, Milton Keynes is renowned as the place where someone decided it would be a good idea to put concrete cows in the fields. It should also be famous today for having the largest purpose-built Indian restaurant in Europe— if not the world. Disappointingly, I didn't see any concrete cows but I couldn't miss the Jaipur restaurant, gleaming as white as the Taj Mahal as we sped by.

I got to know an older lady, who I shall call Doris, on this trip. I heard how Doris was getting on with her knees (not so well), how her husband's chest was (not so good) and how her plans for a little holiday were progressing (quite well). The holiday would not be anything major, what with her knees and her husband's chest and all that. Perhaps a brief coach tour would fit the bill. I also found out about her view of rising prices (dim) and her opinion of the country's immigration policy (low). And I managed to find all this out despite the fact that she was sitting two seats away from me. Some people seem to have faulty volume controls and Doris was one.

We left Doris, Bucks and Bedford behind us and pushed on into the south western edges of the Cambridgeshire Fenlands and I felt that we were entering rural England again after what seemed a long time in its more built-up environs. We passed through the ancient town of St. Neot's and on towards Cambridge itself.

People were fiddling about in these parts long before the Romans arrived, but the Romans were the first to decide to build a proper town here. This was a good point at which to cross the river and you needed to guard such places well. It was also a good site for a service station on the road from Godmanchester to Colchester. The river was also navigable, allowing the town to serve as a port. When the Romans left, the Anglo-Saxons settled in north of the river at Castle Hill. The town was known as Grantabrycge at the time, since the river was the Granta and they hadn't learnt to spell 'bridge' properly.

In the 870's the Danes were back, trying to force their bacon on unsuspecting passers by and the city was another of King Alfred's burhs. Over time the river was spanned in a number of places with King Offa being credited by some with the building of the Great Bridge (later replaced by Magdalene Bridge). The city prospered thanks to trading links with Europe and the property developers moved in. Grantabrycge grew rich, especially the property developers. The Normans arrived and added a castle and a few churches.

The place was variously known as Grentebrige or Cantebrigge as the inhabitants still struggled with mastering the spelling of 'bridge' and resolutely hung on to 'Granta' as the name for the river. At some point which is uncertain the name became Cambridge for reasons which are also uncertain. What is certain is that the river name changed to 'Cam'. Not the whole river though. Further upstream in Grantchester, it was still the Granta.

A number of religious houses were founded and it is good to know that many nuns were settled. In the twelfth century some of these could be found in the nunnery dedicated to St Mary and St Radegund. These buildings were later taken over to become Jesus College.

In the midst of a period of sackings, raids and assorted military activities we also find the beginnings of the university with the arrival of some students from the comparative hustle and bustle of Oxford. This was in the early thirteenth century and after that there was just no stopping them. They sprung up all over the place under the control of various religious bodies until Henry VIII decided he wanted a bit of the academic action and took control away.

Some of the great university buildings went up around this time and colleges were founded off and on until 1594 when it all went quiet. Government targets for getting more individuals into higher education were re-assessed and new proposals were put forward in 1596 and then a three-year review cycle was embedded leading to a complete demoralisation and lack of interest from almost everybody. No new colleges were founded until the 1800s which saw the enlightened opening of the first women's college. There was a small setback in the road to equality—the powers-that-be let the ladies have their college but they were not allowed to gain a degree until the late 1940s.

I made my way along Mill Road in the hope of discovering the Youth Hostel. The street I ambled down was lined with small independent traders and it seemed you could buy anything from a toilet brush to a toaster. I found fruit, chocolate, apple pies and cheese sandwiches. I then found a small park and made a meal of it.

In the hostel, my dorm mates and I were removing items from bags, rearranging gear and making beds. One of them was a man from Holland wearing an inordinate amount of Lycra. The alarm prompted by his choice of fabric was compounded by a request, offered with a hopeful smile: "We will go to bed soon, yes?"

Needless to say, there was a perfectly logical reason for the stretchy clothing and the request for an early night. They were both the result of the individual in question being a long-distance cyclist. Oh, how we laughed. He went on to explain that he was exploring Cambridgeshire and then moving west. He liked the UK for cycling and found it more demanding than his home country. Not completely flat in other words, although much of Cambridgeshire has a pretty good go. As he disrobed and indicated that he would like to do an 'end-to-end' it was once again a relief to hear that this meant nothing more unusual than cycling from John o'Groat's to Land's End.

The other 'dormies' were a father and son doing a slightly less ambitious cycling tour. Our conversation drifted inexorably to the second most popular subject, after the weather, for British conversations—how expensive everything is compared to everywhere else. The usual stuff, you know:

"I was in this lovely village in southern France and we got a bucket of moules mariniere for the price of an egg sandwich here."

"Yes, and we stayed in this lovely pensione in the Pyrenees for a fortnight and the cost of a half-decent cottage in Cornwall was *twice the price!*"

"Oh yes, we travelled on the train in Romania from Bucharest to Oradea and it was only 75p... return!"

Well, I'd travelled from the other side of Newbury to Cambridge for about seven quid and I didn't think that was too bad.

Day 4

From Cambridge to the coast

Breakfast, they say, is the most important meal of the day, closely followed, in my humble opinion, by lunch and dinner. Cambridge YHA offered a very fine self-serve breakfast. I was offered a full English, which is thankfully nothing like a full Brazilian.

I liked Cambridge, probably for the same reasons as the millions of tourists who visit every year—the impressive architecture of the older university buildings, the sense of history, a general charm and tranquillity.

Cambridge has been at the centre of amazing discoveries which have changed our lives and changed the way we look at the world and view the Universe. Newton was weighed down with thoughts of gravity. Darwin evolved his theories of natural science and Rutherford made steps towards understanding radioactivity. Crick and Watson unravelled the spiralling mystery of DNA and Stephen Hawking theoretically plunged into Black Holes and the meaning of Life, the Universe and Everything. You can even ponder existence itself at a lamppost known as 'Reality Checkpoint'.

This name is courtesy of some 1970s students and is something to do with either,

a) the plausibility of holding the truly external 'reality' of physical objects in tension with the idea, as proposed by George Berkeley (1685–1753) that everything that exists is either a mind or is entirely dependent upon a mind for its existence and hence physical objects do not exist outside of the mental ideas which create them, or,

b) too much beer.

The lamppost is in Parker's Piece, a large, manicured open space through which I wandered on a circuitous return to the city centre and buses onward.

Parker's Piece is important as a place for another reality check in a parallel universe—the world of football. Students keen on football played on these grounds but they realised that they all had slightly different rules. A group formed and the Cambridge Rules for football were devised. As well as standardising the rules they introduced the notion that the game should be perhaps more about skill than brute force. Cambridge Rules were influential in the formulation of the Football Association's own rules and consequently on the game we know today. Although the link is real enough, this quiet spot seemed far removed from the razzmatazz, flash and glamour of much of today's football.

I meandered back via Queen's College, down to The Backs, further peaceful spaces where the grounds of the colleges 'back' onto the river, and then along the river itself. It made for an interesting and uplifting stroll. Great amounts of care and attention had obviously been lavished on the construction and presentation of many of the college buildings. They were almost like cathedrals, reflecting a high regard for academic study, education and learning rather than directly for God. God would not have been left out however, but rather recognised, at the time of their construction, as being inextricably linked with all these endeavours. What's more, religious houses and orders were usually the original founders.

The Backs were tranquil and the river unhurried. It's great to find these kinds of places in the middle of what is a fairly densely populated and busy modern city and it's important to think about how much our built environments can affect our behaviour or our mood. Buildings aren't just functional, and the issue isn't simply about appearances either. We are concerned with creating our own habitat as human beings. This part of the Cambridge habitat felt as though it wanted you to relax and enjoy some calm and stillness. I found a similar sense in Christ's Piece, nearer the bus station, but soon realised I could not afford too much calm or stillness if I was going to make any progress with my quest.

Once actually at the bus station, I checked timetables against places on my Tourist Map. I felt that it might just be possible to reach my first cardinal compass point today. Yes, Lowestoft, full of eastern promise, was beckoning.

For the first part of the journey we travelled through parts of Cambridge that did their best to undo the sense of grace and tranquillity conjured by The Backs and Christ's Piece. Dear me, a lot of it was pretty dreadful and I was very glad to finally escape and journey through some truly rural landscapes and the Cambridgeshire Fens.

The fens are flat and if you like hills they are potentially quite dull. But actually they have their own charm and an interesting past. For much of that past they were part of the great area of marsh that stretched out to the coasts and which would have appeared as endless tufts of grass with the occasional lump of high ground standing out above the network of shallow waterways, pools, reed-beds and general swamp. The waterways were a good source of protein, being full of fish and other marine creatures, notably eels. The high ground formed islands and was a good source of income for the property developers. Isolated buildings were constructed but to make more of the opportunities people thought long and hard about draining the fens. The Romans had made a start but decided that the job was too long and hard. Hereward the Wake was glad they had given up when he used the treacherous marshes to organise his resistance to that nasty old William the Conqueror, and nobody else seems to have had much enthusiasm for the drainage idea.

This was partly because, before the seventeenth century, people hadn't really much of a clue as to how to go about draining such vast tracts of land. Then some bright spark thought that a solution might be found through the services of external drainage consultants in the form of the Dutch. They did have considerable experience in this and were obviously fairly optimistic and, let's be fair, successful. The Dutch would survey features that most people would dismiss as being unsuitable for development, for example a lake, and decide to press on anyway. In the Netherlands, they developed a system of polders, dykes, dams and collecting basins known as boezems. And, as the Dutch would say, the bigger the boezems the better. In this way the Dutch proceeded to produce large chunks of their own country from previously submerged areas. So, the thinking went, they could perhaps pull off the same stunt here.

And so began the great fen reclamation, with tens of thousands of acres being drained. In what was apparently an unforeseen consequence, the farmland neighbouring the drainage cuts sank, sometimes by up to six metres, as a result of drying out. You're trying to tell me they didn't see this coming, that similar things hadn't happened in the Netherlands? Anyway, the upshot was that a feature of the Dutch landscape became a familiar sight in the English fens—the windmill. These were used to drive water pumps which kept the land from flooding. As the drainage extended to the Norfolk broads, so the number of windmills increased. A conspiracy theorist might be able to identify the cartel of windmill builders who were behind the original proposals to drain the fens.

Windmills are fine in their way but they do rely on a fairly unreliable power source. Wind, as we all know, is unpredictable and difficult to live with. As a consequence of this unpredictability the windmills were eventually replaced by steam-driven pumps. That technology in turn became obsolete and so steam power gave way to diesel. We are now at a point where burning stuff like diesel is not thought to be a good thing. The pumps will probably eventually be run using bio-fuels. So we can look forward to the day when crops, grown on some of our most fertile agricultural land, are being used to produce bio-fuels to run the motors that keep the pumps running that will drain the waters so that we can maintain our most fertile agricultural soil in order to grow crops that can be used as bio-fuels to keep...

We forged onwards to Bury St Edmunds and another bus station. The historic market town created a good impression on the drive in and I wanted to stay and explore more fully. At the same time I was starting to succumb to the desire to see how far I could get in a day. So I bought a First Eastern Counties 'Day Rover' and boarded a bus for the second leg of my day's journey.

As we traversed the flat lands of the fens, the weather took a turn for the worse. The sky was low and the colour of an old grey face flannel. The flannel was obviously being wrung out at regular intervals and a determined rain set in. Fields rolled out like old carpets as far as the eye could see, and before the view was misted by the rain the eye could see a long way. It really was very flat, some would say in more ways than one. It wasn't breathtaking. It wasn't awe-inspiring. But it wasn't ugly either and, although it was purposeful due to the agriculture, it also somehow managed to possess a certain serenity.

The black, peaty soil looked to be providing whatever was necessary for fruitful agriculture and horticulture. It's what I expected to see in the eastern counties, which are traditionally associated with these kinds of activities. The serenity masks a difficult situation and a hard life. At the beginning of the twentieth century, farming had been characterised by low wages and poor profitability. By the thirties most farmers in Norfolk, Suffolk and Essex were living on bank overdrafts. The formation of the Milk Marketing Board in 1933 is thought by some to have saved the dairy farmers' bacon, as it were, by guaranteeing some monthly income. Sheep were also common here and by 1939 there were hundreds of thousands of them. By 1945 the number seems to have been reduced dramatically, no doubt due to their unsung role in the Secret Army of Sheep or SAS.

In post-war Britain, still reeling from the effects of rationing, food production was top of the political agenda. There was a drive to drain land, remove hedges and plough up grassland. East Anglia became England's breadbasket. By 1986 the cows were basket cases. Mad cow disease struck and there was a huge shift to vegetable growing. Onions, celery, peas and potatoes all did well. Some sought niche markets in asparagus and similar high return crops. With the loss of livestock came the demise of the livestock markets and hardly any remain today. In the twenty-first century, the pressure on farming is still high, with a foot and mouth disaster, issues of genetic modification, sustainability and bird flu. Agricultural employment has dropped although the industry is still important to the region's economy. It's not just a regional issue, of course. Agriculture across the country affects us all when it comes to the food we put on our plate and regarding the notion of national 'food security'.

I wondered what people might be looking at as they travel through this part of the country in 20 or 30 years time.

On the outskirts of Ingham we passed a huge pig farm, not far from Little Livermore, presumably a contraction of the original Little Pigs' Livermore. We stopped at Attleborough, a long-established market town recorded in the Domesday records as Attleburc and yet another place where brave Saxons defended themselves against marauding Danes. There are a number of fine features here, including the Lucky House Chinese restaurant and a kebab shop. There is also a village green, a high school and sixth form centre all neatly bounded by luxurious fields of corn and the A11. We pressed on again, through Wymondham to Norwich, where I needed to change buses.

Another city, another cathedral. Well, two, in fact. These are the snappily named 'Cathedral of the Holy and Undivided Trinity' for the Anglican community and the Roman Catholic 'Cathedral Church of St John the Baptist'. Both of these are no doubt fantastic buildings. Indeed, Norwich has a reputation as one of the most pleasant cities in England, but I would have to return another day to enjoy that because now I was a distance junkie. I needed more miles for my money.

We thundered through Thurton, where there was a foundry, a school and a church; chugged through Chedgrave, and languished in Loddon, before beetling through Beccles, a comparatively sizable settlement with the look of a market town. Someone seems to have forgotten to attach the church tower to the main body of the church although there is probably a perfectly good, rational explanation for this. Not long after leaving Beccles we lumbered into Lowestoft, my first compass point. I'd made it! I was deposited into a mass of milling passengers, disgorging from buses or waiting to board. I wandered to the nearby sea front, which I counted as the position furthest east in England attainable by bus. I spent some time peering out over the choppy waters and decided that this called for a celebration; a very restrained and British celebration. I had a nice cup of tea. I considered my position. This was only my fourth day into the expedition and already I was on the Sunshine Coast! I must admit to feeling quite chuffed.

Lowestoft possibly gets its name from being the toft or

homestead of a Viking man called Lowe or Loth. I think we'll stick with Lowe as Lothstoft is a bit of a mouthful, especially when consuming a sticky bun. There is another suggestion that it has nothing to do with Viking men called Loth or Lowe but instead is a corruption of 'Hloover's toft', the homestead of a man keen on developing the ancient cleaning system of vlacuuming.

Lowestoft is very much on the eastern edge of England and consequently very close to Denmark. You can almost smell the bacon and the Danes weren't slow in capitalising on this proximity. The Vikings had been popping over to plunder from the end of the eighth century. By the middle 800s they were as far south as Kent. Thetford fell in 869 and the king of East Anglia made peace. The rise of King Alfred the Great prevented the complete takeover of England by the Danes but a few generations later Ethelred the Unready was paying Danegeld bribes as a new wave of Danish invasions took place. By the late 1000s, the Danes had morphed themselves into Normans and had another crack at it, but that's a different story.

In the English Civil War Lowestoft took the Royalists' side while the nearby fishing rivals in great Yarmouth took with the Parliamentarians.

A year after the Civil War ended, Lowestoft was caught up in another war, this time with the Dutch. An act of parliament was introduced to ensure that all imports into England were handled by English ships with mainly English crews. This was a deliberate provocation to the Dutch who were busy exporting porcelain and tulips, and probably cheese and out-of-season tomatoes. There were declarations of war and several naval engagements, most of which the English won. The Dutch then got onto the Danes:

"Remember all that hassle you had with Alfred and how he didn't want your bacon? Wouldn't you like to get your own back? How about you close the Baltic to English shipping?"

The English, who by now were predominantly Norman Danish Anglo-Saxon Jutlanders, blockaded the Netherlands in retaliation and starved the Dutch into submission. The Second Dutch War lasted from 1665–1667 and they all waited until 1672 before they started another one. The Dutch resisted, guided by the canny William of Orange, later to become King of England.

Lowestoft endured all of this and more. In the twentieth century the Second World War saw the town evacuating its children and girding itself for invasion and bombardment. The town became one of the most bombed in the country, not least because of the war work carried out in the shipyards. The town has pretty much recovered from the bombs but the shipyards have largely succumbed to a sterner, more relentless foe.

The other once-great industry of Lowestoft, commercial fishing, has also declined in line with the falling catches of what used to be staple British fare: cod, plaice, haddock, herring and skate. There seemed barely a sign of a fishing fleet to me and 700 years of fishing felt pretty much at an end.

I decided to head off again as I still had a ticket with some life in it. Lowestoft had shown me some glimpses of an interesting heritage but I left with an air of sadness, a sense of things lost.

Great Yarmouth, on the mouth of the River Yare, is possibly not as great as it once was either, although that may be a matter of opinion. Its fortunes have long been tied up with the river and the sea.

In fact, the river was more important than the sea in making the place an important port in medieval times. However, you'd expect a place by the sea to have plenty of maritime connections, not to mention the odd naval hero. The famous naval hero in question for Yarmouth is Lord Nelson who is said to have stayed at the Elizabethan Star Hotel on Hall Quay and also to have frequented a pub called the Wrestler's Inn. The landlady of the day apparently asked him if she could rename her pub The Nelson's Arms, in his honour. Nelson supposedly replied that he did not think this was such a good idea, 'being that I have but one.' An awkward moment for the landlady but a nice story and a glimpse of the little-known lighter side of England's most famous naval hero.

Great Yarmouth has had its 'great' moments. It has been an important port and was built on 'silver darlings' or herrings as they are more commonly known. According to tourist information, the average catch in the early years of the twentieth century was 530 million fish. That's a lot of fish and may indeed have been too many, for fishing has steadily declined. The last of the town's special 'drifter' boats was built in the 1930s and made her last catch in 1938. With fishing and its associated industries all but gone, the town is now heavily reliant on tourism. A large part of the attraction for tourists is, ironically, the maritime heritage of the town.

For some, the attraction of the town is that it is a proper seaside resort. All the required features are here. There is a fine promenade and miles of sandy wow-factor beaches. Miles and miles of them in fact. To help you enjoy these there are shops selling beach necessities such as windbreaks, beach cricket sets, lilos, beach balls, buckets and spades. To keep you going you can buy burgers and hot dogs, fish and chips, sweets, ice cream and fudge. If you have had enough of the beach you can check out a games arcade or simply go shopping.

I booked a bed in the Youth Hostel and took a bus that whizzed me up the coast to Caistor, making the most of my day ticket. I was dropped at the back of a Holiday Park of non-mobile mobile homes or 'static caravans'. I wandered around for a while, half-heartedly looking for a beach. I didn't wander far though as I had quickly determined that the best course of action was to return to Great Yarmouth on the first available bus. I took a walk along the almost deserted sands which took on the colour of fresh-baked shortbread in the evening sun. The increasingly subdued light of evening ushered in a general mellowing and a greater sense of calm.

In the peace of the darkening beach I assessed my progress. Following the rubbish second day, caused by the interminable wait in you-know-where, things had gone pretty smoothly and I had made up a lot of ground. The bus journeys had been comfortable and not over-long and, by my reckoning, pretty good value for money. I finally felt a long way from home. I felt too that the notion of joining up bus journeys to travel long distances seemed to be working. I also started to feel that the overall goal of the trip might be achievable.

Day 5

North, by northwest Norfolk

10th August

Although I had my sights on my next cardinal compass point in the North, this was a very, very long way away and simply travelling due north from Great Yarmouth would land me in the sea in no time. My route would, of necessity, be far from direct, and to continue I would have to follow the coast round and along the north of Norfolk. Eventually I would reach a point at which a more northward progress might be possible. On the way there would be some nice scenery to enjoy and interesting places to visit. I reminded myself that, given yesterday's success, there was no rush. These were good feelings for me. I had spent the time dozing off the previous night thinking again about how things were progressing. I had been really hacked off by the Winchester experience and had possibly over-compensated. I had stormed through Bucks and Bedfordshire, Oxfordshire, Cambridgeshire and into East Anglia. I had merely glimpsed Bury St Edmunds and even Norwich had failed to lure me to explore. I thought how much I had missed and decided that I could afford to slow down. It wasn't a race. It wasn't about getting anywhere quickly. It was much more about savouring the sights and sounds and I was in danger of forgetting that. In this new frame of mind I determined to see the north Norfolk coast today and then stop for a day or two.

The first leg of the journey was up to Cromer on a gracefully-aging single deck bus operated by Sanders Bus and Coach Services. For those of you who are interested, the ticket was £3.20. At first glance this may seem rather a large amount compared to an 'All-Day Adult Adventurer Rover Getaway' ticket but the journey was about 32 miles and therefore, compared to a single ticket to my town centre, an absolute bargain. Furthermore, it was, to all intents and purposes, a scenic tour of the Norfolk Broads.

The pace of the journey and the general meandering route suited the landscape—nothing frenetic or super-charged but simply relaxing and pleasant. 'Pleasant' may not sound like much but if more people could be content with things being pleasant then I think we'd all be happier than we are. Consider all the people who live their whole lives in circumstances that most of us would consider deeply unpleasant and then think about what would need to change to make those lives pleasant. That's right, a roof over their head, food on the table, clean, safe water and somewhere to go to the toilet. Hands up all those of you who don't have all those things most of the time. The rest of you, be content.

I was. It may have had something to do with the 'low key' nature of the area which is often put forward as its main selling point. The Broads Authority, for example, states that one of its purposes is to promote 'quiet enjoyment'. It sounded good to me.

But all this peace, quiet enjoyment and relaxation belies a more frenetic history. The locals, the Romans, the Saxons and the Normans were all dab hands at cutting peat turfs. They needed this for fuel to warm their homes and cook their dinners. They needed tons and tons and tons. By the Middle Ages some savvy monks acquired the peat-cutting rights and cleaned up. Demand was huge and over a period of 200 years something like nine-million cubic feet had been cut. All this digging produced large and unsightly holes and trenches which would have remained had it not been for a fortuitous rise in sea level in the fourteenth century which flooded them all. Hey presto! Hundreds of miles of navigable waterways connecting scores of shallow lakes. The monks moved into the boat hire business and prepared to clean up again. They didn't really—they were loaded by then so why would they bother?

The persistent idea that this was an area for peace and relaxation had even permeated the bus driver. He wasn't in a hurry to get anywhere and the roads really didn't encourage high speeds either. I can only assume that the timetable had been worked out to allow for this leisurely pace. One particular incident highlighted the relaxed pace of life. We stopped to allow an older lady on. The driver got out of his cab, stepped off the bus onto the pavement and helped her on board. I hadn't seen anything like that for a long while. I'm more used to reading notices explaining that the bus company will not tolerate any verbal or physical abuse to its drivers than witnessing such positive and human interaction.

The lady had her young grandson with her and as we chatted she explained that they were off to do a little bit of shopping. She enthused about the area and what made it so special. And what was that? It was peaceful and relaxing.

When it came time for them to disembark I took a leaf out of the driver's book and helped her with her bags. She thanked me—and so did the driver. Although they were used to treating one another with respect and being helpful, perhaps they did not expect this from an 'outsider'.

We arrived at Cromer, apparently once a 'lake frequented by crows', and now a small town on the eastern end of the North Norfolk coast. It spent most of its history as a small village of fishermen and merchants until it eventually became fashionable as a resort in the eighteenth century. It was well-known enough in Jane Austen's time to warrant a mention in her novel 'Emma'. Cromer, evidently, was quite superior, at least compared to 'South End'. Mr Woodhouse recommends, "You should have gone to Cromer my dear, if you went anywhere. Perry was a week at Cromer once and he holds it to be the best of all the sea-bathing places. A fine, open sea, he says, and very pure air." We also learn that 'very comfortable' lodgings might be had there.

Emma and others express a number of objections to visiting Cromer, presumably shared by members of Austen's reading public. A primary one was its distance from London and it is pointed out that if travelling the one hundred and fifty miles to Cromer could be achieved with as little expense and inconvenience as the forty to Southend then Cromer would be bang on the money (I am paraphrasing, obviously).

This distance from London was probably the main reason for the town's development being rather slow. The arrival of the railway in the late 1870s changed that and there was considerable expansion in Victorian and Edwardian times. Buildings from this period are therefore well represented in the bulk of the town today and, as a consequence, the town has plenty of the charm and elegance associated with the more refined elements of those eras.

The seas and sandy beaches are below the town, which sits on a cliff top. This gives the place an altogether different feel from resorts which are at sea level. On the cliff tops I certainly experienced Perry's 'very pure air' and also enjoyed the views down towards the pier.

The pier at Cromer is an Edwardian delight from the cupolas that top the circular rooms by the entrance all the way to the Pavilion Theatre that sits on the end. It has seen some dramatic changes since it started life as a humble wooden jetty in 1391. Whatever form the jetty took in 1582 it was important enough for Queen Elizabeth I to grant the townsfolk export rights in certain goods which would allow them to raise funds for its maintenance. Both those earlier structures have long gone and today's pier is based on the one from 1901. Granted, the midsection was removed for the duration of World War Two and the whole thing was pretty much wrecked by gales in 1953, but despite this it is much as it was.

I don't know what it is about walking out along a pier but it is strangely exhilarating. Well, maybe 'exhilarating' is stretching it. But it is fun and surely that's what the traditional seaside piers are all about. I mean, they serve no useful purpose, really. They just allow you to walk out over the sea and eat an icecream or some candy floss whilst peering through the gaps in the planks at the sea down below.

Who was it that first thought that walking out over the sea in this way might be something that people would enjoy? What's more, who thought they might enjoy it enough to be willing to part with cash in order to have the experience?

Back from my promenade on the promenade and up into the town I decided to experience the fruits of another aspect of Cromer life, its fishing industry. Cromer is still a fishing town, although the industry had declined from its heyday, and the catch for which it is most famous is crabs. The crabs here are still reckoned to be amongst the best available. I decided to grab a crab and thought that from now on I should try to eat local delicacies and regional specialties wherever I was. I'd missed a few opportunities for marmalade in Oxford and possibly a Cambridge Sausage but I could make up for that from now on.

In Cromer, crabs were available in any number of small fresh-fish shops in the town's narrow streets. I had a fabulous lunch of dressed, ready-to-eat crab and newly-baked, crusty rolls. The crab had a delicate flavour but tasted mostly of the sea, as all good fresh fish should.

From Cromer I made the journey to Sheringham which was once 'the homestead of the people of a man called Scira'. Originally there had been an Upper Sheringham, which was on the high vantage point where you find today's town, and a Lower Sheringham, probably just a collection of fisherman's cottages. The settlement expanded and its focus shifted in response to the growth in importance of the fishing industry. The current town only really took shape with the arrival of the railway in 1887 which brought holidaymakers in via Cambridge from London, and took lobsters and crabs back.

It was market day in Sheringham which was a blessing because I could buy some bread and cheese and a few pieces of fruit. I had to find these amongst the stalls offering almost anything from jeans to jump leads, car polish to cotton buds and from drills to dry roasted nuts. And there's always someone selling army-style camouflage clothing. Why is that? That day there was another treat. Out by one edge a man was selling CDs. Nothing unusual there you might think. But these were his own CDs. I don't mean he was parting with a treasured collection either. These were CDs he had made. CDs he had made of country and western songs. And to let us know what they sounded like he was playing one and singing over the top of it. To help make the atmosphere complete he was dressed in a large Stetson, suede jacket and cowboy boots. And fair play to him, I say. Where would we be without our eccentrics; people happy to dress up as a cowboy and sing plaintive songs about 'the range', while standing in a car park in Norfolk?

Next to the car park and the market was the terminus of the North Norfolk Railway. This was a fine testimony to the determination and commitment of a group of people who had formed a preservation society. When the government of the day decided to axe the line in the 1960s, because it was uneconomical, the preservation society stepped in. What British Rail seemed unable to manage and make profitable, the group running the North Norfolk Railway have somehow pulled off.

It would have been excellent if the country and western crooner had begun singing 'Who's Sorry Now?' but he didn't.

The streets of Sheringham are lined with a happy mixture of houses, some of red brick, some of pebbles and others clad in timber. Each of these, in their own way, reflected construction using local materials which helps to give the place a real sense of identity. The pebbles seemed to speak particularly clearly of seaside materials and the timber cladding was somehow reminiscent of boats and beach shacks. Wood was probably a plentiful building material, especially compared with stone. The brick houses, rather than speaking of the sea, pointed to the fact that brick earth is readily available and found all over Norfolk.

I spent a happy time wandering round town and then ambled down towards the beach which was bright and windswept. Then I hopped on the 'Coast Hopper' bus.

I'm not sure you could describe the rather nonchalant progress we made along to Wells-next-the-Sea as a 'hop' but we were there soon enough. This 'Wells' was apparently 'Guella' in the Domesday Book, becoming 'Wylla' for the Anglo-Saxons and finally 'Wells' by the 1300s. Wells as a place name is remarkably straightforward. It refers to wells and apparently there were hundreds of these in the town, providing a valuable source of fresh water.

I stood in the shadow of the large granary which dominates the streetscape by the harbour. This large building, with its overhanging gantry, was once an important part of the barley and malting business associated with the town's considerable brewing industry.

On my visit small boats filled the harbour, and across the water lay Wells Salt Marshes. Standing here, the name 'Wells-next-the-Sea' appeared to be a bit of a misnomer in that there wasn't a body of water that you would really call 'sea' anywhere nearby. But that didn't dampen anyone's spirits. And why would it, since the place was bustling with excitement due to it being a carnival day! Bunting-bedecked streets were alive with brass bands and cheerleaders marching about and twirling their batons. Even with all this, there was a sense that the influence of the Broads Authority had reached Wells. There seemed to be a good deal of 'quiet enjoyment' of the proceedings.

I negotiated the merry-making to quietly explore some of the network of narrow streets and alleyways of the town. Shops were dotted about among holiday lets and apartments. Many of these were conversions from old industrial buildings. The shops ran along the quay and up Staithe Street, at the top of which was the Buttlands. This is a small green, lined with lime trees and overlooked by elegant Georgian and Victorian houses. I learnt that the very extensive beach was about a mile away from the town and that I could get there on the miniature railway if I so wished. I decided I would not, preferring instead the refuge of some tea rooms and the availability of tea and scones. Locally made, of course. For once I had actually checked a timetable and was ready when a 'hopper' arrived at The Anchor pub, just down the road.

We made our leisurely way through Holkham and into the quiet backwater that was Burnham Deepdale. After Wells-next-the-Sea, which wasn't next to the sea, it should have been no surprise to find that Deepdale wasn't a deep dale either. Perhaps it's all relative and a shallow dent here qualifies as a deep dale since the surrounding countryside is some of the flattest in England. Opposite St Mary's church, I found the Deepdale campsite. I was allocated the only piece of ground in Norfolk that wasn't completely flat on which to pitch my tent and proceeded to set up my accommodation. I had to decide whether to have blood rushing to my head all night and cold feet in the morning, or to wake warm-footed and light-headed. I decided I would not lose any sleep over it.

Before I faced the prospect of slanted sleeping I thought the beverages available in the nearby White Horse public house might help put things in perspective. The pub was in a fantastic location overlooking the nearby salt marshes and close to the coastal path. For those lucky enough to have booked a table there was an appetising range of delicious-looking food. I comforted myself with a small selection from an appetising range of delicious-tasting beers. The bar was dominated by a group of boisterous young farmers. From what had been happening recently, I felt that I was looking at an endangered species. The farming community was still reeling from the previous year's foot-and-mouth outbreak. The weathermen were predicting rains that would ruin this year's crops and ruin the farmers in the process. The ale, or their own optimism, was masking any obvious signs of fear of impending doom in the young farmers in attendance that evening. They seemed in good spirits and this was encouraging and infectious. I left them to their revelry and returned to my sloping bed where I happily went straight to sleep.

Day 6

A day of rest

11ᵗʰ August

Gravity never lets you down. I, together with my sleeping bag, boots and rucksack had slowly shifted in the night and somehow contrived to be in a huddle in a corner of the tent. It was a surprise to find that there was enough space in my 'one man' tent to actually be in a corner, given the shifting and shuffling that had been required to get me and everything I possessed in there the previous evening. Anyway, we had managed to find the corner thanks to the indefatigable g-forces and I slowly uncreased myself in the growing light. The gentle sounds of snoring came from nearby tents, mingling with the soft murmurs of considerate campers going about early morning tea-making and washing rituals.

It was Sunday morning; a day of rest. It took me some time to reassemble myself and my belongings before going to queue for the shower, housed in what looked like an old outside privy. When my turn came, I put my 20p in the slot and enjoyed my allocation of hot water.

The campsite was in the early stages of development into something much more substantial including new accommodation which was planned to allow for more hostel and backpacking visitors. I don't suppose the coin-operated shower is there now.

To properly cater for the day of rest notion, I headed off to the church for a 9.15 service of Common Worship and Eucharist. It was a quiet and traditional service and would have been approved by the Broads Authority for being 'quiet and relaxing'. A figure of the crucified Christ looked down beneficently on the small congregation as Bible passages were read and expounded, hymns were sung and prayers were said. At the end there was a chance for people to meet and greet and I was made to feel very welcome. An older woman was in a state of some distress over the death of her dog. The church community went into action, people expressing concern and sympathy and showing, sometimes wordlessly, that they cared. It was quite heart-warming really, the sort of thing that's often overlooked. Ordinary people just being nice to one another isn't newsworthy but, bottom line, it's what we all need.

Many people visit this church without coming for a service. They come perhaps because it has a Saxon round tower which has watched over the comings and goings of Burnham Deepdale folk for 950 years. Perhaps they are drawn by the pieces of medieval stained glass or the amazing Norman font. Three sides of this are decorated with panels, four to each side, which show individual characters engaged in a different activity for each month of the year. You can find someone drinking from a horn, another warming his feet, people digging, weeding, binding sheaths and threshing wheat. Each character displays one of the agricultural activities appropriate throughout the farming year. Drinking and foot-warming take place in January and February then there's hardly a break from work until the feasting of December.

The church visit had put me in a very good frame of mind. I set off on a stroll along the coast path to Brancaster Staithe. The tide was out, exposing the salt marshes just off shore. Boats lay at awkward angles, stranded in the muddy channels winding through the grassy banks. Nothing moved in the utter stillness. I reached the Brancaster Staithe Sailing Club and took a left turn, calling briefly at a mobile shop selling tubs of mussels, dressed crabs and assorted fishy delights.

I ate my lunch of locally caught fish in the Jolly Sailors pub. Sitting on the patio, the sun had burnt off any early morning mist and the temperature had risen and it was almost like being in Greece. All that was needed was a grapevine and a couple of old men playing backgammon in the corner. There *was* a Virginia Creeper and it wouldn't have taken much to find a couple of old codgers to play shove ha'penny which would have gone a long way to recreating the scene, but I was in a post-prandial stupor.

So, I had a leisurely afternoon and evening to spend in Brancaster Staithe, Burnham Deepdale and the surrounds. On leaving the pub I passed a small fishing business run by one man, his wife and sister. His eye was mainly on the lobster market but crabs provided a useful sideline. His story seemed to me to be one of strenuous effort and courage entailing, as it did, long voyages miles out to sea in fair weather or foul to set his pots and nets. The hard work did not end with the return to shore since the catch needed to be thoroughly cleaned and prepared for selling on. To make the best of things he timed his trips so that more produce was available for the weekends when more people were eating out or arriving for visits. All this was recounted in a pretty matter-of-fact tone, as if it was nothing extraordinary. It sounded like a pretty hard way to earn a living to me but it was one that seemed to bring a lot of satisfaction. The encounter made me more appreciative and thankful for this man and others like him. I really like the movement towards increasing understanding of where our food comes from and of who is responsible for providing it. It's thanks to people like this that I could enjoy my Cromer crab.

I headed inland briefly, meandering along country lanes before returning to the coast path. There was very little movement in this quietly rural place. The farms gave a clue to the economic base for the area although even these were diversifying their activities, to which the Deepdale campsite gave testimony. All in all, I savoured my time by this tranquil coastline, a world away from the hustle and bustle of so much of what passes for 'life'. From here I would be heading inland and was not planning to touch the coast again for some time.

Day 7

Bourne free and beyond

12ᵗʰ August

I was up early to avoid any rush for the shower and to allow time for grabbing some form of breakfast. I made the bus stop for the 9.23, No.36 service to King's Lynn, a town I thought might be a potential hub for transport out of East Anglia.

We passed through the little village of Titchwell which also boasted a round-towered church, this one being dedicated to St Mary. Here, too, was a large RSPB reserve of the marshes that reached back towards Brancaster. Almost next door was Thornham, an old smuggling village, followed by Holme where a timber circle, or 'Sea Henge' was excavated in 1999. Archae-ological research and dating puts the time of construction as Spring or Early Summer 2049BC. Whatever wood preservative they used it did a pretty good job.

The town of King's Lynn gets its name from a Celtic word for 'lake' or 'pool' and so is another example of people in this part of the country looking at lakes and thinking they would make good places for housing development. The excellently-named Bishop Herbert de Losinga of Thetford, a man keen on throat pastilles, decided to be the first property developer in this area and began by building a church which he dedicated to St Margaret. This building would have created a similar draw to, say, a department store or a super casino today because peo-ple went to church then rather than to the shops. St Margaret's church is one of the largest town churches in the country and has not one, but two, towers. Despite, or perhaps because of, several refurbishments, alterations, tower replacements and accommodations to changing requirements, this is still a lovely piece of ecclesiastical architecture in the heart of the oldest part of town. Other notable buildings are often associated with the town's trading past. The significance of trade here perhaps owes something to Bishop Herbert because, just in case the church wasn't a big enough draw, he also authorised a market from which time the town grew and became prosperous. It was called Bishop's Lynn in 1204, following a charter from Bishop John de Grey of Norwich. After Henry VIII dissolved the monasteries and unsettled the nuns the town became known as Lynn Regis. This was later changed to King's Lynn because too much mail was being misdirected to Lyme Regis, which is a long way off in Dorset.

Another part of the reason for the town's success was the fact that it was on navigable waterways that led inland as well as giving access to the sea. A major overseas influence here came not from the Danes and their bacon but from Germans, in the form of the Hanseatic League. This was a powerful trading group of merchants from North Germany and the surrounding Baltic nations. The Hanseatic League of trading gentlemen built a number of predictably grand houses in the town as well as substantial warehouses. The trading power house was probably the Trinity Guild Hall, dating back to 1421, which today serves as the Town Hall. The pillars and ornate carvings around the doorways, the leaded windows, coat of arms and chess-board patterned front all shout that these guys had cash to splash. It's still an impressive sight today.

I made my way to the Custom House, a landmark building that was built by Henry Bell in 1683. Built into the decoration are symbols of Bacchus, the god of wine, and also wheat sheaves, which signify the two main goods being traded through the town. From the windows there are great views over the River Great Ouse which passes by before emptying itself into the Wash a few kilometres away. There are also interesting exhibitions detailing the town's maritime heritage. As well as having maritime trading links with Europeans, King's Lynn has strong connections to Canada and not just because of the geese which are a common sight. No, the link is more to do with George Vancouver who was born in King's Lynn on 22nd June 1757, the son of an assistant customs collector, John Jasper Vancouver. At the age of fifteen, George began his nautical career with a position serving Captain James Cook. He accompanied Cook on a four-year voyage on the *Resolution* and also on Cook's final voyage on *Discovery*. When he himself set sail from Falmouth in 1791, it was in a ship also called *Discovery*, and his challenge was to map the Pacific coast of America from California northwards to the Canadian border with Alaska. This was generally regarded as a success although he did manage to miss the Columbia River a couple of times.

The Custom House is also home to the Tourist Information Centre and I made enquiries about bus routes vaguely north and east. The helpful staff and I decided that I had two possibilities from here. I could try Spalding or Peterborough. I knew nothing of Spalding apart from the fact that it provided Britain's gardeners with millions of flowering bulbs. It seemed a less likely candidate than Peterborough for being a place with plenty of bus routes. Peterborough it was, then.

So, just like the Danes, I had finished with East Anglia for the time being. They had arrived in various raiding parties with leaders such as Halfdan, Ivarr the Boneless, Thorkell the Tall and our old friend Sweyn who was destined to become King of England. I would perhaps be following in the footsteps of these notorious bacon-purveyors as they made their way to the north of England.

The driver of the X94 to Peterborough had obviously not been having a great day. There must have been a reason for him to be quite so curt with quite so many of his passengers. Still, bus drivers are human and we have to allow them their off days.

When it came to my turn to try and board his bus his chosen point of argument was the size of my bag. He declared that I would not be allowed to take it on board. I didn't feel like arguing or pointing out that I had travelled many miles on even smaller buses than his and my bag had never been barred before. And so my bag was banished to the cargo hold and I sat looking at the empty seat next to me where it could have comfortably rested. Worst of all I had forgotten to remove my chocolate before its stowage. As we re-enacted Keanu Reeves' first *Speed* movie we passed through Wisbech, 'the Capital of the Fens'. This is purported to have been the main base for the 'Fen Tigers', local resistance fighters opposed to the Dutch reclamation and drainage schemes of the sixteenth and seventeenth centuries.

Arriving at our destination, the bus disgorged me in Peterborough. I say 'in' Peterborough but it felt more like 'under'. We were in a cavernous subterranean area beneath the station and a large shopping complex. I set off to explore the possibilities of a) food, b) books and c) buses. I managed to find something to eat quite easily but had more trouble with the book. I wanted a guide to camp sites for future reference. All I had to do was find a book shop. I didn't know what the favourite leisure activity in Peterborough was, but if the number of bookshops was any guide, it didn't seem to be reading. I did eventually find a bookshop and they even had a guide to caravan and camp sites.

As well as being low on bookshops, Peterborough also seemed to offer few possibilities of travelling by bus in anything remotely resembling a northerly direction. After much timetable perusal I established that there was one which made a valiant attempt and so, assured of my means of escape, I went in search of a suitable spot for lunch. Churches and cathedrals had previously proved themselves to be oases of calm and beauty so I sought out the Cathedral Church of Saints Peter, Paul and Andrew. Once again I found myself before an exceptional building. Each of the three great arches of the West Front was topped with a figure of one of the saints to whom the building was dedicated. It was perhaps an even greater joy because of the contrast to the drabness of my earlier impressions formed by the characterless shopping malls through which I had wandered.

Apparently there has been Christian worship on this site for almost 1350 years, with a known monastic church in 665. This was destroyed by some invading marauders who were, what was it now, oh yes, Danes. Knocking down a church is usually a good impetus for building a new one and there was a re-consecration in 972. An 'accidental' fire destroyed this building in 1116 (I don't know how much research has gone into the existence of a malcontent Danish community at the time but it could be worth looking into). This cleared the way for another new build from 1118 to 1238 and this forms the bulk of the present cathedral. It suffered a further desecration at the hands of Oliver Cromwell, but apart from some alterations in the Victorian era that is pretty much it. It had recovered quite well from a fire in 2001.

There are other points of interest here including the fact that Katherine of Aragon is buried here and Mary Queen of Scots was for a time before being moved to Westminster. However, for me I think the truly special thing was the longevity of the wonderful buildings and the faith that inspired them.

Back at the bus interchange, I scanned the bus bays and found the appropriate point of embarkation for the route, operated by the Delaine bus company, that would take me to Bourne. Looking at my trusty Tourist Map I saw that Bourne was pretty much directly north of Peterborough, which was great. I also noticed that it was close to Spalding which was rather annoying. I was effectively travelling two sides of a triangle but if I hadn't I would have missed a great cathedral.

Delaine Buses traces the family business back to the introduction of horse drawn vehicles in 1890. The route between Peterborough and Bourne had been running since 1923! The bus I travelled on was clean and spacious and not pulled by horses.

We passed through the low-lying country of this part of the Lincolnshire Fens. The land was so low-lying, in fact, that it influenced the naming of the villages through which we passed. These were 'The Deepings', places such as Market Deeping and Deeping St James. Safe to say Market Deeping has earned the right to the 'market' element of its name; there has been one there since 1220, after all. Also here were lovely stone buildings and an ancient church dedicated to St Guthlac, an Anglo-Saxon mercenary who took to the religious life and became a hermit. He died in 714 and Crowland Abbey was dedicated to him. I wonder what a man who had opted for quiet religious study and solitude would make of that or indeed of people remembering him through this church nearly 1300 years later.

'The Deepings' have grown around the River Welland, and there is more water in the form of a canal. The presence of these waterways combines with interesting and charming buildings to create a lovely impression for the passing traveller and to plant a desire for a return visit.

A succession of villages appeared and were each left behind, leaving, in their turn, more impressions of pretty rural settlements. Langtoft was stretched along the road and dominated by an impressive spire which belonged to the church of St Michael and All Angels. Baston had a collection of pretty buildings and Thurlby some stunning thatched cottages and the wonderful St Firmin's Church. Here I also noticed the sign to a Youth Hostel. I thought I could always get back here if Bourne turned out to be a dead-end in terms of onward progress.

Bourne didn't let the side down as we drove in. Not to be outdone by its smaller near-neighbours, this market town also had a display of attractive buildings, with both civic and retail functions and some pretty-looking open spaces. However, after such a good first impression it was disappointing to arrive at the bus station. Taking a lead from the bus station designers of Winchester, the one in Bourne was little more than a desolate concrete slab with a small unkempt shelter which provided locals some space on which to indicate who loved who and how they expressed these feelings. Possibly the concrete slab was the foundation of a much more grandiose scheme for which the finances never materialised. Whatever the reason, this is not a place from which to make an assessment of the town. I checked the timetables and was glad to find that there was a bus which would carry me onward. And I mean *a* bus; at 17.25. The continuation of my journey was suddenly dependent on the arrival of a solitary bus.

To pass the time and give the place a proper look, I retraced the route back down into town. North Street, down which I walked, met up with South Street, West Street and Abbey Road in the centre. This looked as though it would have been the market square at one time although this was hard to imagine with all the traffic that now passed through. There were some fine buildings here, not the least of which is the Burghley Arms.

This is the birthplace of William Cecil who became the first Lord Burghley having served Queen Elizabeth I for over forty years. The hostelry is flanked by a Georgian Town Hall and a Victorian bank. There are few signs here of the blandness of many towns. Yes, we can safely say that the town manages to retain the Bourne identity.

I visited shops first, for premises-baked bread, ham off the bone, cheese, and an orange and apple. I figured most of this could count as my regional delicacies for the day. Pig farming seemed to be a local feature and I was told the cheese was from nearby. I wasn't sure about the apple and I knew there was no point asking about the orange.

I took my purchases into the memorial gardens. Sunshine, soft grass, bird song and water. A better place for a picnic you would be hard pressed to find. And what a picnic; good, tasty cheese with what you might call 'bite' and sweet and tender ham.

A stroll after lunch revealed Bourne Abbey, a.k.a. the parish church of St Peter and St Paul, which dated from the twelfth century. Nearby was The Red Hall which was from the seventeenth century. This rather splendid building is a good example of the kind of house a prosperous gentleman of Stuart times would require. The gentleman in question was Gilbert Fisher and he has left us a fine three storey building of handsome red brick, with high gables, stone tiled roof, tall chimneys and an imposing porch. He may have been wealthy when he started but it seems he died bankrupt and in debt in 1633. The Hall is blamed by some for the gentleman's financial demise. At one point it was bought by the Bourne and Essendine Railway Company and served as the station master's house and ticket office until the railway closed, thanks to Doctor Beeching.

Bourne proved to be a very pleasant place, if you ignored the bus 'station'. I passed a few moments of waiting for the bus by glancing at my dictionary of place names.

Bourne: (place at the) spring or streams. OE
burna or Old Scandinavian brunnr.

Scandinavian? The Danes had been here before me.

I chatted to a well dressed and well-spoken woman, who

was waiting for a friend to arrive. She had retired to Bourne (along with quite a few others I shouldn't wonder) four or five years ago and enthused about how lovely she thought it was. Although she then added that in her estimation it had doubled in size since she had arrived and her tone suggested that this hadn't necessarily been a completely good thing.

She wondered if I was from Bourne; she didn't think she'd seen me?

I explained that no, I was just passing through.

She wondered if I had come a long way.

I explained that I had come from Burnham Deepdale in Norfolk today but left Bath 10 days ago.

So I had come a long way then. Was I going far?

I explained my quest. "I'm trying to get round England on service buses," I said.

"Really!" she exclaimed. "How extraordinary."

Was it my imagination or did she edge away from me slightly? The bus arrived. The well-spoken woman's friend disembarked and we bid brief farewells. I was offered a "Good Luck with your travels".

South Lincolnshire wafted by in the greens, yellows and browns of fields and in more cosy-looking villages and in this way we made it to Grantham. I was deposited in an area which seemed to consist entirely of walls of new red brickwork and paving. It was all hard surfaces, functional but not very friendly. I found my way via Wharf Road and the back of the Post Office onto St Peter's Hill and everything was suddenly all right again. The townscape opened out, there were trees and grass and a nice big bronze statue of Sir Isaac Newton; he of the apple on the head and the whole business of gravity. There is a statue of the great man here because he was born in a small hamlet not far from Grantham. That happened in 1642 and he later attended the King's School in the town and left his mark there by scratching his name onto a windowsill. Naughty boy.

The town is obviously proud of its associations with this famous scientist. It is also proud of a certain Edith Smith. And so it should be, for Edith turns out to be the first woman in Britain to be given full powers of arrest in her role as policewoman.

She joined the Grantham force during the First World War and served until it ended in 1918.

My thoughts turned to sleeping, but not because of the town. I just had to think about where I'd rest my head that night. I knew I wasn't going to be camping and I also knew there was no Youth Hostel. In other words, I had the choice of spoiling myself with some bed and breakfast accommodation or sleeping on a park bench. Mmm... What to do? Seconds later I found The Avenue B&B and booked a room. I surveyed the luxurious opulence of a comfy bed and took a long, hot shower. I was blowing several nights' camping fees but I didn't care.

Refreshed and invigorated, I went off to explore. Grantham possibly gets its name from being the homestead or village of a man named Granta, suggesting an Old English heritage. It is believed to have begun life as a Saxon settlement, slowly growing to become a royal manor in the eleventh century. It expanded considerably in the eighteenth century as it was on the main stagecoach route from London to York. The Industrial Revolution changed the face of the town, bringing the canal, warehouses, wharves and factories. A few street names seem to suggest the presence of those fearsome and terrible people, the Danes. Grantham is also the birthplace of another fearsome and terrible person—Margaret Thatcher.

It was still shirt-sleeve warm when I found Mona Lisa making pizza in Castlegate. She sold me a mushroom pizza which I fully understood to be non-representative of local regional delicacies but which tasted fabulous anyway. I consumed it with as much decorum as was possible while studying the civic grandeur of the Guildhall. This is an imposing building right from its colonnaded entrance, up through the stocky main structure and on to the clock tower at the top. It was a multi-functional building in its day having been the town's courtroom and jail as well as housing the governor's residence. They even managed to fit in a ballroom!

I was intrigued by some tourist directions pointing towards 'The Living Sign'. Following the directions led me back to Castlegate and the 'Living Sign' in question, which turned out to be a beehive up a tree. So, you could see that in a sense it was 'living' but what was it a sign for? Why, what is this, just below the tree? Goodness me! It is the Beehive Inn. Well, I had to investigate.

According to the landlady the pub dated from the early 1800's, and was the oldest pub in Grantham. These days pubs are often associated with binge drinkers and health problems rather than with the simple pleasures of a few beers in good company. Perhaps particularly in urban centres they have lost their traditional role as a meeting place and focal point for a community. At the other extreme, there can be difficulties when a pub community focuses too much on itself and is not welcoming to outsiders. I know I'm not alone in experiencing that moment when you walk into a pub and all the conversations, noise and revelry stop as everybody in the bar turns to glare at the stranger.

Nothing like that happened in The Beehive. Halfway down a first pint of the local Little Bytham ale I was engaged in conversation with a local stonemason who explained his recent injuries and their effect on his work. Basically, he wasn't doing any. We were drawn into a small knot of other keen imbibers and were soon swapping stories and woes of the day amid general babble. Finally we moved on to the more serious business of explaining why the government was useless, what to do to sort out education and how to improve the health service. Being included like this doesn't always happen but when it does it's quite remarkable really. It's great that a complete stranger, unknown to anyone and unlikely to be seen by any one of them again, can wander in off the street and become part of a group for an evening. There must be a 'citizenship' PSHE lesson for schools in there somewhere. I left comforted and in good spirits, if slightly befuddled. Fortunately it was not a long walk back to my bed. I needed to get in a serious bit of sleep as I was hoping to cover a fair distance the next day.

Day 8

Farther up and further in

13th August

I liked what I'd seen of Grantham, which was not much I grant you. My impression may have been favourably coloured by the pleasant evening in the Beehive Inn, but even so I was glad I came. By coming here I had cut inland, rather than heading more directly north and would continue this trend today, heading for Huddersfield and a stopover with my sister. This was going to be quite a tall order (the journey, not the stay) for a single day of bus journeys but I was feeling quite optimistic by this stage. I felt the first two-night stop at Burnham Deepdale had recharged my batteries and given me a slightly different perspective. Also, I had almost forgotten the problems I had experienced in you-know-where and felt I was getting to grips with how things worked. Even so, I did have the Peak District to get across, not to mention actually getting *to* the Peak District.

I had been given an old Peak District timetable for buses and trains which I had pored over before venturing out the previous evening. There was a Transpeak service leaving from Nottingham or Derby, heading for Manchester. This looked to be perfect but I worked out a convoluted series of possibilities as a fallback Plan B.

I was looking at using a bus service that, according to the Peak District Timetable, went by the rather poetic name of 'Trent rainbow' or, if you didn't like poetry, was simply the R61. I didn't care if the bus had been named by a New Age hippy or a warehouseman. The important thing for me was that I could get from Derby to arrive in Matlock at 10.07.

The 172 left Matlock at 10.50 and would drop me at Bakewell

at 11.56, to be taken on at 12.10 by the 175 to Grindleford. From here the 65 would get me to Buxton in plenty of time for the 15.30 199 service to New Mills. Then it was a straightforward journey to Glossop on the 361. Thus I would have traversed the Peak District. All that would then be required was a short journey north on the 236 to Stalybridge, joining the 352 to Uppermill and finally the 365 from Uppermill to Huddersfield. I convinced myself that this would be simple enough.

The first leg of the journey was to Nottingham and cost me the princely sum of £2.40. Many of the settlements we passed through gave away their Danish heritage with names ending in '-thorpe', as at Woolsthorpe (Isaac Newton's birthplace) and '-by', as at Barrowby. The Duke of Rutland's house, Belvoir Castle, stood grandly above the distant Vale of Belvoir.

We made steady progress through gently-rolling Lincolnshire. I knew that I was doing extremely well with the weather. It was yet another glorious day and the August summer sun provided perfect lighting for the fields whether they were awaiting harvest or lay in a post-harvested state with great coils of crops dotted about like the abandoned pieces from a giant's game of draughts.

The red brick cottages of Orston gave way to farmland again before we passed through Aslockton. The name of this quintessential English village, with its few houses, pub or two, post office and church, betrays its Scandinavian (i.e. Danish) beginnings as Aslachetune, the farmstead or village of a man called Aslakr. He can't have been that much of a slacker since he wouldn't have owned a farm let alone a village. And thus we blithely pass through the birthplace of Thomas Cranmer, Archbishop of Canterbury and close aide to Henry VIII!

Once again I'd come across another apparently inconsequential place that has an amazing link with the past. I was getting used to the idea that if you stopped and looked, this would happen virtually everywhere you went in the country. You can't turn round for tripping over sites of historic interest. The country is saturated with fascinating places to see and things to do and facts to discover. I think there's a danger we can take it for granted. I know I have.

On this journey the bus felt like a mobile community centre

or a WI meeting, although there was a distinct lack of home-made cakes, jam and cups of tea. There's a thought—a WI-run buffet service on the local bus! The place was buzzing with animated conversation and everybody was having a good time, enjoying the company and the scenery. Here I felt I was witnessing another argument in favour of travelling by bus—people had the time and freedom to talk.

We were passing through landscapes that would perhaps have been trodden by D H Lawrence. He may have agreed with me about the beautiful parts of the countryside but he saw much of the degradation of both nature and human beings in and around the mining towns. He certainly wasn't too enamoured of Nottingham.

In an essay called 'Nottingham and the Mining Country' he wrote about the tragedy of England which he saw as being down to ugliness. Not that he thought the country itself was ugly. By no means, for he said that he thought this was lovely. What was ugly was the man-made element. He lays the blame for this largely at the feet of the Victorians and in particular at those who were in a position to 'condemn' the workers to a life of ugliness. This ugliness, according to Lawrence, permeated all parts of life, from people's surroundings, their clothes, furniture and housing, right through to their love, hopes and ideals. Lawrence sees that the environment provided for the working population does nothing to feed their souls and a 'human soul needs actual beauty more than bread'.

Part of the problem, as he sees it, is an inability in the English character to develop a 'real urban side' to a man. There seem to be two causes of this. Firstly, Lawrence suggests that cities in other countries have proper identities and that the citizens of those places have a proper 'intimate' relationship and connection with their city. He suggests that Siena, for example, is a 'real city' and that its citizens are intimately connected. Nottingham, on the other hand, is an 'amorphous agglomeration'. Secondly, he feels that the Englishman is undeveloped as a citizen and too ready to accept 'hopeless paltriness' in his surroundings. Much of this is due to the 'complete industrialisation' of the English who cannot build a city or don't know how to properly live in one. We are all suburban and 'pseudo-cottagey', and happy with our own little suburban plot.

It is quite sobering to consider that we might, as English nationals, be rubbish at making cities and urban landscapes. I'm not sure I can wholeheartedly agree with D.H. though. We have some tremendous towns and cities with some wonderful urban landscapes and some of them are great places to live. Admittedly, for my money, the best of these are the old ones. I do think he might be on to something though, when he talks about knowing how to live in a city. Perhaps it's even more important to know how to love a city. For some there seems to be little or no 'civic pride' and perhaps that's just a very old fashioned idea. I wonder if the individualism that's developed recently in our society is being reflected to a degree in some people only being interested in their own 'little home' and their little patch of garden. I wonder, are too many of us still ready to accept the 'hopeless paltriness' of our surroundings?

Nottingham was to be my first truly 'industrial revolution' town and D.H.Lawrence hadn't done a tremendous job of PR for the place. It seemed to be making strenuous efforts to be more than an 'amorphous agglomeration' but as with other established places it has to work with what has gone before. Things may have been tough from the beginning, given that the settlement's name originally meant 'the home of Snot'. The unhappily-named Snot family were Anglo-Saxons and the kids must have had a rotten time at school. The '-ham' ending, combined with the possessive 'ing' gave us Snottingham. As soon as was feasible this was changed to Nottingham, for obvious reasons. After all, would Robin Hood be that scared of a man called the Sheriff of Snottingham?

Although it has a long history as a settlement before industrialisation, it was industrialisation that kick-started a rapid growth, with the town becoming a centre for lace-making and a hub of a wider-spread mining community. This growth perhaps helped a certain John Boot's decision to open a herbalist store here in 1849. This was the beginning of what would become, under the guidance of his son Jesse, Boots the Chemist. I had a lightning tour of a small part of town. I'm sure DH Lawrence wouldn't recognise it now. They certainly seem to be working hard at livening up the place and there were plenty of shops, bars and what appeared to be refurbished warehouses. I guess that a certain grittiness and functionality still pervades the place. From my first impressions, it didn't strike me as being 'pretty', but at the same time I wasn't inclined to think 'ugly this', 'ugly that', 'ugly the other' and I think there were clues that there *was* a Nottingham, much in the same way as there *is* a Siena.

The fact that I had a tour at all, speedy and brief though it may have been, was due to the graciousness of the driver. I had told him of my intentions regarding onward travel. He informed me that the bus I would need to catch would leave from another part of town. Then he actually took me there. He was going there anyway; he didn't take me on a special journey on his bus or anything like that. But he didn't have to 'go the extra mile' as it were. It was another example of a bus service employee simply being helpful and I really appreciated it.

The onward travel I had in mind involved a bus to Derby. I wanted to get there because this is where I could avail myself of the promising Transpeak service, courtesy of something called a Derbyshire Wayfarer. This sounded like the proverbial 'dream ticket'. It would, apparently, provide for my conveyance right across the Peaks and I wouldn't need my rather tortuous plan B.

Derby has attracted many other people for different reasons, completely unrelated to the availability of buses. The Romans, Anglo-Saxons and Vikings have all carelessly left evidence of their periods of settlement here. This long heritage as a settlement is no doubt due in part to its location on the banks of the River Derwent. The river also played a part in the changes brought about by the Industrial Revolution, and specifically by the silk and cotton spinning industries. It was this period which really put Derby on the map.

I confess I really only saw bus stations and had my attention far too focussed on my trans-Peak attempt.

However, as we left Derby we effectively followed the Derwent River upstream and saw more evidence of how this water course was responsible for shaping the economy of Derbyshire, and indeed much of the country, in the eighteenth and nineteenth centuries. This crucially important role for the river was as a power source, its energy being harnessed by a series of entrepreneurs to drive the machinery in their cotton mills. The first such mill was established by Richard Arkwright and his partners at Cromford in 1771. As we travelled north another of his mills appeared—or perhaps more appropriately 'loomed'. This magnificent 5-storey structure dates from 1783 and the statement it makes about the scale of the cotton spinning and cloth-making industries of the time is emphatically, 'We are in business and business is booming.'

We breached the high limestone defences and entered Matlock Dale, and within this stunning deep gorge sat the equally stunning Matlock Bath. Hotels, villas, houses and gardens sat quietly by the river or clung precariously to the rising limestone ledges. This pretty town had developed during the Regency period as a result of the discovery of warm springs in 1698. People began to arrive to 'take the waters' and also to enjoy the dramatic scenery. Today there are numerous shops and cafes catering for the tourists who still flock here, mostly to take in the views rather than the waters. Here was another place offering a sense of seclusion and sanctuary.

As we passed on towards Matlock itself, the towering rock above recalled John Betjeman's observations recorded in his poem named after the town:

By cool Siloam's shady rill—
The sounds are sweet as strawberry jam
I raise mine eyes unto the hill,
The beetling Heights of Abraham;
The branchy trees are white with rime
In Matlock Bath this winter-time. *

For me it was gorgeous summertime and the leafy trees were green with life.

We navigated our way in and out of the larger and slightly

* From 'Matlock Bath', from *Collected Poems*, by John Betjeman, © 1955, 1958, 1962, 1964, 1968, 1970, 1979, 1981, 1982, 2001. Reproduced by permission of John Murray (Publishers).

less picturesque Matlock. The town can't help not being in quite such a beautiful setting as its diminutive near-neighbour. It has some attractive buildings and is perhaps proud of the fact that it displays a bit more 'grittiness' than straightforward gentility. The onward journey plunged me into the midst of the wonderful scenery and landscapes that have earned this area the right to be designated as the Peak District National Park.

We are greatly blessed in Britain to have such varied and exciting areas of countryside so freely available to us. The places have always been there and for a long time perhaps nobody cared. Once people did start to care they realised the continued existence of these places was not assured and neither was open access guaranteed. This situation was addressed through the creation of National Parks.

The National Parks Authority traces the beginnings of the National Park phenomenon to the romantic poets of the early nineteenth century, such as Byron, Coleridge and Wordsworth. The latter, for example, loved the Lake District and claimed that this was a "sort of national property, in which every man has a right and interest, who has an eye to perceive and a heart to enjoy."

By the late nineteenth century, the MP James Bryce was fired up enough to introduce the first 'freedom to roam' bill in 1884. Rich and powerful people owned lots of land and didn't like the idea of people wandering freely (that is, going where they want and not paying for the privilege). Coincidentally, rich and powerful people also occupied many seats in parliament and the bill was defeated.

The beginning of the twentieth century saw a massive increase in interest in the great outdoors. More and more people sought the benefits—physical, emotional and spiritual—of time spent in recreation in the open air. People from the industrialised towns and cities had often escaped to the 'lungs' provided by surrounding countryside. At the same time as the expansion of the cities and their encroachment on the countryside, landowners had been enclosing vast tracts for farming and sport. The public demand for access increased steadily and by 1932 feelings were running high enough for a mass trespass on Kinder Scout. Yes, this radical move actually happened in England and involved English people! The original trespass had involved about four hundred ramblers from Manchester and another group based in Sheffield. The subsequent arrest, trial and imprisonment of five trespassers aroused a good deal of public sympathy and perhaps motivated others who had been passive. Suffice to say that another trespass a few weeks later at Winnats Pass attracted ten thousand.

Several groups including the Ramblers' Association, The Youth Hostel Association and the Councils for the Protection of Rural England and Wales lobbied the government and argued the case for National Parks. The pressure produced results in 1945 when the government issued a White Paper on National Parks as part of the country's post-war reconstruction and again in 1949, which saw the passing of an Act of Parliament to establish National Parks. The Peak District was the first to be designated in 1951. Looking around me at the glorious scenery I thought they all deserved a big "Well done".

We motored on through Rowsley, hurried past Haddon Hall and bowled into Bakewell, home of the famous tart and also of that delicious tea-time treat made with pastry, jam, eggs and almonds. The town sits well in the landscape, not surprising perhaps given that many of its buildings are constructed from the local sandstone. The three-storey Rutland Arms Hotel in the centre is a fine example and a grand-looking place.

We soon passed through Ashford-in-the-Water, a village on the River Wye for which the word 'picturesque' is hardly sufficient. The Sheep Wash Bridge is a main feature here. This ancient structure was on a medieval packhorse route and its name has come about from the practise of washing sheep nearby. You should have worked that one out. The sheep washers had a cunning plan. They would pen the lambs on one side of the river and throw their mothers in at the other bank. The anxious parents did all the work, crossing to their bleating offspring. Hey presto! Nice, clean sheep, ready for shearing. It is hard to believe that the pretty village on show today was once a centre of 'heavy' industries based on lead mining and a material called 'Ashford marble', a material once highly prized for its decorative qualities. It was made into just about everything you can make from marble and was used in everything from cathedrals to stately homes. The industry had a life span of a hundred and fifty years and ended in 1905.

A pioneering lady, Celia Fiennes, had been this way—riding side-saddle—in 1697, which was long before what you and I would call 'roads' existed. She toured Britain extensively in this manner and when describing part of her journey from Bakewell to Buxton, explained:

It is very difficult to find the Wayes here for you see only tops of hills and so many roads—by reason of ye best wayes up and down—that its impossible for Coach or Waggon to pass some of them, and you scarce see a tree and No hedges all over ye Country, only dry stone walls that incloses ground no other ffence. Buxton we saw 2 or 3 tymes and then lost ye sight of it as often, and at last did not see it till just you came upon it—that 9 mile we were above 6 hours going it. [*]

If she's trying to say it's very hilly you can't fault her. We made for Buxton, across:

*those Craggy hills Whose Bowells are full of mines
of all kinds off Black and white and veined Marbles,
and some have mines of Copper, others tinn and
Leaden mines, in wch is a great deale of silver.* [†]

For me it was the first proper dose of rugged upland scenery on the journey so far and it was a pronounced contrast to the flat lands that I had grown used to in Cambridgeshire, Norfolk and South Lincolnshire. Although the 'wayes' may have been up and down, the bus coped admirably and it took us nothing like 6 hours. I confess I was enjoying myself considerably more than if I'd been riding side-saddle on a horse.

Buxton is all elegance and sophistication, as befits a spa

---

[*] Celia Fiennes, *Through England on a Side Saddle in the Time of William and Mary* (London: Field and Tuer, The Leadenhall Press, 1888)
[†] *ibid.*

town that has had centuries in which to develop. The Romans first established the spa baths around the hot springs and gave the place the snappy name of Aquae Arnemetiae. My *Dictionary of Place Names* suggests that Buxton as a name has derived from Buchestanes, meaning the rocking stones or logan stones, which in turn comes from the Old English 'bug stan', a misspelling of the phenomenon caused by sitting on a small, soft insect.

The Sixth Earl of Shrewsbury had one of his eight principal houses at Buxton Hall. An interesting visitor was Mary Queen of Scots who was brought there in 1573 when she was under the guardianship of the Earl and his then wife Bess of Hardwick. Mary apparently suffered badly from rheumatism so was perhaps here in the hope that the warm spa waters would bring her some comfort.

Much of the architecture which gives Buxton its current air of refinement is from building programmes from the late eighteenth century when it was developed by the Dukes of Devonshire. What the Earl of Shrewsbury and the Dukes of Devonshire are doing creating all these buildings in Derbyshire I don't know. But if they were all up to it I suppose it's all right. Perhaps the Earls of Derbyshire reciprocated by developing the delightful seaside town of Appledore in Devon. There was another surge of interest in Buxton during the Victorian period when large numbers of people were convinced of the efficaciousness of the waters with a resultant crop of architecture from that period.

This was another place in which I could have happily lingered if I hadn't been careering across to New Mills in the hope of catching a bus to Glossop to connect with the service to Upper Mills and so on.

Having ensured I would have a timely arrival in New Mills I was thrilled to discover that I had just missed a bus to Glossop. There was nothing for it but to check out the nearest pub, located close to the station. Within its small confines I had half a pint of 'dark mild'. I counted this as one of my 'local delicacies' for the day since, although not limited to the east Midlands, it is not generally available in the South. It was a lovely, near-black brew, with a good, malty taste and dangerously drinkable. I sensed I was also a bit of a curiosity here, in that it didn't look like the sort of pub that enjoyed a great deal of passing trade. Much more, this was the usual haunt of a few regular locals. A pub as a pub should be, in other words. A place of meeting and sharing.

I never got to Glossop. Not because of too much dark mild, I hasten to add. In fact, I would really have liked to go and see what a place called Glossop looks like. It sounded rather wet and soggy. Or perhaps it could even be the word for a small amount of clear honey or syrup.

"Would you care for some syrup on your pancakes?"

"Just a glossop, thank you."

I didn't get there because when I told the driver of the bus to Glossop where I eventually wanted to go, he very helpfully suggested I go to Ashton-under-Lyne instead. There, he said, I would have more choices of onward routes and therefore more chance of getting where I wanted to go.

So I got off his bus again and waited. I waited half an hour. It was a quarter past five and I was beginning to get a little edgy about making my connections. Then two buses to Ashton arrived. Finally, after over a week of almost continuous bus travel, I could utter that almost mythical phrase:

"I dunno, you wait ages for a bus and then two come along at once."

We journeyed on through what was still very much industrial England. The new mills of New Mills, which I had just left, had been for the cotton industry and they replaced even older corn mills. Eventually, when I'd crossed the county boundary into Lancashire and arrived at Ashton, I was still in the thick of industrialisation. Ashton-under-Lyne is thought to have grown from a small hillock by a crossing-point on the River Tame. Its name seems to derive from a place (ton) were ash trees grow or perhaps a Celtic name meaning 'elm-tree region'. Sounds like somebody doesn't know his ash from his elm trees.

A house near the hillock became a village and over time grew into a small market town. The town eventually found itself at the junction for the Manchester and Ashton canal, the

Huddersfield Narrow Canal and the Peak Forest Canal and these had a huge impact, in combination with tramways and later railways. These transport systems freed up the movement of coal, other raw materials and finished goods around the area and beyond. Freight movement was the significant factor driving growth and development here. Improved transport of raw materials helped production and better access to markets led to increased sales, all of which meant more job opportunities and a need for housing. Back then, people wouldn't have come to admire the scenery. This is in contrast to other places in the country, such as resorts like Cromer. These places grew precisely because they weren't 'industrial' and allowed for a bit of rest and relaxation.

The transport concerning me at that moment was the bus for my onward journey. Despite the thoughts of the driver of the Glossop bus there was not a great choice of routes onward. I took my chances with Uppermill and reaching here I discovered that there was one final bus to Huddersfield that evening. Once again, the continuation of my quest relied on this last available bus. All I needed was for the vehicle not to break down and for there not to be a shortage of drivers. Allowing my head to fill with all the other possible things that could go wrong helped to pass the time until the bus for Huddersfield calmly arrived, as scheduled, as if to prove that there had been nothing to worry about.

This journey took me into my third county of the day and across the Pennines. Somewhere below me were some of the longest canal tunnels known to man and around me a mixture of terraced housing marching up the hillsides, redundant chimneys rising from valley floors and a scattering of communication masts. Ahead lay a similar mixture of elegant townscapes, industrial heritage, open country and micro-breweries. I was looking forward to spending a day or two exploring all that this fascinating area had to offer.

Days 9 and 10

Exploring Hudraed's Lands

14th and 15th September

And so I had a couple of days to explore in and around what must once have been, if I was getting the hang of this place-name thing at all, 'a field belonging to a man called Hudder'. 'Open land of a man named Hudraed', as it turned out from the Dictionary.

A lot has happened on Hudraed's open land and he would be forgiven for not recognising the place if he turned up today.

Humans were active in the area long before Hudraed arrived, with some evidence of this dating from over 4000 years ago being found on Castle Hill. This was also the site of an Iron Age hill fort. A fort suggests the need for security and a propensity towards war and violence. It's probably fair to say that the tribes in Britain had such a propensity. When the Romans arrived in this part of the world they certainly found this to be true, especially since this was Brigantia, the territory of the Brigantes. If you wanted to pick on a pre-Roman Celtic people to mess with, the Brigantes would have been a bad choice. As far as the Romans were concerned the Brigantes were revolting in more ways than one.

So, how do we get to the arrival of a chap like Hudraed? At some point, the Romans had had enough of Britain, or perhaps it's better to say that Britain was proving to be a bridge too far. The Roman Empire was corrupting and crumbling from the centre. There were attacks on various fronts in the East and at some point the troops here were pulled out. With them gone, the North of England was prone to attacks from the Picts from Scotland and the Scots from Ireland. The locals still sought help from Rome but when this was not forthcoming they turned to Angles, Jutes and Saxons. These people agreed to help see off the Picts and Scots but they liked the place so much they decided to stay, effectively conquering the very people they had come to help. Don't worry though; it wasn't long before their plans went pear-shaped thanks to our old friends the Norsemen.

Hudraed, or Hutthare, is possibly an Englishman of that name or he may be a Scandinavian called Hather. Whoever he was, at some point he must have marked off a desirable portion of open land. Following this there would have been the familiar growth and development into village and market town. However, we should really thank sheep for Huddersfield's continued prosperity and certainly for the admirable town we can see today. That is not meant to suggest that the sheep were trained architects, builders and masons. No, sheep were pretty much the same: they stood around eating grass for most of the time. What they did in return for this free food was provide wool. This would have been used for clothing for centuries and was at the heart of early 'cottage' industries. But the eighteenth and nineteenth centuries saw a real boom. The cloth trade became a hugely profitable and global industry.

Huddersfield was where the money was and this is still evident in the fine civic buildings and public spaces. As an indication of the extent of this significant architecture, the town claims the third highest number of listed buildings of any town or city in the UK. Huddersfield had a good reputation for its architecture early on. Friedrich Engels wrote in 1844 that it was the 'handsomest by far of all the factory towns in Lancashire and Yorkshire by reason of its charming situation and modern architecture.' What was 'modern' for Engels is 'Victorian' for us and the many buildings from these times are certainly very fine. The positive attitude to architecture seems to have continued into later periods too.

A few significant buildings were drawn to my attention. In order of age they are the railway station, built 1846–47, the library and art gallery (built 1937–1940) and Queensgate Market (1970). The station, on St George's Square, is an imposing neo-classical building with a wonderful façade and portico. The façade was 'the most splendid in England' according to the poet John Betjeman. Outside is a statue of former Prime Minister Harold Wilson, who was born here. The art gallery is in the 'stripped classical style' and is adorned with some wonderful stone figures and relief panels. Among the delights inside are works by L S Lowry, Francis Bacon and Henry Moore. The much more recent Queensgate Market is an intriguing structure with its own adornment—an extensive ceramic sculpture called 'Articulation in Movement'. The building has many admirers, and who can blame them, considering that the interior has 21 free-standing asymmetrical hyperbolic paraboloids?

Huddersfield has plenty to offer in the town but there are also many delights to be had along the Huddersfield Canal up the Colne Valley with plenty of variety along the different stretches. At certain points are reminders of the boom years of the textile industry such as the imposing Titanic Mill near Linthwaite. The word 'Titanic' has become virtually synonymous with the ill-fated passenger liner and the mill acquired its name partly because it was completed in the same year as that ship was launched. However, even without the ship, the name would suit because this truly is a 'gigantic' structure. Rows of twenty or so large windows climb solidly up its generous six storeys creating what would have been the closest achievable equivalent to a wall of glass. This abundance of windows was needed to allow in the maximum amount of light so the mill workers could see what they were doing. All this ingress of light perhaps helps to persuade developers that old mills are perfect for conversion into modern, luxury apartments. It seems that such a transformation is what the future holds, at least for the Titanic Mill.

There were a few canal boats on the waters but none more interesting for me than the "Moonraker" at Slaithwaite. This is not just a boat but a floating tearoom and a cup of tea and a bun set me up for the walk on to Marsden, a large village at the head of the valley. If anywhere could be said to 'nestle' in the hills, Marsden would surely qualify. It is in a great setting and has lovely features, many enhanced by the fact that the Colne River variously glides, burbles, drifts and tumbles through town to be crossed here and there by dark-coloured sturdy bridges. Amongst the town's smaller shops and houses, two buildings stand out. The first is the Mechanics Hall with its distinctive red and white clock tower. This fine building opened in 1861, the cost of £2,500 having been found through public subscription. It reminds us of a time when education wasn't the universal experience it is today. The institute provided an education thanks to volunteer teachers. They taught a range of subjects including reading and writing, maths and science, geography and singing.

There would have been singing, too, in St Bartholomew's Church, the second dominant building. This dates from the turn of the twentieth century and was built to accommodate 800 people, which hints at how strong church attendance was at the time. It is a substantial affair sitting quietly in peaceful grounds at the end of town.

Above the town is Butterley Reservoir and beyond that Marsden Moor, lovingly cared for by the National Trust and described by them as 'a vast swathe of unspoilt valleys, reservoirs, peaks and crags'.

Make your way across the moor and you are back in Lancashire, and for a very long time that was the way to get there. Then somebody had a cunning plan. To find out about the plan we needed to carry on past a series of locks up to Standedge.

All was revealed here as the canal disappeared into the longest (at 5029m), highest (at 196m above sea level) and deepest (at 194m) canal tunnel in Britain. The construction of such things as the Standedge Tunnel tend to leave me somewhat in awe. Looking into the darkness of the tunnel I wondered at the hardship of those who were actually at the rock face as this hole was slowly bored through the hill. I wondered too about the boatmen who had to get barges through it once it was operational. To keep costs down, there was no towpath. The horses that pulled the barges were taken over the top of the hill. This left only one other means of getting a barge from one side to the other. The boatmen had to 'leg' it. This involved lying on boards laid across the boats and 'walking' on the tunnel roof.

To find out how bad that is, lie on the floor for a few minutes and 'walk' with your legs in the air. It's pretty dreadful, even without having to propel a fully laden barge. It's best to do this in private as anyone who sees you will think you are weird. There's plenty to see and do at Standedge, including a wander round the Visitor Centre and, if you time it right, a trip through the tunnel. It's a fascinating insight into what is a bit of an engineering marvel.

Back in Marsden, the wood-panelled interior of The Riverhead pub provided a comfortable setting for another chance to experience something locally produced. And you can't get much more local than a beer brewed in the cellar downstairs.

Day 11

To Danish Yorvik

16*th* September

I'm on the road again, on the X6 to Leeds at a cost of £1.20.

We soon passed through Fartown. You don't need a dictionary of place names to work that one out. Here was the intriguingly named Slubbers' Arms pub. 'Slubbers' Arms' sounds a bit like a complaint, similar to 'Housemaid's Knee'. "I can't come into work today, I've got Slubber's Arms". Slubbing is, apparently, the ancient art of drawing out and twisting fibres before they are spun. A few hours of that and I should think it would be more than the slubbers' arms that would need resting at the end of the day.

The surroundings became increasingly built-up courtesy of residential property developers, industrialists, retailers, storage providers and restaurateurs. The gentle transportation of the Huddersfield canals has given way to busy roads, and we crossed over the M62 on our way to Brighouse. Images slipped by in quick succession: a glimpse of a river between the buildings, a glint of sun from the surface of a canal, the broad sweep of car park before the shiny Sainsbury's supermarket, the desolate façade of a boarded-up carpet warehouse, weeds and vegetation encroaching on disused railway lines, and the bizarre giant-turtle shape of the Richard Dunn Sports Centre. Suddenly we were in Bradford. As a welcome, Sahib's Restaurant tempted me to eat as much as I could for a mere £5.50 but sadly the offer was only available between 5 and 7pm.

Bradford was originally a Saxon settlement around a 'broad ford' which crossed a stream called Bradford Beck. As far back as people can remember there have been sheep covering the countryside around Bradford. Anyone who's done any walking around there will know what the sheep have been covering it with. The locals have been able to forgive them because they have provided plenty of wool, not to mention the occasional roast dinner. As was the case with Huddersfield, the wool has been the making of Bradford. The sheep that have always been there and always provided the wool meant that the early settlers could make nice warm clothes to keep out the Yorkshire cold. They could make so many that they could sell them elsewhere. They could also make woollen cloth and begin import and export businesses and so on. The place became increasingly important but it was biding its time, waiting for the industrial revolution. When this finally arrived Bradford was ready. By the middle of the nineteenth century it had gone from being a quiet rural market town to become a thumping great industrialised urban area.

And thumping great industrialised urban areas were full of confident, optimistic and prosperous people who wanted to build things that showed how confident, optimistic and prosperous they were. Bradford has several examples, including the impressive St George's Hall. This was built as a concert hall and meeting rooms and was officially opened on 29th August 1853 by Queen Victoria and Prince Albert. A year later Charles Dickens gave his first reading of Bleak House here and 149 years later I went past it on a bus. Amazing!

Bradford is often said to have been 'the wool capital of the world' with estimates of two-thirds of Britain's wool production happening here at the industry's high point. Amidst all this prosperity and confidence it is easy to forget the workers, often children. In the nineteenth century the Earl of Shaftesbury was a leader in campaigning for shorter working hours, and in a speech calling for a bill to relieve the conditions of textile workers in India he referred to his experiences in Britain. Amongst other things he refuted the argument that the work was light:

Light! Why, no doubt, much of it is light, if measured by the endurance of some three or four minutes. But what say you,

*my Lords, to a continuity of toil, in a standing posture, in
a poisonous atmosphere, during 13 hours, with 15 minutes
of rest? Why, the stoutest man in England, were he made,
in such a condition of things, to do nothing during the
whole of that time but be erect on his feet and stick pins in
a pincushion, would sink under the burden. What say you,
then, of children... children of the tenderest years? Why, they
become stunted, crippled, deformed, useless. I speak what
I know—I state what I have seen. When I visited Bradford
in Yorkshire, in 1838, being desirous to see the condition of
the children—for I knew that they were employed at very
early ages in the worsted business... I asked for a collection
of cripples and deformities. In a short time more than 80
were gathered in a large courtyard. They were mere samples
of the entire mass. I assert without exaggeration that no
power of language could describe the varieties, and I may
say, the cruelties, in all these degradations of the human
form. They stood or squatted before me in all the shapes of
the letters of the alphabet. This was the effect of prolonged
toil on the tender frames of children at early ages.*

*When I visited Bradford, under the limitation of
hours some years afterwards, I called for a similar
exhibition of cripples; but, God be praised! there was
not one to be found in that vast city. Yet the work of
these poor sufferers had been light, if measured by
minutes, but terrific when measured by hours.*[*]

George Orwell would later point out the invisible nature of
miners in his *Road to Wigan Pier*. They provided the energy for
the nation to function but did so in terrible conditions and at
great cost to their health. Yet they were invisible. Out of sight
and out of mind. The same could be said of the child labourers
in the mills of Bradford and elsewhere in the 1800s. We have
sorted that out now. There are no child labourers in Bradford's
mills. There are no working mills. Bradford's silent mills made

---

* From "The Benefit of the Factory Legislation" [Hansard's
Parliamentary Debates, Apr. 4, 1879, 3rd Series, vol.CCXLV, *pp*.355–356.]

me wonder where in the world today's textile child labourers are, working 13 hours bent over a loom. We haven't really sorted out the problem. We've moved it.

By the 1970s the industrial ground beneath Bradford's feet was severely shaken. The textile industry declined and there was a need to diversify. Today the town seems to be reinventing itself, taking advantage perhaps of the proximity of places like Ilkley Moor which is on the doorstep, and the fact that here we are in 'Bronte Country', where the famous sisters lived and wrote.

I was not destined to experience the wild and windy moors but rather the delights of Leeds, with my expectations raised by H.V. Morton.

> *When a man looks at Leeds he realises what a*
> *blessing a really big fire can be to a city.* *

What can he mean? Henry Canova Vollam (H.V.) Morton was a journalist and travel writer and this observation on Leeds was in a small pamphlet published by the Labour Party in 1933. It was his frank opinion that:

> *the whole of Leeds should be scrapped and rebuilt. It is*
> *the creation of the big commercial booms of the nine-*
> *teenth century, when no one cared for anything but profit*
> *and exploitation. It is a nasty, dirty old money box.* †

That didn't sound promising. He was, of course, describing a different Leeds, a Leeds of row upon row of back to back housing—'slums'. His horror was partly due to the poor quality of the houses and sanitary provisions and partly due to the scale of the problem. He notes that in 1920 there were 72000 of these 'horrible houses', and a commitment from the local authorities

---

* "What I saw in the slums", a Labour Party Pamphlet from 1933 by H V Morton. Reprinted in *Writing Englishness 1900–1950: An Introductory Sourcebook on National Identity*, Judy Giles and Tim Middleton, Routledge, 1995.
† *Ibid.*

to remove 400 a year. He pointed out that the plan, if adhered to, would lead to a far healthier-looking town 'in about 180 years'.

Now, I admit that I didn't do an exhaustive tour of Leeds and there could be plenty of substandard housing but I determinedly readjusted my rose-coloured spectacles and made sure they wouldn't slip down my nose as I explored the city centre. There was a grand scale to the predominantly Victorian architecture and a sense of space and freedom enhanced perhaps by the almost traffic-free feel to the centre. Not much sign of a 'nasty, dirty old money box' here. The confidence which must have inspired the architects and designers, and indeed the municipal officers, of the past still emanated from the grander buildings, including the Town Hall. Even shopping, or more correctly in my case walking past shops, was uplifting in the elegant and magnificent covered arcades and the corn exchange. Actually, I did need to do some shopping, searching as I was for a new sleeping bag.

I had with me a rather sad and depressed (as in flat) Moon Bag. This item had been a good and faithful servant but was now doing little to keep me warm at night in the tent. I had experienced the cold in both Newbury and Burnham Deepdale. My soft southern brain told me that my equally soft southern body would not fare well as I headed into the frozen north.

At the camping shop I told the assistant my problem and showed him my Moon Bag. He was thrilled to see one of these, as if it was an exhibit from a camping museum.

"Great in their day," he mused, "but not much good to you now."

"Would you get rid of it for me?" I queried.

"I could do that," he offered, "but why don't you hang on to it? It would make a good cover for your surfboard."

In the glow produced by the fact that this guy could think for one moment that I looked like the sort of person who would not only own a surfboard, but also use one and therefore need a cover for it, I failed to indicate that I was neither. I left him deluded by saying simply, "Yeah, good idea."

Now, you may think I was almost lying. But the idea was indeed a good one. A Moon Bag would undoubtedly make a good cover for a surfboard. The fact that I would not be using it in this manner is a completely different issue. Having been given the notion that the Moon Bag could have an alternative use, I decided to keep it and use it as a mattress, another layer between me and the cold, hard ground.

I liked the shop man a lot, after all he thought I looked like a surfer dude. Personally, I think I probably looked more like a serf; a person who may have wandered around in the eighth century when the local area was known as Loidis.

The name changed over time to Ledes, which gets a mention in the Domesday Book. By 1207, the Lord of the Manor was establishing a New Town. This was hardly anything like other new towns such as Telford or Stevenage. For a start, people quite liked it. It was centred on a river crossing and a bridge and didn't have miles of winding footpaths going nowhere or endless rows of bland housing. In fact, we might say calling it a town at all was pushing it a bit. There would only have been a few houses, a church and probably a pub or two. On the other hand, all the services you'd need would have been there, such as a butcher, a baker, a candlestick maker. Probably a 'Clogs the Apothecary' as well. There would *not* have been a post office, but where can you find one of those these days, anyway?

The familiar northern-town story of a booming textile industry follows, along with the construction of the Leeds to Liverpool Canal which effectively joined up the East and West coasts, courtesy of navigable rivers including the Ouse, Humber, Aire and Calder. Before you knew it Leeds was a water-based communications hub and a centre of commerce, textiles and engineering. After the boom years came the bust and Leeds suffered as the industry nose-dived. It is making a brave recovery and I'd really enjoyed my time here. To me the town felt lively and vibrant, busy and almost, dare I say it, exciting.

My next trip would be to the ancient estate of yew trees, which was once home to the Brigantes, had become a strategic Roman garrison, then an important town for our friends the Danes, a centre for the medieval wool trade, a hub for the railway system and now, thanks to all this rich heritage, a major tourist destination.

The day was going well. The journey from Huddersfield to Leeds had been straightforward and the next proved to be equally easy to arrange and was smoothly executed courtesy of the Yorkshire Coastliner service. This is a fantastic service, with frequent buses. As the name suggests, most of these will take you to the coast at such places as Whitby, Scarborough or Bridlington. I planned to disembark before reaching the coast. Perhaps by way of compensation, we first sailed through Seacroft, although the name seems to have been stretching the use of the word 'sea', since it seems to mean 'an enclosure by a pond'. Next we took in Tadcaster and cruised through Copmanthorpe, and after only fifty minutes or so of leaving Leeds, I disembarked near the station in the fabulous city of York.

I bought a street map from the Tourist Information Centre and perused this over an expensive but very welcome cup of coffee, searching out possibilities for accommodation and, ideally, camping. As my gaze wandered over the cartographic streets and down the river, my eye fell on Rowntree Park and then just above it the unexpected words 'Caravan Park'. This seemed to be remarkably close to the city centre and, if they allowed tents, would be an ideal base for an overnight stop.

I hot-footed down the River Ouse and found, to my delight, a small caravan *and camping* site. I established a pitch tucked into a cosy little field, hedged off from the surrounding houses and yet just metres from the river. It was a fantastic location being such a short walk from the city centre. On talking to the manageress I discovered that I would not have been so keen had I been here just two weeks earlier. Apparently the whole site had been under two feet of water following a flood. I let my gaze rest on the river for a while and decided it didn't look like it was going to repeat this performance, so happily left all my stuff in the tent and went to explore.

I needed to eat and an obvious choice for local food would be chocolate since this had long been manufactured here by one of the UK's favourite household names, before it was taken over by another household name.

Rowntree's was founded in 1862 by Henry Isaac Rowntree who was joined by his brother Joseph in 1869. Joseph was a

Quaker and a philanthropist who combined his ability to turn the company into the fourth largest exporter in the country by 1904 with his desire to see improvements in the life of 'the common man'. He translated this desire into reality by providing good working conditions in his factories, establishing the housing 'experiment' of New Earswick garden village, introducing adult education to combat illiteracy, and founding one of the first company pension schemes. A number of charitable trusts ensure the continuation of these great works.

These are great legacies indeed, but I was currently concerned with the edible variety. I could have chosen from any number of delights that have a long and distinguished heritage of their own such as Fruit Pastilles (available since 1881!) or KitKat, Aero and Smarties which have all been around since the 1930s.

Chocolate may have been an obvious choice but perhaps not all that sensible. I decided I needed something slightly more filling.

The taking of afternoon tea is perhaps our closest equivalent to the oriental tea rituals, since both serve as occasions which focus the senses and heighten the pleasure. It's a fairly elaborate, whimsical and even slightly eccentric process which surrounds the otherwise mundane business of having a cup of tea and a bun. The whole experience is further enhanced when it happens in a place like Betty's Tea Rooms which I found nearby. I wasn't sure who Betty was or if she even existed. All I knew was that I was ready for a bit of nostalgic indulgence. Drinking tea and eating cake is elevated to an altogether higher plain when consumed amid art deco elegance, wooden panelling and ornate mirrors. The experience was one of finding a little anachronistic haven within a more complicated and worrying reality. Who needs Class A drugs when you've got English Breakfast tea and a slice of Lemon Drizzle?

After the treat it was time to find out about York. It has Roman remnants from its time as Eboracum. This was a garrison town and later a provincial capital. Under the Saxons the town became known as Eoforwic and was the capital of the Northumbrian kingdom. Any fortifications set up by the

Romans had been rather neglected by the time the Danes turned up in 866. They didn't meet much resistance when they took the city. They were led by Ivar the Boneless, whom you may remember as the marauding warrior who led an invasion into East Anglia. He had wandered North with his army doing what they did best: raping, pillaging, conferring strange-sounding place names on innocent villages and establishing retail outlets for pork-related products. He had with him his brother Halfdan or it may have been his half-brother Dan. They were heading to Northumbria desirous of laying their hands on Aella, the King of Northumbria who had made the unwise move of murdering their father, Radnor Lodbrok, the famous bokmaker. When they found Aella he apparently endured 'the blood eagle' ritual execution. This elaborate piece of brutality seems to involve having an eagle drawing carved into your back before your ribs are removed from your spine and your lungs cut out. I don't know about Ivar being Boneless but his victims would have been.

So in 866 the Danes captured and plundered York or Jorvik, which became the capital of the Danelaw, the half of England where Danish law held sway and everyone ate bacon. This period of the town's history is extensively covered in the Jorvik Centre.

The Danes were in charge pretty much all the way into the tenth century when they were finally expelled by Anglo-Saxons who in turn took a hiding from the Normans in 1068 when William entered the city and built a castle. The Danes weren't done yet and they returned in 1069 along with local rebels. The Normans took the inspired step of saying "If we can't have York, you can't either," and they burnt it to the ground. The period between the end of 1069 and early 1070 saw 'The Harrying of the North' in which William laid waste to pretty much the whole region, burning farmland and property and killing all who got in his way.

The medieval period saw York thriving as part of the wool trade and elements of York's layout and architecture from this time can still be seen. As it was on a major route between London and Edinburgh it developed a long-term relationship with transport and became a centre for associated industries, especially the railways.

After my tea I explored the maze of little streets nearby whose names are somehow so evocative of the past: Little Stonegate, Swinegate, Patrick Pool, and Shambles. This last is a narrow, medieval street complete with half-timbered housing whose upper storeys reach out to one another across the thoroughfare. This was once the 'street of butchers' and the building design reflects this. The wide window ledges at street level allowed for the display of meat and the overhanging buildings kept it all out of the sun. One assumes all the blood and gore was occasionally washed down the street. This and the interlacing streets in the surrounding area are now tourist heaven with all manner of gift shops and eateries. I like these places. There's a human scale and intimacy sometimes missing from larger, planned, modern precincts.

York is also famous for the Minster, its cathedral church, and this was another real treat. Like other great cathedral buildings, York Minster stops you in your tracks. Well, it did me. Its great Gothic edifice rises up stone on stone, carving upon carving, until the details are lost in the high reaches of the towers. I did the only appropriate thing. I stood and stared. Then I did some more standing and staring. Then I went inside to be silenced again by the high vaulted ceiling of the nave, the carvings of the quire screen and the apocalyptic vision of The Great East Window. Added to these visual treats was the soundtrack provided by a choir rehearsal. It was, well, heavenly.

Outside it was yet another splendid evening and the sun brought out the best in the stone of the buildings. I bought fish and chips which I counted as another local regional food. You might think this was stretching the definition, but my justifications were firstly that there was a lot of fishing going on off the Yorkshire coast and, secondly, Harry Ramsden. He opened his first stall in Guiseley, West Yorkshire in 1928 and so a fish and chip supper has a long and proud association with Yorkshire.

I watched the impressive River Ouse gliding through the broad channel it has steadily cut to divide the city. The sinking sun was leaving the waters a steely blue-grey but was still managing to bring out the best in a terrace of three-storey, creeper-embraced town houses. In the dimming light the quietness of the evening took over. The river tour landing stages were empty and a few well-mannered diners populated the eateries under the Ouse Bridge. I made my way back to the camp site, my tent, my new sleeping bag and sleep.

Day 12

Gannin furtha north

17th September

I was awake quite early and into the now familiar camping routine of groaning, stretching, showering, shaving, breakfasting, tent taking-down and bag packing-up. With all this done quite quickly I had time to make my way into town and explore a small part of the miles of city walls with which York is blessed.

The walls have risen and fallen along with the fortunes of the city's inhabitants. There are still some sections dating from the residency of the Romans although much of this had been neglected by apathetic Anglo-Saxons. The determined Danes developed the defences but the majority of the walls available today are of medieval masonry from the twelfth to the fourteenth centuries. Walking the city walls is another treat and I enjoyed the opportunity to take in some of the exclusive views, which provide a completely different perspective on the city, and the chance to rise above the hubbub of the streets.

York was somehow different from other northern towns I'd visited or passed through. Although the city prospered from the wool industry this was perhaps more as a place of trading than of manufacture. Consequently the great mills that can be found in some other industrial towns are absent here. There was manufacturing, especially of chocolate, and also engineering related to the railways. Even so, York doesn't seem to have such an industrialised feel. Perhaps it was just that the older history of the town—the walls, Minster and medieval streets— left a greater impression on me than marks left by the Industrial Revolution and the reign of Queen Victoria. I liked it all the more for its subdued, almost provincial air. It may not inspire the use of words such as 'vibrant' but perhaps there is a greater possibility for long-term enjoyment here than in places that are constantly lively and racy.

I was developing early morning rituals involving the scanning of timetables which still managed to instil a certain mixture of excitement, anticipation and apprehension. It would start with looking at my Tourist Map and deciding on a place that it would be good to get to. The possibility of managing this was exciting. Next would be the business of finding out how that might be achieved on my chosen transport. This was when apprehension could set in. What if I couldn't get where I wanted to? Simple. Go somewhere else. Get to the next place another way. There were always possibilities and solutions. Today I had envisaged a fragmented progress of connecting journeys punctuated by waits at bus stops or in soulless bus stations. I was hoping to make Newcastle, and this was quite a distance. To my delight I discovered that the Stagecoach X90 would take me straight there, quite painlessly in one simple journey. The bus was due to leave at 11.35 and in the interlude I took a coffee at Coopers near the station and had a brief look at a model railway exhibition.

I am not ashamed to admit to having a period of railway modelling in my past which, to the uninitiated, means more than having a train set. No, being a railway modeller means much more. I, with plenty of help from my father, spent hours creating scale worlds of fields, moor and mountain out of crumpled newspapers, chicken wire, papier-mâché and what we decided could be classed as 'old' towels from the airing cupboard. So my modelling past helped me appreciate the exhibition and I happily filled in the time before catching the bus.

I paid my £5.50 and settled down for the 2 hour and 40 minute journey.

I experienced again the rather pleasant feeling that was becoming increasingly familiar, once all possible apprehension had gone. I was safely seated on my bus, I had no more responsibilities or concerns and I knew where I was going. What added a certain *frisson* was that I didn't know the exact route we would take to reach the final destination. The choice of towns and villages through which we would pass would be entirely out of my hands, and I enjoyed the 'pot luck' feeling.

To begin, we headed off on the A19. It was another hot, blue August day and the agricultural community was out in force, harvesters and bailers tracing their regular paths up and down the fields. A tractor pulling a grain-laden wagon slowed our progress for a time before we turned off the main road on a detour to Stillington, originally an estate associated with a man called Styfel. The impression from the bus was of an archetypal English village. Small dwellings gathered around a centrally-placed parish church. There were areas of grass, graceful trees, a pub or two. We pressed on to the market town of Easingwold, formerly known as the high forest land of the family of a man named Esa. The forest may have disappeared but the (now) Georgian town sits comfortably amid the Hambleton Hills and there were good views of these from the bus.

Glorious images of rural England drifted by: rolling hills, neatly partitioned fields, dry-stone walls, distant horizons and patches of woodland. The clear light of the summer brought out the different shades in the predominantly green palette. Even from inside the bus the sense of health and well-being made available by such expansive open areas was palpable.

We were passing through the Vale of York, between what is now the Yorkshire Dales to the west and the North York Moors to the east. The vale was patiently cut by the persistent River Ouse and its tributaries including the Rivers Ure and Swale, and then altered by several glaciations. This has left a mainly flat and wide valley bottom layered with rich alluvial deposits, making it perfect for agriculture.

Large parts of these two upland areas are designated as National Parks, not least because they offer some of the best scenery in the country. They are incredibly popular areas for visitors but are becoming victims of their own success. Most people still visit in the car and this is causing general pollution and also more specific problems for the countryside itself. Cars are parked on road sides causing damage to the verges. To avoid this there is pressure to turn more of the open land into car parks, eating away at the very thing people have driven all that way to see. Views of the scenery itself can be marred by continuous reflections from windscreens and so on where there should be nothing but dry stone walls, sheep, grass and moor. There is an obvious answer of course, and I was sitting in one.

As we approached Thirsk, the White Horse carved into the hillside at Kilburn on the edge of the North York Moors appeared to the right. What is it with these giant chalk animal drawings? This one was dreamt up by a grocer called Thomas Taylor and carried out by John Hodgson, a local schoolmaster who marked it out with the help of his pupils. I can't imagine him getting away with that today. He might be able to justify it if he could identify a 'raft' (I think that's the favoured term) of national curriculum targets that the exercise would meet, and it may even count as a 'cultural' endeavour. But I think the health and safety issues would defeat him. Preparing a risk assessment that didn't give the head teacher heart failure or get the parents lining up at the solicitors would be a real challenge.

Location: Steep embankment on edge of North York Moors
Risk to pupils: Allergic reaction to grass pollens, exposure to pathogens in recently deposited rabbit droppings, falling to their death.

No, it wouldn't happen today. However, the enlightened (or foolishly reckless depending on your HSE stance) Victorians and their schoolchildren went ahead and the horse was completed on 4th November 1857. Will there be any school-pupil assisted artistic monuments for travellers to admire in 150 years time, I wonder? Perhaps not, but historians will be able to look back and marvel at the meteoric rise in educational 'standards' (whatever they are) and teenage pregnancy rates.

The apparent calm and serenity of the distant hills belies the fact that they were once, and still are to a degree, the engines that drove local industries and powered the prosperity of places like Thirsk. The original settlers would have recognised good grazing land when they saw it, not to mention the possibilities for a bit of arable farming as well, despite the fact that the name derives from an Old Scandinavian word *thresk* meaning 'a marsh'. Thirsk not only hosted thriving livestock markets but also boasted many associated traders and craftspeople. The animals provided meat and other produce for sale. They also gave skins and hides for leather and tanning industries. Here also were blacksmiths, farriers and wheelwrights together with carpenters and joiners, all of whom would have found work from the farming industry and the growing population. There were jobs for corn millers too, together with brewers and the public houses that dispensed their products. As the town grew, builders and labourers would have been gainfully employed, and where you have inhabitants you have shops.

It was hard to picture all this activity as I came into Thirsk. Its wide centre, dominated by an impressive clock, announces that it is a market town, and there is no doubt plenty of activity on market days. It seemed as though most, if not all, of the older industries and crafts had disappeared. Thirsk had a saviour in the person of James Herriot who lived and worked here and immortalised the town and its surroundings in his famous 'vet' books. His veterinary surgery is now a popular museum.

We made our unhurried way North beneath ever-blue benevolent skies in and out of places with wonderful names. We even passed through Thornton-le-Beans (bury Bill here!).

The human activity and settlements in this area are so attractive and seemed to 'fit' so well, partly because they have grown almost organically from the land in response to human needs. The dry stone walls are created from material literally taken from the ground and so they do not jar the way bright wooden fences would. The villages and towns are often created from local materials and their streets and buildings have a scale and obvious sense of purpose that relates directly to us as humans. There is nothing overwhelming or 'cold'; the places almost embrace you and welcome you.

This is so different from the situations where we as humans are relegated to a secondary role, subjugated by the demands of traffic flows and freight transportation. Rather than originating, growing and evolving in response to natural demands, so many created environments today seem to be imposed from above or from 'outside'. Market research may show that there is a demand for a hypermarket but the resulting metal box is often plonked onto a former playing field (nice and flat) or uncomfortably juxtaposed with existing architecture. It may be essential to facilitate the movement of 40-tonne articulated juggernauts from the coastal ports to the centrally-located distribution point but we must pay with the loss of open land to a bypass or watch ancient villages, designed to accommodate horse-drawn traffic, slowly blacken and crumble. I'm afraid I fall into the camp of those who dislike much of what 'progress' has produced.

We reached Northallerton, a busy, bustling market town that owes its existence and growth to its position. It was an obvious place for produce to be brought to from the surrounding countryside, and this has been happening for centuries. The town has also found itself on the main route between the north and the south. Roman soldiers marched up and down through here as did the Danes, the Normans, the Scots and the armies of Royalists and Parliamentarians in the Civil War. In more peaceful times, and once personal travel had moved to a certain level of sophistication, the town took on a role as a staging post and 'watering hole'. In the 1700s the town catered for a burgeoning stage coach trade through the provision of inns and hotels which would have enjoyed good business until the coaches were replaced by the railways in the 1840s.

Another group who had marched this way were Scottish. This particular bit of marching was part of a troubling episode from our history involving King David I of Scotland. He was storming down, ostensibly in support of his niece Matilda but also with an eye to increasing his boundaries. You may remember Matilda, she was the one who escaped from a snow-bound Oxford castle in a white dress. To explain further why some angry Scotsmen were marching through Northallerton we need to get a bit more background. Matilda was struggling to assert her claim as rightful heir to the English throne. She had previously done fairly well for herself by marrying Emperor Henry V of Germany. Although this would have produced a few perks, the union did not produce any offspring. Emperor Henry died in 1125 leaving Matilda as a childless widow. She was recalled to the court of her father Henry I. Henry's barons were made to swear to accept her as heir if he died without a male heir. While waiting for Henry I to pop his clogs, she married Geoffrey Plantagenet. This move, combined with the fact that she was a woman, made her an unpopular choice as heir in some quarters. Henry I departed this life in 1135 and things looked set for Matilda to become queen. Henry's nephew Stephen had other plans, namely to be king himself. He achieved this just before Christmas in 1135 but ruled a country with divided loyalties. The Battle of Northallerton, or the Battle of the Standard, was fought on nearby Cowton Moor on 22nd August 1138 as part of the furore surrounding these events. Today the area is more like a nice place for a picnic rather than a pitched battle. If you did spread your blanket on the ground it would be atop the blood of possibly 12,000 Scottish soldiers said to have died that day.

Northallerton itself looked perfectly pleasant and we stopped briefly by the fifteenth century All Saints Parish Church with its imposing, stocky tower.

Pressing on north we passed through predominantly rural landscapes where settlements such as Great and Little Smeaton were dotted around the area along our route. Through Dalton-on-Tees we passed under the railway, the other great transport link to the north. Pulling into Croft-on-Tees, St Peter's Church loomed into view. Nearby, the Croft Rectory has a garden in which Lewis Carroll played as a boy and where he later wrote *Alice in Wonderland*. Another wonderful little curiosity can be found inside the church itself—a carving of the face of a cat. Was this the inspiration for the Cheshire Cat in Carroll's story? If so, it has become part of a story that has permeated popular culture around the globe, an idea which would seem as weird to the sculptor originally responsible as anything Alice might have encountered in Wonderland.

Darlington, our next prominent place, has a special place in history for very different reasons. In the early nineteenth century, Edward Pease, the head of a local Quaker family, decided, with a remarkable piece of prescience, to turn down the idea of constructing a canal for coal shipment. Instead he set in motion events that would lead to Darlington being the birthplace of the railways. Pease employed George Stevenson to design steam locomotives that would run along the railway he sought in preference to the canal. History was made on 27th September 1825 because the train, pulled by Locomotion Number 1, carried not only coal but passengers, the first time this had ever happened in the world. Darlington did not fail to capitalise on the success of the railways and became a major centre for locomotive works, including the North Road Shops. The works opened in 1863 and managed to stay in production for just over 100 years, finally closing in 1966, a testament to the longevity of the railway concept. How much longer the concept will survive remains to be seen. Perhaps we are approaching a time when the true costs of private car ownership, of road freight and the associated road-building programmes will be counted. Perhaps other forms of transport, including the railways, will have a greater role to play.

Next up was Newton Aycliffe, which has its origins in a Saxon settlement amongst an oak forest. From that point it quietly developed as a village with little, perhaps, to draw anyone's attention. This sense of remoteness and lack of notoriety led to its being chosen as the location for two periods of construction which make it quite remarkable.

As the country descended into the depths of war with Nazi Germany, it was clear that the armed forces needed munitions. To provide these you need munitions factories. The government realised that such facilities must be located in places that were away from the threat of aerial bombardments which were such a major part of Nazi strategy. Such places, although remote, also had to be accessible by rail. Aycliffe was chosen because it met both these criteria. Furthermore, local climate and topography meant that the area was often shrouded in mists and fog, providing further protection should the location ever become known to the Germans. Upwards of 17,000 workers, mostly women, made the daily journey to Royal Ordnance Factory (ROF) 59 where they would undertake the dangerous and life-threatening task of filling bullets and shells with explosives and fitting detonators. The 'Aycliffe Angels' may be largely unsung heroes but the factory in which they risked their lives went on to provide an interesting impetus for shaping a new Britain after the war.

The ideas behind turning Aycliffe into Newton Aycliffe were driven by feelings as intense, and aims as laudable, as those of any of the nineteenth century philanthropists such as the Rowntree brothers or Titas Salt. The wartime government needed an encouraging vision of how Britain could be rebuilt after the war as a boost to morale and as a reinvigoration of commitment to success. Lord Beveridge was an economist and social reformer who was asked to prepare a report which would guide just such a vision. He saw that five great 'giants' oppressed the people and stood in the way of reconstruction: Want, Disease, Squalor, Ignorance and Idleness. In his vision, these giants would be defeated through the provision of Social Security benefits, a National Health Service, free education for everybody, high quality council houses and full employment. The Social Insurance and Allied Services report would later be developed into what we know as the Welfare State which has shaped life in Britain since the end of the 1940s.

Beveridge's ideas needed physical expression and this was provided in the shape of new towns with the one in the north being built here at Newton Aycliffe. The choice of location was perhaps a mixture of the pragmatic (there were these large redundant factory buildings and poor farmland on which to build houses) and the principled (the area having a good deal of poor quality housing from which residents could be rehoused). Beveridge was the first chairman of the Aycliffe Development Corporation and he hoped his dreams of a classless welfare state would be realised here. The new town would see the end of unemployment and its miserable bedfellows poverty and squalor. The Master Plan envisaged workers and managers living happily side by side in well-constructed council properties, set in areas of green where children could happily and safely play away from the roads. Nurseries would mind children while mothers shopped. Obviously, those were the days when that was what mothers were expected to do. Residents could keep fit in the parks or at the sports stadium, be entertained in the theatre and cinema or enjoy themselves in the dance hall. Visitors would be able to stay in the city centre's luxury hotel or relax in one of the state-run pubs. It was a 'dream town' and 'a bold experiment', according to the newspapers of the time. It is still there but is perhaps not quite a 'dream town', as originally envisaged. For example, I don't know how well the workers and managers get on and how close to one another they live.

The towns where we had stopped off earlier—at Northallerton, Darlington and our next, Ferryhill—were all also stopping off points of one of the most iconic workers' actions of all time. They were all on the route of the Jarrow crusade.

In the 1930s the world was burdened with a depression. Heavy industries were among the hardest hit in this country and areas that depended largely on these for employment suffered most. Jarrow, north east of Newcastle, was being brought to its knees. By 1936 unemployment was running at 70% here, mainly because the major employer for the town, Palmers shipyard, had closed down the previous year. The population was trapped in poor housing with little money for food or fuel and faced greater risks of illness and premature demise. It is perhaps hard for us and all our instant communication to conceive that this situation could be happening in one part of the country while other parts, notably the south, seemed to be in ignorance. And yet that seems to have been the case and it was partly to bring a greater awareness of the situation to a wider group that a march was organised that would see 200 men walk the 300 miles to London. As well as drawing attention to the plight of the people of Jarrow, the marchers would be presenting a petition which sought government intervention. The marchers successfully reached London and won general public sympathy but failed to provoke a useful response from the government. Rejuvenation would have to wait for the outbreak of a World War.

It was market day at Ferryhill and it appeared busy and vibrant as a result. Its history and development are down to local coal deposits and mining. The Dean and Chapter Colliery and Mansfield Colliery were together employing over 5000 men in 1941, providing fuel for the war effort. You wouldn't have known, looking at the place today. Evidence of similar industry showed up in the spoil heaps of the Aycliffe quarry and later the Thrislington Lime works. We reached the village of West Cornforth where the view towards Spennymoor hinted at the agricultural landscape that we would pass through on our way north. The balance of rural and urban landscape was in favour of the former, until Chester-le-Street and the built environment began to gain ground. The battle was completely lost by the time we approached Gateshead under the watchful gaze of the Angel of the North, Anthony Gormley's steel icon. Rail yards and industrial units lay beneath Victorian warehouses as we pushed through, bounded the Tyne with a brief view of the famous bridge to our right and finally entered Newcastle.

It had been a long journey but a very straightforward way of travelling across so great a distance. I was saddened, though not particularly surprised, to hear that the service was soon to be discontinued. I could understand why; I had not been alone on the bus but it had hardly been packed out. Here was a case of the common 'use it or lose it' prophecy bearing out its unfortunate fulfilment.

Newcastle and its neighbour across the river, Gateshead, are being transformed into a new vibrant 'visitor destination' imaginatively called NewcastleGateshead. This clever re-branding involves moving the name of the town on the southern bank of the river (Gateshead) into a position such that the beginning abuts the end of the name of the city on the northern bank (Newcastle). Very clever. And very exciting. NewcastleGateshead is full of an exciting blend of the modern and the historic, exciting shopping and exciting nightlife. You can hardly move for exciting architecture, pubs, restaurants, galleries, clubs and public art. Wow! Zing! Capow!

Actually, I was largely ignorant of this most famous town and I was looking forward to remedying that, if only to a small degree. I knew Newcastle had a bridge, I had heard about the pointlessness of 'taking coals to Newcastle' and I had enjoyed Newcastle Brown Ale off and on for many a year. I did not know much more than that when I stepped off the bus outside the Eldon Square shopping precinct.

The city takes its name from a New Castle which stretches the meaning of the word 'new' to extremes since it was constructed by the Normans in 1080. The history-insensitive railway entrepreneurs of the nineteenth century demolished most of it to make way for their tracks.

There *is* history here but I sensed that the current burghers were not pressing this in their advertising. Perhaps they felt that the area needed regeneration and rebranding, and this should not be begrudged. Like many other places in the north, Newcastle has seen the rug of traditional industries pulled from beneath its feet. One such industry was coal.

A clue as to the long-standing significance of coal to the area is in the fact that a 'pointless exercise' was first described by reference to the futility of taking coals to Newcastle as long ago as 1538. Newcastle was already shipping 15 000 tonnes per year in 1378! The Northumbrian coal field was the driver for the mining and associated industries and it kept it all running until June 1994 when the Wearmouth Colliery closed. The extraction industry that had taken Newcastle into the top five of the 1372 chart of "England's Wealthiest Towns" and helped the city (along with shipbuilding, iron and salt-making) to develop vibrant ports, was no more. Losing all those crucial economic foundations must have been a pretty heavy blow. The sterling efforts of the city at making a come-back inspire admiration and deserve support.

Having found accommodation in the YHA annexe at Gurney House I was able to explore a bit of the city. Celia Fiennes seemed to think that Newcastle 'most resembles London of any place in England' because its buildings were 'lofty and large' its streets 'broad and handsome' and many of them had 'fine Cunduits of water'. I don't know about resembling London but it was certainly lively, there were broad and handsome streets, even if they were now devoid of cunduits.

I retraced my steps back down Haymarket and Percy Street to Eldon Square and its associated Shopping Centre, an obvious focal point for the town. If we've always been 'a nation of shopkeepers' it seems we are keeping up the tradition. Shopping centres are not necessarily top of my list of places to see in a town and for some they are an anathema but if you have to shop there are worse places to do it than here. It's bright and clean and conditionally aired. It's easy to be a bit sniffy about this sort of facility but there was a relaxed feel to the place, people were socialising as well as shopping and it wasn't simply about consumerism.

In Eldon Square is a fine statue of St George slaying the dragon. As an indication that the local people do not simply accept blanket modernisation, there was apparently an outcry in the 1970s when the council wanted this monument moved. Another popular landmark is nearby at the head of Grey Street. This is Grey's Monument, Newcastle's answer to Nelson's Column. The monument takes the form of a statue of Lord Grey which stands on a 41 metre column. It was erected in 1838 to commemorate the Great Reform Act of 1832. And what a great reform act it was. It dramatically altered the representation of the people through a new voting system. It altered the places which would be eligible for putting forward an MP. All very worthy stuff, I'm sure, but whether this alone is sufficient cause to build a monument to the man is perhaps questionable. However, think of his Lordship's contribution to the tea drinking fraternity and there can be no doubt, for he has given his name to 'Earl Grey', that popular black tea delicately flavoured with oil of bergamot. Name me one of our politicians today who can lay claim to as great a contribution to society as this. You can't, can you? Is it any surprise that we get ourselves into such a national mess when our MPs aren't thinking enough about tea?

The area around the monument is apparently a popular spot for buskers, other street performers, activists and religious speakers. While I was there a young woman was explaining how her faith had freed her from a heroin addiction. I think her faith had also given her considerable bottle since her audience consisted of a small group of unreceptive and apparently quite angry young men who spent the time shouting abuse at her.

The urban setting around the monument is generous and expansive, with three and four storey terraces radiating out from a wide, open area. The impressive three-domed Central Exchange Building forms an important part of the streetscape and houses the Central Arcade, a lovely example of this kind of shopping facility, complete with tiled floors and a high glass barrel-vaulted roof. It all looked clean and cared for and spoke of a civic pride. I walked down Highbridge and through Groat Market before passing by St Nicholas Cathedral. Although this may not have competed with larger cathedrals such as York or Wells, it still struck me as a fine building, especially in view of its main feature—the Lantern Tower built in 1448. Hard by the railway are the Black Gate and Castle Keep, the remnants of the Norman 'new' castle. The Keep is a strong square tower and is enough for the imagination to begin a reconstruction of the original building. It must have been an impressive and imposing sight as it stood guard over the strategic river crossing below.

Down to the Millennium Bridge, a great structure whose walkway is a sweeping curve, balanced by another which stood out against the sky. The whole thing can tip to allow for particularly tall river traffic. From here I admired the newly converted Baltic Centre for Contemporary Arts across the river in Gateshead. This solid industrial building, once the Baltic Flour Mills, has classic lines that were somehow reminiscent of Battersea Power Station. It was a landmark building and made a bold statement about regeneration and renewal. Having taken in modern shopping centres, bits of old castle, a converted flour mill, ancient bell tower and fragments of the old town walls, I reassessed my first impressions of the town. It was seeking to be determinedly modern but was perhaps not completely oblivious to the treasures of its past.

As the afternoon light faded and turned slowly into evening I realised that all the activity and 'life' that I had witnessed in the afternoon was simply a warm-up act for Newcastle's 'big number'—a neet oot on the toon. As the working day ended and the evening out took hold, greater numbers of young ladies appeared in their posh frocks and mini-skirts, clip-clopping on high heels down the streets. Their male counterparts appeared in shirt sleeves, smart trousers and shiny shoes. All were

111

looking suitably well-groomed to comply with the required dress codes displayed in the bars and pubs to which they were heading, flowing down to the Quayside almost as if caught in one of Celia Fiennes's Cunduits. When Celia was here she had looked down on the 'whole river and shipps in the harbour'. The Quayside which would once have been the stevedore's domain was now bright with bars and belonged to those in serious pursuit of a 'good time'. The bars' doors were invariably open, though guarded by large men in sharp suits. A hubbub of animated chatter drifted out over thumping bass lines.

I stood on the Millennium Bridge as walkers and cyclists made their separate ways to and fro. This is a good spot from which to view the river and the older bridges: The High Level Bridge and the Tyne Bridge. This latter is the city's most iconic structure, instantly recognisable, drawing visitors from far and wide. It must also be the sight that stirs a returning Geordie's heart, letting them know they are home. The shapes shifted in the changing light, patterns of shadows deepening and darkening. Lights were illuminated and began to cast a different kind of spell.

After gazing at the river and the bridges long enough to feel the chill of evening and the beginnings of hunger, I retraced my steps towards town. The animated atmosphere held out the promise of an enjoyable evening. To help things go with a swing, Mr Fireman, the 'Ultimate Party Machine', arrived on the Quayside. Mr Fireman's vehicle of choice was a retired fire engine from which a group of girls emerged. They tottered off to a nearby bar to top up their alcohol levels.

I was hungry and was tempted away from my 'regional speciality' idea by El Torero, an attractive-looking Spanish restaurant that promised me all manner of delights. Britain has been very open to culinary influences and ideas from far and wide. Indian and Chinese restaurants are found in almost every town of any size. The Yellow Pages now divides its restaurant pages up into regional categories: Italian, Thai, Turkish and so on. A benefit of this is that we can experience all these wonderful foods on our doorsteps. You can eat a fabulous Spanish meal in the heart of an English town.

It doesn't seem to work the other way round. Find an English restaurant in a Spanish town and you will realise it is not there to entice the locals to try out tasty delights from the finest of English cuisine. No, it will more than likely be there to satisfy the holidaying Brit who cannot go for a week without some keg beer and a meal of pie and chips, preferably consumed while watching football on a widescreen TV. I'm sorry, I know I shouldn't reinforce erroneous and grotesque stereotypes.

El Torero, where I sat and savoured, would have adequately met the needs of chorizo-starved or paella-deprived Spanish nationals. It also offered me a brief taste of Spain. I enjoyed *Papas a lo pobre*, *Lomitos con ajos* and *Arroz con pollo "Mama Antonio"*, which were as delicious and unusual as they sound. I opened myself up to the whole experience; the lighting, the décor, the wine, the lovers sharing tapas, the music. All in all it was a rather exotic way to pass the evening as Newcastle slowly faded from my consciousness and eventually seemed a very long way away. At day's end, I returned, heavy and happy, to my YHA bed.

Day 13

The only way is up

18ᵗʰ September

My next target destination lay 56 miles (91 km) to the north as the crow flies and considerably more as the bus drives. I needed to cross Northumberland and in my mind this was remote and rural. I was not sure how many buses there would be and where they would go. I feared I might struggle to find connections or wind up in places where there was one bus every two days.

The news in the modern, bustling bus station could not have been better or more remarkable. My timetable perusal revealed that once again, I would need to catch only one bus which would carry me all the way to my most northern destination in England. I took the opportunity to make up for last night's retreat to Spanish cuisine by buying the local staple of Stottie. This was the local variation on the basic theme of 'bread'. According to some, it gets its name from the Geordie dialect for 'bounce' because if you dropped it this is what it would do. It certainly looked as though it would provide sustenance and some good exercise for the jaw muscles.

The crowds were doing a good job of milling. There were rumours of problems with broken down vehicles or a shortage of drivers. Inspectors were popping up here and there and official-looking individuals engaged one another in serious conversation. You could tell it wasn't amusing conversation because no one was smiling. The number of potential passengers continued to swell and a man in Arriva company uniform began bellowing something like, "Enny wun fre Annick ernly cum ower heor!"

I worked out that he was offering people a chance to get on a particular bus that was going to 'Annick'. This was of no interest to me since I was going somewhere else. It was rather confusing, however, since the bus he stood in front of clearly proclaimed from its destination board that it was going to Alnwick which read to my soft, southern mind like 'All'n'wick'. Plenty of people did want to go to 'Annick' and seemed quite happy to board a bus going to All'n'wick and this reduced the numbers who were preparing to squeeze onto the bus for Berwick. Not that there was any real hassle, you understand. We were all English and we know how to queue. Alnwick, I soon realised, was one of those awkward place names in England that sound nothing like they look. Places like Bicester ('Bisster' not 'Bi-cester') or Alciston ('Aston' not 'All-ciston') and even Quernmore (inexplicably pronounced 'Kormer'). Now we had Annick, not All'n'wick.

I managed to secure an upstairs seat on the bus going beyond Alnwick. The upper deck, which offers the best views, slowly reached capacity and, given the amount of time from when this point was reached and our actual departure, I can only assume that the lower deck was similarly full. Most of my fellow passengers, including an older gentleman opposite, were taking the bus for pleasure, for the day out. The front seats, however, were occupied by a family with young children heading off on a short holiday, and all seemed in suitably high spirits. I asked about the choice of transport and the possible inconveniences. The parents made it plain that the fact that they were going on the bus meant that the holiday had already started for them. They could relax and enjoy the scenery with their children and there would be a greater degree of cordial relationships. Having to lug suitcases and rucksacks a bit at either end was seen as a reasonable pay off.

We made our way out across Northumbria. The area is charming, remote, peaceful and the scenery gives no clue to the fact that this is blood-soaked soil.

The fearsome Brigantes ruled the roost here in the north-east before the Romans arrived. They did this by shedding lots of blood. Other people's blood, usually. The Romans had arrived in the south of Britain in 43AD but it took them almost thirty years to get enough bottle to have a bash at the Brigantes.

It took them about eight years to finally subdue the area, which they did by shedding lots of other people's blood. That seems to be the way of things. Then there were the Picts and Scots to deal with. The Romans shed lots of Pictish and Scottish blood but they kept coming back. The Romans thought a very large wall might help to keep them out.

The Romans themselves left in about 410AD when the Goths started shedding Roman blood in other parts of the empire. The northern Britons were now only a wall away from the northern invaders who were Picts, or Scots or Celts, it's hard to tell. In fear of having their blood shed by the wild men of the north, the Britons decided to ask some friendly Anglo-Saxons to come and help. They gladly did, shedding some blood in the process. Rather than returning home (which the Britons had probably hoped would be the case) the Anglo-Saxons decided to stay.

Northumbria (North of the Humber) became an Anglo-Saxon kingdom which amalgamated two smaller ones, Bernicia, north of the Tees, and Deira to the south. Amalgamating kingdoms is never easy and various royal houses jostled for control. This led to a very unstable situation which in turn brought about a collapse of leadership and unity, not to mention serious amounts of blood-shedding. The Danes realised that this was a good opportunity to get in on a bit of the blood-shedding action and so they attacked the Northumbrian coast in 793AD. It wasn't long before southern Northumbria became the Danish Kingdom of York.

To the North of the Kingdom, the Scots/Picts/Celts continued to cause trouble, that is, shed blood. Later on, the Normans, having shed considerable amounts of other people's blood, divided the area into the County Palatinate of Durham to the south with the remainder of the Earldom north of the Tyne and Derwent rivers being known as Northumberland. Northumberland was carved up and given to Norman Barons who had to protect themselves from the Scots who still wanted to shed other people's blood. The Normans built castles in which they hoped they would be safe.

The area was border country and so the English and the Scots, as they now were, continued to shed one another's blood.

The Battle of Otterburn, fought on 19th August 1388, saw the mighty Percys of Northumberland face the equally impressive Douglas family of Scotland. The Scots had invaded England, travelling south, leaving hamlets and villages burning, with their inhabitants mostly killed. As 'The Border Ballad', a poem collected by Sir Walter Scott, would have it:

And he has burn'd the dales of Tyne,
And part of Bamburgh Shire;
And three good towers on Redeswire fells,
He left them all on fire.

The Scots were returning home and were encamped at Otterburn when an English army under Henry Percy set upon them. More bloodshed, and at day's end two hundred Scotsmen lay dead while the English lost over a thousand.

In 1513 it was James IV of Scotland who led an army south, winding up at Flodden Hill. The Earl of Surrey led the English army as the two forces joined in battle. By now the armies had weapons such as an 18 foot pike, the equally nasty 'bills' as well as artillery. Larger armies and more sophisticated weaponry meant larger amounts of bloodshed and loss of life. An estimated 4000 Englishmen and 10 000 Scots perished.

Almost as if attempting to expunge this troubled and turbulent past, Northumberland now offers itself as a place of peace and tranquillity. It certainly looked expansive, calm and beautiful as we passed through. There is a generosity in the open space, and a lack of 'pace' which even seemed to pervade the bus. We made good, steady progress and there were no indications that anyone wanted things to speed up. Bordered to the East by a beautiful coast and to the West by a National Park that includes the Cheviot Hills, the scenery makes for a wonderful bus journey, especially from the vantage point of the top floor of a double-decker.

The A1 'Great North Road' carried us serenely on and I enjoyed chatting to the holiday-bound family and the daytripper gent. He apparently made this trip quite regularly, explaining that it made for an easy sightseeing tour along this wonderful stretch of coast. It would have been a nice enough experience alone but it was also good to enjoy the scenery together. Amid the open spaces were numerous castles and fortified buildings serving as reminders of the turbulent past. In fact, Northumberland claims more of these than any other English county. Castle-hunters would have good quarry along our route, with opportunities to alight and explore at Morpeth and Alnwick and later at Bamburgh. Our raised vantage point offered unrivalled views over enclosed farmland and along the coast, which was happily displaying the justifications for its official designation as an Area of Outstanding Natural Beauty; the gently rolling landscape fell gently away towards numerous wide, sweeping beaches. Eventually, Holy Island, complete with yet another castle, came into view just a little way from the mainland.

Holy Island, also known as Lindisfarne, was home to Aidan and his fellow missionaries who sought to bring the 'good news' of Christ to the pagan English. These guys were in for the long haul, as was the person responsible for producing the Lindisfarne gospels. This remarkable object is now in the British Museum and is deemed to be one of the most beautiful and most important artistic and religious treasures we have. Such gospels were often the work of several scribes whose careful work would be augmented by equally talented illustrators and illuminators. The Lindisfarne Gospels are all the more remarkable because a note added at the end of the manuscript indicates that they were all the work of a single man, Eadfrith, Bishop of Lindisfarne from 698 to 721. The idea of peace, serenity, quiet contemplation and study in a monastery is in stark contrast to much of the area's history. The monks would not be allowed to enjoy this peace uninterrupted, and faced a deeply unpleasant visit from the Vikings in 793.

Meanwhile, twenty minutes or so after passing Lindisfarne we were making our final approach into the place that was my second cardinal compass point—picturesque Berwick-upon-Tweed. Berwick sits on the northern bank of the river Tweed, where this waterway empties into the North Sea. At certain points in history I would have been wandering in a

Scottish town since Berwick has changed hands more times than a second-hand car with 'one careful owner'. These frequent exchanges between England and Scotland have given the town some of its most interesting features, including barracks from the early 1700s built to house soldiers whose job it was to keep out the Scots. The barracks are now home to a museum. There are also some old walls. Not any old walls, mind you, but 1½ miles of Elizabethan walls, extending and improving those from the fourteenth century begun by Edward I. If you're not interested in history then I guess they *are* just some old walls.

I enjoyed a walk around the walls with their weathered stones and grassy tops, partly because they offered such good views of the town and the river. Once back in the town I found a number of impressive civic buildings like the Town Hall (from 1760) and pretty street scenes like those of Bridge Street and Marygate. There was also a collection of bridges which could almost rival those in Newcastle. The Old Bridge dates from 1611 and on my visit its fourteen arches of red sandstone stood out against the blue water of the Tweed and against an equally blue sky while families of swans made their leisurely way in and out of its shade. Beyond this was a more modern structure of concrete and behind and above both soared the 28 arches of the Royal Border Bridge, built between 1846 and 1850, which carries the railway.

I wandered to the coast to find a quiet beach layered with rock ledges that sloped away into the clear blue water. For a while I contemplated the proximity of the Scottish border, just a couple of miles north, while I worked my way through the Stottie bought in Newcastle. As well as contemplating Scotland, I assessed my progress. Here I was in Berwick, the most northern English town and my second compass point. I had reached another milestone in my journey but still had plenty of the day left. It was time for another decision. Nice though Berwick was, I decided to head inland in search of a spot for a night or two camping and I had a particularly charming place in mind.

Munro Coaches provided the transport out of town, in the shape of the No.23 to Kelso. We made steady progress through a landscape of enclosed fields and quiet villages. As we cleared

Cornhill-on-Tweed, the road was carried over the river. We swung left along a tree-lined road and when the trees finally gave way to houses we were on the outskirts of the small town that would be my final destination for the day and a stop-off point for two.

I was now out of England, happy to be in Scottish territory, and in the pleasant town of Coldstream. I had established in Berwick that there was a camp site here and was directed by a local inhabitant down a lane towards a field by the river which described a graceful arc below the town. A small sign informed me that this was indeed a camp site and that someone would collect money at some point. I would also be able to obtain a key which would unlock the toilets and showers. I pitched my tent close to the water's edge and then wandered into town. A shopkeeper gave me the address of the person who would have the keys and would be collecting money. I walked round to the appointed house but could get no reply. The shopkeeper had also told me not to worry if there was nobody in as they would turn up eventually. It was all very relaxed and set the tone for my time in this peaceful place.

I later returned to the shop to buy a few edibles. Another man entered and the shopkeeper explained who I was. The new man said he had just seen the person I needed to obtain the key from and told me to accompany him. We found the young man in question, who said he would see me down at the camp site in a short while. I thanked them both and made my way back to the tent. Sure enough, the keeper of the keys appeared and money (50p) and keys changed hands. I was now sorted with food, accommodation and sanitation. All I needed now was for the pub to open.

The Besom offered a good pint of the suitably Scottish Mc-Ewan's ale, as well as a very friendly atmosphere. Indeed, there seemed to be a real sense of community in here just as in the rest of the village. Some teenage boys appeared. There was some discussion about hanging baskets. In my experience objects such as hanging baskets and social sub-groups such as 'teenage boys' are normally only found together in sentences describing how the said sub-group has been responsible for the vandalising or unlawful removal of the stated object. Imagine my surprise when it transpired that the discussion was to do with the hanging-basket watering and maintenance for which the young people of Coldstream were responsible. This was part of their efforts towards the town achieving a place in a Scotland in Bloom competition. I thought that I had inadvertently stepped back in time to the 1950s or at least wandered on to the set of one of those cosy TV family dramas, scheduled for transmission on a Sunday evening. But no, I just seemed to be in a place with a genuine sense of community, where people knew each other, cared, felt valued and took on responsibilities. It was great.

Coldstream is famous for its guards. Not that they are there much. In fact, they do not guard Coldstream at all. They do guard royal property in London and Windsor and perform ceremonial duties such as The Changing of the Guard. These are the guys that Christopher Robin went down with Alice to watch. As well as these familiar ceremonial roles, soldiers from the regiment also see active service in dangerous places. I wondered where the name Coldstream Guards came from. Well, Coldstream of course, but what was the story?

This is: The regiment has its origins in the Civil War when Oliver Cromwell gave Colonel George Monck permission to form his own regiment as part of the New Model Army. He duly did this, deciding to call it Monck's Regiment of Foot from which point we can understand why they were looking for a change of name. The Coldstream connection came following Cromwell's death when Monck, perhaps sensing a change in the air, turned royalist. On the 1st January 1660 he marched the regiment across the River Tweed at Coldstream and began a five-week march to London to assist in suppressing unruly behaviour and in restoring Charles II to the throne. They became the Coldstream Guards in commemoration of their walk from the town of that name.

I hooked up with another lone traveller at the camp site who seemed to be just as keen on the idea of exploring the delights offered by The Besom as I was, and an evening spent largely there proved to be most convivial and a suitable prelude to a good night's sleep.

Day 14

We will not wander more

19th September

I woke to a still, warm morning and opened the flap of my tent. As I was pitched just above a bend in the river I could watch it glide almost noiselessly by. Early sunlight caught the ripples and a group of swallows patrolled the air space a few metres above the surface. Back and forth along their allotted stretch they dipped and turned, making sudden insect-snaffling twitches before reaching the limit of their patrol, making a high and graceful turn and then resuming a fly-past in the opposite direction. This was an idyllic start to the day and set the perfect tone.

Coldstream became to me what the Island of the Lotos Eaters was to Odysseus and his mariners in the poem by Alfred, Lord Tennyson. I allowed its restful colours, calming nature and sense of peace to seduce me into relaxation. Here indeed was 'music that softer falls than petals from blown roses on the grass'. I concurred with the mariners who wondered why are we so often 'weighed upon with heaviness and utterly consumed with sharp distress, when all things else have rest from weariness?'

Here was a place where you could get all the rest from weariness you wanted. I could stay here, perhaps even longer than my planned two nights, I thought. Now you have to watch this sort of thing, of course, because if you're not careful you get to thinking that you've been away so long that the fires at home will have long gone out, your wife won't recognise you, and your children will have inherited all you own because everyone thinks you're dead. While here,

on Coldtream's lush grass,
beside the ever-gentle waters of the Tweed,
propped on beds of speedwell, moss and even moly,
the warm air lulls you, blowing lowly,
with half-dropped eyelids still
beneath the Besom dark and holy,
you watch the long, bright river drawing slowly
His waters from the—

You see what I mean? "I'd better not hang about here too long," I concluded. "I may never leave."

But I could not rush away. I had a lovely, lazy day enjoying the intimate quality of the High Street and the slightly more spacious Market Square. From Henderson Park, opposite the Town Hall, the land dropped away dramatically and I sat for a long time drinking in the fantastic views over the river and beyond. The gardens were very neat and tidy, easy and friendly with numerous flowers scenting the warm air. I bought a paper and had the luxury of reading it, found succour and sustenance in the Besom and took another amble round the town, one more turn around its lanes, a gentle stroll along to the bridge across the river to watch the swallows, some time just breathing in the summer on the breeze.

All too soon it was a final evening visit to the Besom followed by a long stretch beneath the stars, watching that glorious heavenly display in the ever-darkening sky before a deep and restful sleep. For tomorrow I would move on. I must, I must, I thought with half-dropped eyelids and half beer-fuddled brain.

Day 15

Left a bit and down

20th September

It was time to wrench myself away from this wonderful spot. My stay, although brief, had been long enough to give me a real sense of relaxation. I felt much further removed from the bright lights and excitement of Newcastle than a mere day's bus ride. It was almost another world and yet the divide between the buzz of the one place and the serenity of the other could be breached quite simply using good old public service buses. Now it was time to see where else they would take me and to make my way along the borders, before beginning my descent down the western fringes of England towards my remaining compass points.

We drifted along, following the Tweed upstream through border country towards Kelso. When I say 'drifted', I am not casting aspersions. I'm sure the bus was being diligently and purposefully driven by a diligent and purposeful driver. But *I* drifted, freed still from any responsibilities regarding driving and able therefore to take in all the views of the countryside afforded by the elevated position and the large panoramic window. I had also drifted in another sense, since I was off my original brief. I was now firmly across the border in the Scottish Lowlands. The landscape through which we travelled was, however, a green and pleasant land much like that of the Sassenach territory just to the south, topography being no respecter of boundary lines drawn by cartographers at the behest of bureaucrats and politicians.

Our progress was eventually interrupted by Kelso, a rather special place which stood solidly at the joining of the Rivers

Tweed and Teviot. The largely stone-built town featured an attractive cobbled square flanked by shops, bars and restaurants with an almost French feel, which is in no way intended as a criticism and should perhaps be no surprise, given the Auld Alliance between these two countries. The main aims of that alliance may have been mutual military support but cultural exchanges also grew from it. The French influence on the architecture in this area is proof of this. Church buildings proliferated in the town and grand-looking municipal and financial buildings were matched by equally elegant hotels. Nearby was Kelso Abbey and, across the Tweed, Floors Castle, home of the Duke of Roxburghe.

The town has links with a number of important and famous people. One of these is Sir Walter Scott—his great grandfather was born here and the man himself stayed with an aunt while attending school in the town. Another is one William Murdoch. No, I didn't know who he was either. But why didn't I? Was I not paying attention in the history lesson that day at school? Perhaps my 'British' history was heavily biased toward England. Whatever the reason, William had been off my radar despite his being a gifted and prolific inventor and engineer, even to the point of being in there at the beginning of steam engines with the likes of Watt and Trevithick. Apart from allegedly wearing a wooden bowler hat, which he had turned from a piece of wood, Mr Murdoch (sometimes Murdock) is credited with inventing the use of coal gas as a fuel for lighting. The Kelso connection comes from the claim that his invention was first tried out, at least as a domestic application, in a house in Bridge Street.

My book of English place names was no good to me when confronted with the Scottish town of Jedburgh, in which I was deposited some time later. The burg(h) suggested a stronghold yet it was in fact a royal burgh, the 'Jed' coming from the 'Jed Water', a tributary of the Teviot on which the town stands. The ruins of a fine abbey, first established as a priory by David I of Scotland in 1138, made for a good focus of a visit here. There seems to be evidence of a place of Christian worship on the site from the early 700s but a church was definitely established here by Bishop Ecgred of Lindisfarne in 830. The Abbey ruins are impressive enough, being in an elevated position that makes them even more imposing. The great arches rising in tiers above look imposing and speak of former grandeur long gone. Nearby is Mary, Queen of Scots House. Here she stayed for a number of weeks in October 1566 and here her life story is told through the exhibitions within.

Munro's coaches had brought me this far and they would take me on. We were destined for Hawick. Just as the locals will send you to 'Jeddart' if you are looking for Jedburgh, so you will be directed to 'Hoik' when enquiring about Hawick. I was having similar problems to those encountered at 'Al'n'wick'. Despite embarrassing attempts at pronouncing place names properly, I was delivered safely having travelled through more wonderful, pastoral scenery. The bus was comfortable and well-used which was encouraging to see.

Hawick was a point of arrival and departure for me and little else. There was just time to gaze in wonder at the multi-turreted Town Hall, more Bavarian castle than municipal offices. Had I been here a couple of centuries earlier, I would have been in the middle of a thriving, pulsating mill town where, in the late 1800s, upwards of half a million kilograms of wool was being processed into all sorts of garments, socks and undies. The River Teviot is joined here by the Slitrig and these two powered the town's mills. Woollen cloth from these parts is still world famous. I'd never really thought where tweed might have come from.

I was focussing on finding the X93 for Carlisle. A bus so numbered appeared at the stop over the road. I realised with a panic that I could be standing at the wrong place. The stop I had been loitering by *was* for the X93 but it was, I now saw, for buses travelling in the opposite direction. The queue on the opposite side of the road that I had languorously observed as it gently diminished had suddenly grown unnervingly short. In fact it seemed as though the last person had boarded and was in the process of buying a ticket. I had to get across the road, and quick.

All I needed was for that person to be a fumbler, looking around in the recesses of a deep, dark bag to locate the purse that held their change. Or perhaps they would be unable to locate sufficient funds in coins and have to run the gauntlet of offering the driver a note. He in turn might then be reluctant to accept this and take a few precious moments explaining the difficulty that receiving notes of such a denomination posed to him, given the limited amount of change at his disposal. All I didn't need was for that person to have a bus pass or a season ticket which they simply had to pass under the driver's nose before he waved them on while simultaneously activating the mechanism that closes the doors.

I arrived somewhat flushed of face and definitely flustered at the still-open doors. I bought my day ticket and took a seat with a sigh of relief. That had been a bit close. Then I watched bemused as the driver quietly read his paper for a few minutes before the appointed time for departure.

When we eventually did leave town we took the A7, following the course of the River Teviot upstream. Lorries laden with hay bales and tractors working the fields here and there were signs that the agricultural year was turning. The sun shone and the glorious landscape seemed to hint that it owed its features to the same forces that have shaped the Lake District. Here were impressive hills, their forms softened and rounded by ancient glacial action. Distant views and far horizons created a sense of space and, although the heights were not as awe-inspiring as some of the hills in the Lakes, the area still looked as though it offered great walking.

We called briefly in Langholme, birthplace of Hugh Mac-Diarmid, Scotland's most famous modern poet. No, I hadn't heard of him either but that says more about me than about Hugh. He is remembered with a memorial above the town. Langholme has settled itself very nicely, thank you, between the confluence of the River Esk and Ewes Water, although it has spread itself beyond these boundaries here and there. The usual uplift, for me at least, of seeing attractive architecture in close proximity with water worked again. There was a pleasant feeling of enclosure or enfolding as the surrounding hills provided a comforting horizon for this nicely isolated settlement. Before 1788 the only bridge across the Esk was Skipper Bridge almost a mile south. This changed when the Duke of

Buccleugh founded what was effectively New Langholme on the west bank of the river and connected this to the existing town with a bridge. Running west from this bridge is Telford Road, named after Thomas Telford who was born nearby and apprenticed as a stone mason in the town.

We passed by The Reivers' Rest Hotel. Who, I wondered, were the Reivers and why did they need a rest? The Reivers ruled the roost back in the sixteenth century all over the border country, which was known as 'The Debateable Lands' since neither Scots nor English law held sway. When I say the reivers 'ruled' I obviously mean they terrorised, and this was seemingly a common interpretation of the word 'debateable' when it came to deciding who controlled what. The reivers were feuding families and clans such as the Armstrongs, the Maxwells, the Elliots and the Grahams. If you wanted to experience a bereavement or simply to be reaved yourself, these were the chaps for the job. To reave, a variant of which is reive, means 'to make raids' or 'to plunder', 'to forcibly deprive', 'to take by force' and 'to carry off'. You get the idea. So this was how the merry reivers passed the time; raiding and plundering, forcibly depriving whoever happened to be about of all of whatever it was that they happened to have on them and from thence carrying it all off. Obviously there was a considerable amount of death and maiming along the way. No wonder they needed somewhere warm and cosy to rest at the end of a busy day.

The countryside as viewed from the bus was stunning in its own rugged way and dotted here and there were castles, towers and fortified houses which would once perhaps have offered the locals some hope of protection from marauding reivers.

While still in The Debateable Lands we, along with the River Esk, arrived at Canonbie. It was through here that the dashing knight of Sir Walter Scott's Lochinvar is said to have dashed. Well, he had stolen a bride from a wedding at Netherby Hall and those in pursuit were Graemes, Fosters, Fenwicks and Musgraves; Reivers to a man, I'll be bound!

We were soon to pass Scotch Dyke and Ginger Bank, who make an unlikely couple, you have to admit.

On the border and across the River Esk lay Longtown, so

named because it is a town or tun and it is long. The main features are a handsome bridge, the Graham Arms and a massive livestock market.

The area has seen its times of trial for, as well as being in the midst of The Debateable Lands, Longtown is on part of the site of the Battle of Solway Moss. This all came about because of a dispute between Henry VIII and his contumacious nephew James V of Scotland. Henry sent his troops to attack Scotland and, as you would expect, James sent Scottish troops into England. Three thousand men under the Englishman Sir Thomas Wharton met the fifteen to eighteen thousand men of James V on the 24th November 1542. It wasn't a good day for the Scots. The dubious command structure seems to have failed and they were routed with about 1200 prisoners being taken. The English lost very few men during the fighting and the Scots killed in battle only amounted to about twenty. In what feels like a bit of a tragedy, hundreds of Scots are reckoned to have drowned trying to escape through the fast flowing waters of the Esk.

The English would have set out from Carlisle Castle and this should be a part of any visit to this northerly town. It should be, but it wasn't to be for me. I had time only for the briefest look about the town centre and a glance at the impressive cathedral, a building begun in the twelfth century which boasts a fabulous stained glass window from the fourteenth.

My attention was rather focussed on where I would be going next. I fancied a lightning tour of Cumbria and to this end arranged the purchase of an Explorer ticket with an agreeable and accommodating bus driver, for which he requested the sum of £7.00.

I knew it wouldn't be easy but my training over the previous weeks meant that I was as prepared as I would ever be for the gruelling business ahead: sitting in a fairly comfortable seat from here to Cockermouth and watching the world go by.

The route took me across the low lands between the Solway Firth and the Cumbrian Mountains, which are the big draw for many people coming to this part of the world. But mountains are not the only feature of The Lake District. No, there are lakes too.

We passed through Wigton on our way. Unassuming and unpretentious it may be, but it has a quiet attractiveness nonetheless. The market square has Georgian architecture but the Romans were here earlier. They have left their mark in the form of Maglona Fort, sometimes referred to as Old Carlisle. This is beside the main A595 which itself follows the route of a Roman road.

We passed through Bothel, famous for its postitutes, just outside the Lake District National Park. This is an attractive rural village and there were good views from this area south to the Lakeland hills and north over the Solway Firth. 'Firth', now there's a word. A lowland Scots word, in fact, for a body of water. If the Danes had had their way it might well have been Solway Fjord. 'Solway' too is of interest. It is Anglo-Saxon and appears to mean mud ford. So, I could well be looking over mud ford fjord.

Solway Firth and the Irish Sea share a lot of water, water being what it is and behaving as it does. This is not normally a problem of course, and in fact it's probably rather jolly for all the fishes and things to go from one place to another as the fancy takes them. However, there could be some things in the Irish Sea that you don't want drifting into the Solway Firth and equally there might be some things in the Solway Firth that you don't want drifting out to the Irish Sea.

You see, Sellafield is nearby. This is a site of nuclear fuel production based around a site originally used for the production of weapons-grade plutonium, and there are some who worry about what's in the water and where it's going.

I pressed on to Cockermouth at the mouth of the River Cocker, a Celtic name meaning 'crooked'. This is the birthplace of William Wordsworth, and the house in which he was born is now run by the National Trust. The house and contents are presented with the usual panache of this organisation, providing a perfect balance of information to complement the items on display. As always the experience was enhanced by having enthusiastic and passionate guides on hand who are there because they care, not because they're being paid. In fact, they're not being paid. The Wordsworths were in residence in the 1770s and here you can begin to imagine what life was like for them.

Apparently, we're lucky to have the house at all because in the 1930s they nearly knocked it down to make way for a bus station. Now bus stations are important, of course they are. I've said so myself, and would even argue that in some cases they should be more important than they are. But you don't need to go around knocking down perfectly serviceable buildings, especially ones of historic or architectural significance, in order to create them. And you certainly don't need to knock down the birthplace of one of our best-known poets. 'They' saw sense and it's still there.

Wordsworth is not everyone's cup of tea but his poems speak across 200 years with such relevance, recognising the power and inspiration available in natural landscapes. We may not be able to articulate our responses as eloquently as Mr Wordsworth but, if we give ourselves and the landscapes adequate time and space, his thoughts might resonate with ours when he says he is:

...well pleased to recognise
In nature and the language of the sense,
The anchor of my purest thoughts, the nurse,
The guide, the guardian of my heart, and soul
Of all my moral being.

You don't have to go all soft and start quoting poetry to enjoy this area but its popularity suggests to me that Wordsworth was on to something. For many people, striding over the hills is how these features are best experienced. Walking is not just undertaken in fair weather but in all weathers. People wrap up in several layers of high tech waterproof, windproof, breathable clothing, armed with sticks and compasses and supplies and emergency rations, and head off in driving rain and swirling mists and... enjoy themselves. How come? Perhaps even in such extreme and inclement conditions they find in the nature and language of their senses the anchor of their purest thoughts.

Cockermouth is a charming little market town with a predominantly Georgian look to the architecture. It also boasts Jennings Brewery. Beer is not everyone's cup of tea, I know. Neither is religion, but many people admire and even love our religious buildings and churches even though they only set foot in one for a wedding, baptism or funeral or, if you really push it, for a Christmas carol service. In the same way, even if you never touch a drop of beer (seek help) the small-scale breweries that are dotted up and down the country are an intrinsic and important part of our national heritage and they need to be treasured. If not, they will disappear, and many have. So, support these local breweries however you can. I know it's hard, but someone's got to do it. You can buy Jennings beers in handy take-away containers called 'bottles' which fit quite easily into a rucksack.

The next stage of the bus journey took me back out through the Lake District, at a fairly cracking pace I must admit, but it made for a very enjoyable trip. It could hardly fail to with all this wonderful scenery to drink in. I made it first of all to Keswick and from there boarded a bus that would eventually get me to Lancaster. This was a useful, frequent service which would allow for stopping off at a number of places along the way and catching a later bus for the onward journey.

I was struck once again by the potential problems caused by cars in a sensitive area such as the Lakes, and also by the possible alleviation of some of these problems that is offered by buses.

The problem for the Lake District, like other National Parks, is that it is a victim of its own success. As a stonkingly beautiful area of mountains, rivers and lakes it is hard to beat. Understandably, for this reason alone, people flock here in their thousands. Add to this the other attractions such as associations with famous dead poets and it is easy to see why the place is 'rammed' (to use the current vernacular), especially in high season. The problems arise because most people find their way here in a car and then use the same vehicle to get around. We all know why—it's by far the most convenient. However, all the cars clog the roads and when they stop they need somewhere to park. More of what people come to see has to be covered in tarmac as a result. So, people are encouraged to leave the car wherever they're staying and get about by bus. Within the area there are plenty of opportunities to do this and to combine bus journeys with walking to create a long distance round trip. Great stuff and more power to their elbow! How about taking this one stage further? Could you actually go *to* the Lake District on the bus? It had been a doddle from Carlisle and, reversing my present journey, would be from Lancaster.

Keswick itself is a small market town centred on a Market Square surrounded by shops and hotels. It is another good place for a visit as it sits on Derwentwater and acts as a good starting point for exploring on foot or indeed by rowing boat. Similar attractions await you at the other places on the route.

Although there is a similar feel and look to most of the towns and villages in the area, each has its own particular features and attractions. Grasmere, for example, is famous because it was another home for William Wordsworth. He lived here in Dove Cottage with his sister and they also moved to the larger Allan Bank where Coleridge joined them. Today it is a tourist's paradise with scores of gift shops, eateries, historic buildings and even a Wordsworth Daffodil Gardens. There would be many walks from here, around the lake and on to nearby Rydal Water or, for the more adventurous, a hike in the hills. Stone Arthur is a popular vantage point from which to look down on the village.

Ambleside was bustling and flushed with colour thanks to being bedecked with bunting, filled with flags and hung with hanging baskets. It was fairly packed with tourists and seemed to offer the usual delights of a Lake District settlement: proximity to water and hills, views of these, reasonably attractive architecture and plenty of places to eat or to exchange money for things to put on your mantelpiece.

As we drew past the lake at Bowness-on-Windermere a breeze ruffled the surface of the water as a lone cormorant pierced it in search of food. The sky greyed slightly and a pleasure craft pulled away. More of what the Lake District does best is on offer here with the additional attraction of the largest natural lake in England.

The bus passed through the curiously-named village of Ings where you can find the Watermill Inn and brewery. We pushed on through other villages such as Nether Staveley. Staveleys are so called because they were woods where staves were obtained. 'Nether' I've always associated with things a little dark, mysterious and even a bit saucy. Don't you wonder what happens in the 'nether regions'? Come to Nether Staveley and find out!

The destination for this stretch approached and I disembarked in the fairly substantial settlement of Kendal and immediately set about finding some of the local delicacy—Kendal Mint Cake. Kendal Mint Cake is the stuff of legend. The tale goes that, back in the 1860s, a confectioner preparing glacier mints took his eye off the pan at a crucial point. On returning his gaze (it is not clear what was of such interest as to distract him in the first place) he noticed that his preparation was 'grainy' rather than clear. He poured the mixture out and was presented with what we now know as mint cake. The man in question was one Joseph Wiper. From such fortuitous beginnings, the production of Wiper's Mint Cake continued, with most being sold locally or to places in the North of England. Being a sugary confection, the product supplies a good source of quick-release energy; a 'sugar rush'. As such it was supplied, by Joseph's canny son Robert, to the Transarctic Expedition in 1914–17 and also to the first Everest expedition. Wiper's was sold to George Romneys Ltd in 1987. This company had been started by one Sam T Clarke who had been making mint cake since 1919. His company supplied the 1953 Everest expedition and the product received a predictable boost when it emerged that it had been enjoyed by Edmund Hillary and Sirdar Tensing at the top of the world's highest mountain. So, Mint Cake has put Kendal on the map. It is rather wonderful stuff and quite rich in its own way—so too much of it will see you running round like a hyperactive night clubber on speed. I say that, but it's probably just as likely to make you feel ever so slightly queasy.

There's more to Kendal than Mint Cake of course. It's an attractive market town of predominantly Victorian buildings. It has a long history of market trading which really took off with the granting of a charter in 1189 by Richard I to Baron Gilbert

Fritz-Renfried, inventor of Renfried beans, a dish exported successfully to the Texas/Mexico border. That is not true by the way, but it is true that Kendal is in a good location as it is easy to go west to the Lakes or east to the Pennines and Yorkshire Dales or, as it happens, south to Lancaster.

The sun was beginning to set as the last stretch of this journey drew towards its end. I noticed signs for Bolton-le-Sands and knew that there were beaches along Morecambe Bay which would doubtless have camp sites. The sunset would have been excellent from these places I'm sure. But I hesitated and we all know what happens to he who hesitates. Yes, he misses his bus stop. Actually, I wanted to make the most out of the Day Ticket and if I disembarked here I would be required to buy another ticket in the morning just to get into Lancaster and then another one to get out again. So, my hesitation and deliberations meant that I was not deposited near the expansive sands of Morecambe Bay but at Lancaster Bus Station with the dawning realisation that I had nowhere to stay for the night.

The evening was shutting up shop and proper night-time was setting out its stall. It was getting dark and that always seemed to heighten my sense of anxiety. Logically, places that offer a bed for the night would presumably be open at times when this service might be most needed. That is, at night. That logic doesn't always seem to apply though. Look at tea shops. They almost always shut at tea time. What would I do if I couldn't find anywhere to sleep? In the back of my mind I sort of knew that, of course, I would be able to find a bed somewhere but I also didn't relish the idea of spending a large wodge of money for the privilege of lying down.

I needn't have worried because I soon found a pub that had the wonderful word 'Accommodation' over the door, near to the equally wonderful word 'beer'. The accommodation normally took the form of Bed and Breakfast and the rate was quite reasonable. When I expressed an interest I was informed that the chef was ill and consequently the 'Breakfast' part of 'Bed and Breakfast' would not be available. I wondered if the 'Bed' part was and indeed it was—and at a suitably reduced rate. A deal was done and I was given keys and directions to the room.

Having deposited my gear I set off in search of a food outlet where the chefs were well. Having refuelled on some fairly basic English cuisine involving filleted sea creatures and fried stick-shapes cut from potatoes (you get the idea) I returned to the pub that was to be my home for the evening and partook of a pint before retiring. I felt tired but satisfied. I was pleased to realise that I had woken up in Scotland that morning.

As I drifted into sleep there was a knock on the door. I couldn't quite make out what was being said as I gingerly set the door ajar. Someone, who had enjoyed rather more pints than me, was enquiring after Alice and whether I had her in my room. I assured the gentleman that I did not. He asked if I was sure because he could have sworn she said she was in this room. I confirmed that unless she was very thin, very quiet or hiding in the wardrobe, Alice was not in the room. He went away mumbling. I checked the wardrobe and then got back into bed, worrying about where on earth Alice could be.

Day 16

To Shropshire, lad

20th August

I was up early and out, there being no need to hang about for breakfast. I found that in a small café nearby. I'd like to say that I feasted on local organic bacon and free range eggs with artisan-baked bread washed down with hand-picked and fairly traded tea but I can't promise that I did. All I can say was that the food was well cooked and nicely presented and the place was clean and, let's be honest... cheap. I think I parted with £3.75 and I was well and truly set up for the morning.

I didn't do Lancaster justice. It's an attractive market town and it has a fascinating castle and many other good things besides, I'm sure. But for me it was just a passing-through place. After breakfast I was soon heading to the bus station to see where I could get to next.

It turned out to be Preston, as it happens, at a cost of £4.35. We meandered through most of Lancaster and its environs before finally breaking free and making more apparent progress to somewhere else. We passed through Garstang, which sounds like a town in Bavaria or some such place but apparently derives its name from something meaning 'spear post', whatever one of those is. It could be a spear stuck in the ground as a sort of post or it could be a post against which you can rest your spear.

Garstang welcomes you with a sign declaring it to be 'The world's first fair trade town'. It is in an attractive setting at a crossing over the River Wyre. The choice of location was obviously a good one regarding transport. The river was no doubt first but the topography has lent itself to subsequent transport developments. So, there are former coaching inns, a canal, a railway and roads. The roads are not an attraction particularly and a lot of people don't like railways either, but Garstang looked like an attractive market town complete with historic buildings and the possibility of pleasant ambles along a canal.

The journey from Lancaster to Preston took about an hour altogether. The bus station at Preston was amazing and it looked like anything but a bus station. For a start it was a proper building and not a space between other buildings with a few plastic shelters dotted about. It wasn't hidden away like an embarrassing relative but displayed for all to see. Here at last there seemed to be an indication that someone, somewhere, thought bus transportation was anything but second best. It looked distinctly modern and almost like an airport terminal. Light streamed in through the high glass frontage. The concourse was open and expansive, tiled throughout with various colours and textures. Information was easily accessible and bus bays clearly marked in eye-catching designs. Purpose-built and well designed, full of durable materials and details like the simple-faced clocks, here was a place that would allow you to believe that travelling by bus could be efficient, attractive and perhaps even 'happening'. The bus station was actually built at the tail end of the 1960s and is hailed by some as a great example of 'brutalist' architecture while other people think that it is just in the way and needs to be pulled down. One of the arguments in favour of pulling it down, let me point out, is that it is not used enough.

I was looking for my next destination, trying to head in a generally southward direction, to a place where there would be onward buses whilst avoiding the potentially difficult conurbations of Manchester and Liverpool. Wigan presented itself as a good option, poised as it was between these two vast places, and I felt sure the necessary routes further south would be found there.

I had a bit of difficulty explaining to the nice person at the enquiries place why I didn't want to avail myself of the speedy and efficient services offered by a certain well-known express coach company, but I managed eventually. I also finally established that The Blue Bus would take me to Wigan and that I might be able to get from there to Chester.

I bought my single to Wigan and settled back for the ride. Preston's a big place and once again we struggled to free ourselves of the built-up area, finally escaping out over the River Ribble. We followed this for a while and criss-crossed the main-line railway until we arrived in Lostock Hall, another settlement with an industrial past, little evidence of which remained. Mills and rail yards may have dominated the place at one time but no more. We briefly breached the built up area and were surrounded by agricultural land, but this was a short-lived respite. We pressed on through to Leyland, calling in at the Tesco store. Finally the built up area began to peter out and agriculture took up the dominant position once again. Thus it was we made our way to Eccleston.

Eccleston would, you might reasonably suppose, be a tun or town associated with Eccles, whatever they are. Yes, what are Eccles, I wondered? Eccles cakes I know. They are a delightful confection of buttery puff pastry encasing a filling of prepared dried currants and sugar, the lot topped off with a delicious sprinkling of demerara sugar. They are named after the town of Eccles near Manchester and they are said to have originated there although their true origin is lost in the mists of time. One J. Birch is proposed as the first person to sell them on a commercial basis. They can be referred to somewhat disparagingly, or 'dissed' if you prefer a modern word, by giving them the name of 'dead fly pie'. This is really an affectionate term of endearment as the Eccles cake is felt to be a grand example of local British cuisine, as iconic as a French croissant. This doesn't really help us in establishing what an Eccles might be and why a place might be called this. Obviously Eccleston can't simply be named after Eccles because this would mean 'The town of Eccles town'. Fortunately for us, someone has been here before and wrestled with the question. A quick glance at the place names dictionary reveals that 'Eccles' means 'Romano-British Christian Church' and that putting a 'ton' (tun) on the end signifies a 'farmstead'. So, Eccleston is the shorthand version of 'farmstead near a Romano-British Christian Church' which, you have to admit, would be an awful lot to get on a road sign as in 'The Farmstead near the Romano-British Christian Church Welcomes Careful Drivers'. This does have some serious implications regarding the wonderful Eccles Cake. Are these, strictly speaking, 'Romano-British Christian Church Cakes'? If so, isn't it time we saw this wonderful baked delight taking its proper place amongst those other fine examples of Church-calendar inspired foodstuffs, the Christmas cake, the Easter biscuit and the Harvest Crunch?

However you choose to refer to it, Eccleston is pleasant enough and a good base for exploring the surrounding area. It certainly has a name to conjure with, and believe it or not we were only a wand-wave away from The Magical Kingdom of Camelot. Now, I'm no expert on the legends of King Arthur and his Knights of the Round Table but I don't recall Camelot being on the edge of Preston. However, who's to say and I don't want to be accused of being a killjoy. If you want a wizard day out I'm sure The Magical Kingdom is the place to go.

My mission allowed me no time for such a pleasant diversion. We passed through undulating landscape with views from the high points across the plain and to distant hills. Thus we passed through Wrightington Bar, Hungers Hill and into Standish, a reasonably friendly-looking place, unlike the slightly larger but less welcoming Standoffish. Standish actually derives its name from past people who struggled with spelling 'stone' properly, it being a 'stony pasture' and originally 'stanedis'.

We made our way finally into Wigan, famous for containing 'Wigan Pier'. This seems to have been a jocular reference to a coal-landing jetty on the Leeds-Liverpool canal at the base of a set of locks. It found itself in the title of *The Road to Wigan Pier*, by George Orwell, published in 1937, in which he descries a winter afternoon in Wigan's 'dreadful environs'. He paints a vivid picture of a landscape dominated by slag heaps with views through these mountainous waste piles to the smoking factory chimneys. We are presented with a well-worn, if not almost worn out environment, with a canal tow path ground to cinders and frozen mud by innumerable clogs, and everywhere are the 'flashes', pools of stagnant water collecting in the depressions caused by the subsidence of old workings. It might have been better if he'd been there on a nice sunny afternoon, but as it is he saw bargemen covered up to their eyes against the cold in layers of sacks and a landscape from which vegetation had been banished and there was nothing but 'smoke, shale, ice, mud, ashes and foul water.'

It's not like that in Wigan now but it is quite salutary to think that it was within living memory. Again, as a soft southerner, used to endless leafy avenues and parks and streets paved with gold, I wondered what a place like Wigan might have to offer a tourist. As I'd discovered in other old industrial towns there had been a good deal of re-invention and a pragmatic approach to the local heritage. I was only looking at tourist brochures (which obviously give things a positive spin) but as well as talk of a varied history and heritage there was also mention of attractive countryside, lakes and canal towpath walks. It seems that the vegetation has been allowed back and the slag-heaps, flashes and foul water have been banished.

On the business side of things, the bus station was off Market Street, on the other side of which were, appropriately enough, markets and The Galleries shopping area. Wigan Pier and the Treacherfield Mill were a bit too much of a walk away for me and my timetable-driven life. A Day Rider (not quite as exciting as The Night Rider but only £2.99) enabled me to leave town. I caught sight of The Anvil public house (CAMRA Pub of the Year at the time of my visit) which would have been a short stroll from the bus station and therefore reachable but I hadn't spotted it until I was on the bus on my way out of town. Next time.

We wound through the red-brick streets to Abram, then finally broke cover again and were in something a bit more like open country. We had to negotiate railways and the M6 and the M62 before we could reach Warrington. There are many places to embark and disembark a bus in Warrington but the bus station is near the grandly named Golden Square shopping centre. Golden Square? Mmmm. In Warrington is the Warrington Museum. The museum is in Museum Street. This good, solid honest and straightforward naming of things acts as a counterbalance to calling something 'The Golden Square'. The museum has exhibitions explaining the town's past industries including soap-making, tanning, clog-making, wire, steel and beer. And I thought they just made vodka. At one time or another almost every place in England of any size seems to have had a brewery. Warrington is no exception and there have been several over the years. Perhaps the largest in Warrington's brewing history is Greenall's, established in the 1780s, which had over 1000 tied pubs by 1900, making them the biggest pub chain in the country. Beyond this, Warrington was pretty much another transit stop for me. I confess to the beginnings of industrial-town fatigue and longed for a change of scenery or at least a change of townscape. The X30 promised a speedy-sounding service to Chester. I thought this would serve me well, sending me further West and ready to drop South through the border counties.

En route, our way was blocked by the Manchester Ship Canal and we had to wait near Walton at a swing bridge while an extremely large vessel made its stately progress inland, an oddly surreal sight since I felt we were in a thoroughly inland location. We pressed on, over another canal and on to Daresbury, the birthplace of Lewis Carroll. The village is a draw because of its associations with the man who dreamt up *Alice's Adventures in Wonderland* and *Through the Looking-Glass* and the nineteenth century All Saints Church has memorial windows.

The road carried us high over what appeared to be a retail or light commercial area before we entered the suburbs of Runcorn and the streets bore romantic, pastoral and unintentionally ironic names such as Osprey Close and Goldcrest Close in amongst the other Groves, Avenues, Ways, Crescents and Rises. We ducked under the M56, or 'Lesser Spotted Woodpecker Highway' as it is affectionately known hereabouts, and crossed the River Weaver before entering Frodsham. This was a small attractive market town which was originally the home of a man called Frod. Should you have time to disembark and take a stroll you could do worse than climb Overton Hill which overlooks the town. This would provide good views across the

Mersey Estuary if you enjoy looking at heavy industry. Raise your gaze and Liverpool should be visible. You might prefer to turn round and try to see Wales.

Once again we travelled through predominantly agricultural landscapes and passed through Helsby ('a village on a ledge'), crossed the River Gowy and through a couple of Traffords before ducking under the A55 at Hoole ('a hole' or, as they say in the Northeast, a 'hoole'). From here we were swallowed by the suburbs of Chester.

That makes Chester sound like a great, sprawling metropolis which is hardly the case. It is a charming town, encased by Roman and medieval walls and full of historical treasures. Had my bag and I stumbled here in Neolithic times the chances are we would not have been alone. The sandstone plateau above the River Dee on which the town sits was probably seen as an advantageous location even then. Subsequent arrivals obviously spotted this potential too, not least the Romans who probably had to wrest it from the grasp of some barbarians. Who were all these barbarians anyway and were they really all that bad? We've only got the Romans' word for it after all. I mean, if you were a Roman posted over here and you had to send reports back to explain what you were doing and why it was taking you so long to take control of more land or keep order amongst a conquered population you could hardly describe your foes as 'quite decent chaps, really'. The Romans patently decided that the locals were dangerous and so they built a fort. Through superstition or in deference to the locals, they named it Deva or Deoua after the goddess of the local river. We would call her Dee today. The Roman fort had the name of the legion added to it to make Deva Vitrix which sounds like something you might buy from the chemist to rub on your chest if you had a nasty cold.

The Romans seem to have deserted the place and it was left... well, deserted. There is some doubt about the sequence of inhabitants but it looks as though the Saxons pushed west and reached here in the seventh century, booting out any Welsh tribes that may have taken up residence. The Saxons suffered at the hands of the Danes after they arrived in the ninth century but they took it back later and made it a burgh. This was fortified and therefore reasonably secure and people were encouraged to move here and settle and given a suitable relocation package no doubt. The package might have included a small degree of safety from marauding Danes, Welsh and later, Normans. The city did eventually fall to the Normans but was the last city in England to do so.

When the Saxons had taken it back they set about renaming the place. It had been a city with legions of soldiers in it for a long time, so it can't have taken them long to plump for Legacaestir, 'City of the Legions'. After the 'Lega' was dropped they were left with Caestir which slowly became Chester. Its strategic position close to North Wales meant that the city continued to be important militarily. Since it was at a crossing point of the river, it would have controlled a major trade route between England and Scotland. It was also a significant port. They seemed to have it all and the trading aspect certainly contributed greatly to Chester's continuing success during the Middle Ages. The port diminished in importance as the river silted up but it remained an important market town. The river was dredged in the mid-eighteenth century, a canal reached here by the beginning of the nineteenth, and there was something of a revival but it never 'boomed' industrially like many of the other northern towns. It is rather charming and genteel as a result.

I walked a small section of the fabulous City Walls. Chester claims the most complete Roman/Saxon/Medieval Walls in the country and they offer a great way to see the city and appreciate its setting. Walking along such structures always makes me stop to wonder about things like who patrolled this spot two thousand years ago and who made their way home via this route in 1279.

Chester's other great attraction is the shopping area known as The Rows. As shopping areas go, this is pretty darned good. The buildings are half-timbered black and white constructions joined by continuous covered galleries. Most of this is 'mock-Tudor' but who cares? To see what Chester may have looked like in the thirteenth century, I checked out the Three Old

Arches in Bridge Street dated 1274AD. I could easily have spent the day in Chester, if not more, but I couldn't and I was left with a tantalising impression of a town that would pay great dividends to those with time to explore.

Back at the bus station I surveyed options. Chester still stood as a gateway into Wales. Had I but world enough and time I would have considered a longer foray into that great country. I had set myself a time limit of one month for my overall journey and, although I had absolutely no idea really, I felt that I would not be able to fit in a Welsh tour. That would have to wait for another time. Looking at possible destinations to the south, my eye fell upon Shrewsbury. That seemed to be a sensible option on a number of levels. It was in the right direction, it was a good number of miles away and it had a youth hostel.

We breached Chester's town walls at Little John Street, passed by the racecourse and crossed the Dee. The weather continued to hold as we made our way out of town and I waited for the familiar change in scenery from urban to rural. We passed through Lache, once a hamlet but now a housing estate. The houses, roads, streetlights, benches, bushes, gardens, pedestrian crossings and street signs of the urban landscape gave way and settlements gradually separated themselves as exemplified by Cuckoo's Nest, a tiny collection of farm buildings, which would certainly qualify for the category of 'remote'. Apparently this was the site of a repair yard for the narrow gauge railway that served the nearby Eaton Hall estate. I had a railway once too, but mine fitted in the loft.

We crossed the border and I began a brief, unplanned excursion into Wales. At Rossett we were treated to a glimpse of the Mill. This was a new-build in 1588 and replaced a former structure. It looked well-preserved although hard to tell if it was functioning. My dictionary was not particularly helpful in regard to the origins of the village's name, excusing itself by pointing out that I was actually in Wales and it was, after all, a dictionary of *English* place names. It did indicate that 'Ross' is a hill-spur, moor, or 'heathy upland'. So perhaps a Rossett was a smaller version.

Subsequent investigations have revealed that this has

nothing to do with it and that the derivation is Welsh. One suggestion is that it is made up of a word for horse (hros) and settlement (set). Another is that it has come from Yr Orsedd, meaning 'The High Seat' or The Judgement Seat.

We climbed to the more sizeable Gresford and enjoyed good views to the north east.

Inadvertently I was traversing the area of my birth and early years as we headed towards Wrexham.

Q. What's the effect on towns when you take away the industries that have helped them grow and flourish?

A. 'Wrexham'.

Although this is the largest settlement in North Wales, all its main supporting industries, such as mining, seemed over and done with by the time I arrived and the area looked in need of regeneration.

We passed through Ruabon. I lived here until I was about five years old. I don't remember much about it from those times but we returned often and I can still see through my child's eye the vast slag heaps which looked like mountains to me, albeit accompanied by pit-head wheels and gantries rather than ski-lifts or cable car stations. Of the village itself I have images of fields which needed to be traversed in order to reach the local shops and of my grandparent's home just off the main street. From an upstairs landing here you could, if you stood on a stool and craned your neck out of the window, catch a glimpse of trains calling at the station far down below. From the stone terrace, a flight of steep, covered steps led down to the walled garden. Although a few houses, like that of my grandparents, were made of stone, red brick seemed to dominate. This is not surprising given that the large clay deposits in the area supported at least three brick works during the twentieth century.

Chirk boasts a castle and some fantastic examples of industrial architecture which resulted from the need to get a canal and a railway from one side of a valley to the other. When Thomas Telford and William Jessop designed the means of conveyance for these they did so with style. The aqueduct carries the Llangollen branch of the Shropshire Union Canal 70 feet above the ground. Less than fifty years after the completion of the aqueduct you could argue that it was almost obsolete. The railways had arrived and a viaduct was needed. I am pleased to say that both these structures have remained even if the canal is in use more for pleasure than for trade. Together they make for an awesome sight. At the same time they seem quite at home in this setting and don't jar on the senses, they have become a part of the landscape rather than obliterating it. Crossing either of these would take you across the Welsh/English border and my own brief sojourn into Wales ended as we headed on towards Oswestry.

Oswestry in Shropshire is a frontier town on a troubled border. Frontier towns in my mind are usually inhabited by men in large hats who gallop into town on horseback, dismount with consummate ease from their stallions, push open the swing doors of a saloon and stride over to a bar ordering two fingers of whisky before either passionately embracing a red-lipped harlot or gunning down a no-good, two-bit varmint. If Oswestry was going to be anything like that then I was in for an exciting time. Oswestry wasn't anything like that. I didn't really expect it to be and it's just as well because I can't ride a horse, I don't have a gun and my mother warned me off red-lipped harlots. Well, harlots of any description come to think about it.

Oswestry has had its moments, of course, but if you'd been here in the 1860s, when the frontier towns of the Wild West were 'wild', you would have found people quietly building reservoirs and developing market places, founding a football club and opening a railway station amongst other rather genteel activities. However, there is a rather bloody and turbulent episode from the more distant past, which some claim to be the origin of the town's name, said to be a corruption of 'Oswald's Tree'. The Oswald in question is traditionally believed to be the Christian King Oswald. He is said to have died at the hands of the pagan King Penda who had his body hung in a tree to show he meant business. A more sedate interpretation merely suggests that there was a tree owned by a man named Oswald. Well, there's no photographic record so we can't be certain. What *is* certain is the ongoing struggle between the Welsh and English to determine who should have the land and the town. In the course of these disputes Oswestry has been burnt down, rebuilt and burnt down again on more than one occasion. The cycle obviously ended with a rebuilding rather than a fire otherwise there would be nothing to see but ashes and burnt timber.

As part of the military defences between the Anglian kingdom of Mercia and the Welsh kingdom of Powys, the Saxon king Offa built a dyke that ran from 'sea to sea'. There is a National Trail based along the dyke which runs from Chepstow to Prestatyn and passes quite close by. Happily, on my visit Oswestry was a calm and peaceful place. No-one seemed to be intent on invading or claiming land or burning the place down in frustration. It is a lovely example of a country market town with handsome buildings as well as a few reminders of the more turbulent past. High on this list would be the remains of a castle which has Norman origins and connections with all sorts of people from Alan Fitzlaad, an ancestor to the FitzAlan Earls of Arundel, through Henry II to the mysterious fifteenth century Welsh nationalist, Owain Glyndwr.

Railways too played a more peaceful but nonetheless important role in the development of the town, and the town, in turn, became an important hub for the railways. It is only fitting, then, that there should be a transport museum to visit. Oswestry proved a good place to pause; but pause is about all I could do.

The last leg of the journey allowed me to savour this beautiful part of the country. It is full of lovely scenery and the bus was not in any hurry. It was a good feeling, if hard to identify. There was no anxiety because I wasn't wandering as though lost or purposeless. Neither was I hurrying as if late for an appointment. I decided that I wasn't even simply going to Shrewsbury. No, I was 'wending my way' there. I think that's about the best description and one that could be applied to most journeys on a bus. I drank in the wonderful views of the Shropshire Plain with distant vistas of Wales providing a fantastic backdrop in the west.

Shrewsbury is another frontier town which does a very good

job of disguising itself as a charming medieval market town. There is a charming market square and plenty of charming narrow streets lined with charming black and white buildings. I have to admit, I was charmed. In addition to all the architecture there is the River Severn coiling round the town like a brown snake. It may not always be brown but it was when I saw it. It was still churning away after a recent attempt at flooding the town, a habit towards which the river is predisposed.

I viewed the waters from the safety of The English Bridge. This spanned the river at the site originally taken by a structure thought to date back to Norman times, and which also had a gate tower, a drawbridge, accommodation for the gatekeeper and even shops. That bridge eventually fell down. A replacement was built in the 1700s but this, with an unutterably forgivable lack of foresight, was built in such a way that it was unsuitable for 'modern traffic'. It was too narrow, too steep and had a hump. And so it came to pass, in the 1920s, when 'modern traffic' had had enough of squeezing itself across this narrow, awkward crossing, the bridge was demolished. It sounds dreadful but there is a happy ending to the tale because the bridge was very carefully demolished. In fact, 'demolished' sounds altogether too harsh a word to describe the painstaking manner in which the structure was disassembled. This was accomplished stone by stone with each one being numbered with scrupulous attention to detail. All this was done because the old, original stones were to be re-used in the construction of the new bridge. How refreshing to hear of such an approach to renewal and 'modernisation'. In my limited experience it is far more usual for those concerned with such matters to explain that this kind of reclamation and refurbishment is highly uneconomic and a far better method is to bring in the bulldozers and start again. The new bridge was wider, less steep and humpless and, it seems, everyone was happy.

Shrewsbury also boasts another listed bridge on the other side of town. This is the Welsh Bridge, also from the 1700s and also a very fine structure. The Welsh Bridge is confusingly still in England but on the Welsh side of town and the original was again fortified with an imposing gatehouse.

Shrewsbury Youth Hostel accepted me and my huge rucksack. I left the rucksack and briefly explored some of the town in the gathering evening. I was charmed by its charms once again and by a couple of pints of local beer.

Back at the hostel I fell to chatting with a couple of girls from New Zealand who, like me, were travelling the country. They, unlike me, seemed to be very well-organised with a pre-planned itinerary. They, like me, found the country immensely varied and predominantly attractive and so completely full of amazing history. They, unlike me, seemed to have boundless reserves of energy. I soon began to feel rather sleepy due to circumstances entirely unrelated to the couple of pints of local beer.

I retired to my dorm. When I say 'my dorm', this time I mean it. I was the only male guest that night. This was a good thing in that I didn't have to worry about there being a snorer in the room but bad since it also suggested that business could have been better. It was August after all, the height of the holiday season.

It was, understandably, very quiet in the dorm. I assessed the day and mentally ticked boxes for satisfactory distance covered (must be more than 100 miles, I reckoned) and of sights seen (Chester, Oswestry, the place of my birth, countryside, rolling hills) and so on through the drowsiness and into sleep.

Day 17

Dropping down the borders

21ˢᵗ August

I perused my Tourist Map before breakfast and vaguely plotted a course, knowing that I was at the mercy of bus routes and timetables in a similar way that people in sailing boats depend on favourable winds. The sensible thing seemed to be to drop down, almost due south, to Ludlow. I noticed that this would entail traversing a large area of pale green, signifying high ground, and possibly passing through Church Stretton and Craven Arms as well as passing by the Long Mynd. On my map this had a star symbol next to it. This meant it was an 'Other Place of Interest'. As I was discovering, applying that criterion, you could pretty much cover the whole map with stars.

Before leaving town I took in some of Shrewsbury's Tudor houses and visited Shrewsbury Abbey. The present building here is all that remains of a once great Norman structure. For all that, there are Norman bits and pieces here and there together with plenty of other items of interest, including the font which is made from the inverted base of a Roman column. Working onwards through time there are Norman arches from 1083, twelfth and thirteenth century tombs brought in from other churches, the west window from about 1380, blocked walls in the side aisles marking the effects of the Dissolution in 1540, evidence of demolition during the Civil War, the rebuilt Choir and Chancel from 1886–7 and the war memorial containing the name of the poet Wilfred Owen, who lived in Shrewsbury and died in the last days of the First World War. At one time the place would have thronged with pilgrims, perhaps visiting the Shrine of St Winefride, but not during my visit. I shared the space with a few other members of the public respectfully speaking in hushed voices that echoed softly round the nave. Perhaps their reasons for being there were different from the pilgrims of long ago but perhaps, like them, they hoped for some spiritual uplift, even if this simply took the form of a time of tranquillity away from the busyness of the world.

As I boarded an Arriva bus I was beginning to feel more confident about achieving my ultimate aim. In a little over two weeks I had managed to get as far east and north in England as one could reasonably expect using buses and I was well on the way south. I thought this was pretty good going, especially given that I had opted for almost no research before my departure. The lack of research meant I had little clue as to which company would be running the buses I would need on any given day and where they would actually go. That was part of the fun for me but could be overcome by proper planning and use of the internet. Even with my reckless approach, the bus transport system, although operated by separate companies, had sufficient overlap between 'rival' territories to allow for some 'joining up'. It had worked very successfully so far and so with these cheery, confident thoughts in mind I happily boarded a bus for Ludlow. Although I knew it was hardly what could be described as a heaving metropolis I felt sure that there would be connecting buses from there. I bought a single and, with my rucksack safely stowed in the luggage rack, took a seat nearby and settled down.

We passed over the Severn via the English Bridge and were soon out of town. A few miles south we came to Bayston Hill. Bayston was recorded as Begestan in the Domesday Book, and meant 'the stone of a woman called Beage', with the appendage of 'hill' coming from the Old English 'hyll'. Beage's stone hill has obviously continued to be a source of interest for many, including the operators of a large quarry. Take a sharp left up Sharpstone Lane and you will find Bayston Hill Quarry from where up to 800,000 tonnes of gritstone aggregate are extracted each and every year. Getting this much rock out of the ground obviously results in a pretty big hole—apparently 1km by 300m by 95m. The hole was not visible from the bus and you have to wonder what the journey would be like without something like Brayston's greywacke gritstone surfacing the road. If we want roads, the material to build, maintain and repair them has to come from somewhere. I suppose the question is, how many roads do we want and what do we want them for? Surely predictions of car ownership levels from, say, 2006, will look a bit shaky in light of the world-wide financial catastrophe of recent years, and particularly its effects on the car manufacturers, not to mention the issues surrounding oil supplies and climate change. Yet the loudest voice still seems to be shouting "Build more roads, build more roads!"

We drove through spacious countryside, the feeling of space resulting from a low population density. In Manchester there are over 9000 people for every square mile while people in Inner London share the equivalent space with over 22000 people. In Shropshire, each square mile only has to accommodate 235 people. Through the bus window I watched largely unpopulated and empty hills rolling gently into the distance above expanses of fields strewn with straw bales.

We detoured from our determined push south and fell straight into the arms of Condover, a substantial village for this rural setting. The streets were lined with pretty cottages either of brick the colour of the local sandstone or rendered and painted. Small windows were tucked under steeply pitched tiled roofs. Condover Hall is an Elizabethan Manor built in the 1590s for the family of one Thomas Owen MP. Apparently Mark Twain stayed here on visits in 1873 and 1879. Some may also find delight in the lovely church of St Mary and St Andrew while others may be drawn to the remains of an RAF base from the Second World War. It makes for an interesting little juxtaposition of two longstanding threads of our country's 'narrative'—faith and war.

The lanes through which we passed were lined with trees whose leafy fingers brushed against the windows. Out in the sunshine, cows and sheep grazed the fields as we wound our way to the tiny but very 'cool' Ryton and then to nearby Dorrington. The Bridge Inn looked inviting, and tempting foods were on offer at the Netley Fruit Farm where potatoes, raspberries, strawberries, carrots, cabbages, cauliflowers and runner beans were all available. Minutes later yet another charming village of half-timbered houses appeared. This was Leebotwood whose historical pedigree is evidenced by the thirteenth century church and the fifteenth century, thatched, Pound Inn.

The village is in the shadow of the Long Mynd, the 'Other Place of Interest' marked on my Tourist Map. The curious name means 'Long Mountain' and people have been busy up there since the Bronze Age. From the bus it seemed imposing and appealing with the bright sun bringing out all the shades of green, brown and purple with which it was clothed. The colours come partly from the rock but also from the covering of bilberries and heather. The Mynd is within the Shropshire Hills Area of Outstanding Natural Beauty and is also an area of special biological and geological interest. I gazed, rather longingly, at the heights and remembered the clean freshness of hilltop air. Although the walking was denied me this time, the bus service could bring others to a useful setting-off point for just such a venture.

The bus was full of conversation and there was an almost jolly atmosphere. It was plainly not a bus full of commuters on their way to work. Nor was it a bus displaying the national trait of 'being reserved' so often associated with the British or, perhaps particularly, the English. People can travel on the same train or bus for years and never speak. Not so the Shrewsbury–Ludlow bus on this glorious summer day. We were having a rare old time and it was more like a mobile coffee morning... minus the coffee.

Church Stretton was a farmstead or village on 'the Street' and the street being referred to was Watling Street. The 'Church' prefix distinguishes it from the other nearby 'Strettons' which were also on, or at least near, this important Roman road. Church Stretton is yet another reason to fall in love with the area and to write it in your list of places to visit. The backdrop of the Long Mynd obviously helps but even with glorious hills surrounding it, any town could be a little less than special. Not so Church Stretton, which has plenty of charm and historical character. I got the sense that here was an unhurried and peaceful place, where the pressures and urgency of much of the modern world were paid little heed. Carding Mill Valley wound its way from here back up to the heights of the Long Mynd and there were further walking opportunities on the Caradoc, Hazler and Ragleth Hills to the other side of town. To underline the fact that this was definitely a rural area, we passed near to Acton Scott Historic Working Farm and soon had to negotiate a number of horses being ridden down the road.

Wistanstow came and went with its church, post office and Plough Inn conjoined with the Woods Brewery. I must admit there were times, and this was one of them, when I regretted whizzing past things on a bus. Craven Arms looked worthy of closer inspection, too, as did the nearby fortified manor of Stokesay Castle. However, time was not on my side. 'Time is not on your side,' I told myself, as we traversed a level crossing and the River Onny at Onibury.

My compensation took the form of the wonderful town of Ludlow. It's not all wonderful, of course, but most of it is. From a distance the tower of the central church rises above the rooftops. You need to avert your eyes from things like supermarkets and the railway station on the way in but otherwise the town's a treat. The bus carries you up Corve Street to the top of town, past the seventeenth century Feathers Hotel and the Bull Ring along to Market Square. Once off the bus you can't turn round without tripping over history. Nor can you go far without finding somewhere great to eat or purchase food. Market Square is adjacent to Ludlow Castle, a marvellous medieval ruin perched on a cliff above the River Teme. While invoking everything romantic and chivalrous, the castle had a serious job to do as a fortress on the border with Wales and also as a royal residence.

Ludlow became a walled town in the thirteenth century and the gateway on Broad Street remains to give a clue as to the size of these constructions. At the bottom of Broad Street the road crosses over the river via the Ludford Bridge. Just past the Charlton Arms Hotel, a right turn takes you to The Bread Walk, so called because some of those who laboured in its construction were paid in bread. This path leads round above the river to Dinham Bridge and another climb back to Market Square. Just off the square is the church of St Laurence, mostly rebuilt in the fifteenth century. There were plenty of special things to see here including some wonderful carvings on the misericords, those little projections beneath an upturned seat that allowed for some support for a standing person. You would be forgiven for thinking, when looking at these narrow perches, that the name derives from 'misery' since they look extremely uncomfortable. Just the opposite is true, however, as the meaning comes from 'compassionate', itself stemming from 'pity' and 'heart'. The ashes of A.E. Housman, who wrote the poem 'A Shropshire Lad', are buried against the wall and there are great views from the tower, too. I loved the way different periods of Ludlow's past were in evidence through its architecture. In addition to these treasures the town had proper tea rooms in de Greys, and cheesemongers, fruiterers, butchers and bakers. It was a whirlwind visit and there was far too much to take in during my brief stay. Even so, it's small enough to quickly gain a good sense of the place. It's quiet, calm, and, let's not forget, a 'foodie capital'.

Buses left from Mill Street by the Assembly Rooms, another lovely building, this time from 1840. I'm sorry to inject potentially boring stuff about tickets and timetables but they get to be quite important when you're travelling by bus. It's really about trying to get the best value for money, rather than being the first signs of becoming a nerd. I wondered about a 'Rover' ticket (£4.60) but was not sure how far this would get me beyond my next port of call. It would have been great if I wanted to spend the day exploring some of the 'black and white' villages in the area but would not necessarily suit my purposes if the relevant bus operator did not provide services beyond Hereford. I took my chances with a single on a First Midland Red service at £3.15.

It was a restorative journey through tranquil and beautiful scenery. There was turmoil and unrest just below the surface. In 2002, many in the farming community were still reeling from the poorly-handled outbreak of foot-and-mouth disease the previous year. Things were also gearing up for the 'Liberty and Livelihood' march which was billed as a protest against the fact that a distant, ignorant and predominantly 'townie' government was passing legislation that affected rural life in ways they did not understand. This wider range of concerns had grown from an initial reaction to the proposed ban on fox hunting, and the strength of local feeling was in evidence through the numerous Liberty and Livelihood placards on show. It was a sign of a schism in the land.

Another schism had occurred locally when somebody decided to build nearby Richard's Castle. Richard, having a castle and all that, would no doubt have owned most of the wonderful countryside over which I gazed and would have had fellow castle-owners over for a spot of hunting, shooting, fishing and whatever else was the rage in the 1050s. The Richard in question was one Richard FitzScrob who had been granted the plot by Edward the Confessor. After Richard's death, the castle passed to his son Osbern Fitz Richard and from him to his grandson Osbern Fitz Hugh. When he passed on, the castle passed on to his brother-in-law Hugh de Say who died in 1190, leaving the place to his son, another Hugh Say. I would love to be able to tell you that he married into a family of market gardeners and it was thus that the castle finally passed into the hands of Hugh Say Tomatoes. Sadly, this is not possible since it actually went to the Mortimers and thence to the Talbots who were still living there in the fourteenth century. In the succeeding 200 years it all went pear-shaped and the castle was in ruins. Interestingly, Richard's Castle was 'Norman' despite being built before the Norman invasion. At the time of its construction there were no castles in England because no-one had heard of them. This one was only built because it was built by foreigners and its arrival caused outrage, shock and offence. It was an eleventh century 'monstrous carbuncle'. The monk who described its construction and the effects on the local landscape had referred to it as a 'castle' since that was the foreigners' word for it.

In the Domesday Book, Richard's Castle is associated with

the name Alretune, the modern equivalent of which is Orleton, a village through which we soon passed. Of interest here was The Boot Inn, a black and white public house built when Richard's Castle had become a ruin. The bus was travelling through an area renowned for its black and white villages and there were more of these attractive buildings at Luston.

Luston may not hold a candle to Lord Hereford's Knob in the 'saucily suggestive place-name' stakes, but it's fun to think for a few moments that it might have been a 'town of Lust'. Such thoughts are short lived and sent packing when the place-name dictionary reveals a meaning of 'insignificant or louse infested farmhouse'. Oh well.

After a few more small settlements at Hope-under-Dinmore, Moreton-on-Lugg, and Upper Lyn we reached the outer limits of Hereford, 'Historic City of the Marches'. I must admit to feeling that it looked more like a Historic City of the Hypermarkets as we passed car dealerships, huge stores and light industries. You need to ignore the outskirts and find Hereford's heart. In fact you need to ignore quite a lot and search out the history and associated buildings. They are there, but I felt they were rather overwhelmed. Take the bus station. Please, please, take the bus station. Oh, it's hard, I know, we can't have it both ways. I've already suggested that if bus travel is going to be elevated to anything other than a last resort or Hobson's choice, the associated facilities need to be upgraded. And Hereford's bus station is quite modern. You know, clean, efficient... soulless. Perhaps you can't have everything.

To be fair to Hereford, I wasn't giving it a particularly close examination. I was once again more intent on my onward progress. It was getting to that point in the day, mid-afternoon, when I would begin to consider whereabouts I might be laying my head that night. Looking at my trusty Tourist Map I was presented with an obstacle which called for a decision about onward routes. The obstacle was the Severn Estuary. From Hereford I could attempt to drop down to Monmouth and Chepstow and follow this with a crossing on one of the Severn Bridges. Alternatively, I could swing east to Ross-on-Wye then to Gloucester and from there begin to move more directly south. I wasn't sure how many buses would traverse the Severn Estuary per day, if they did at all. I was more confident about buses in and out of Gloucester so I plumped for that route.

So my survey of Hereford only really consisted of a walk along the High Street with its varied collection of buildings from different periods. Some of these were quite plain but still handsome enough. One or two were rather more ornate and grand, embellished with columns or arches and in one case even topped off with a clock tower. I like the half-timbered Old House and the impressive but rather stolid Shire Hall. Any normal person would ensure that a visit to Hereford included a good deal of time at the Cathedral, which has twelfth century origins and is home to many treasures including the Mappa Mundi. Not me; I was on my way again just after 3.30, courtesy of a County Rider at £4.00 from Stagecoach. Once again we passed through gorgeous countryside and there were good views to the Welsh hills. We passed a little village called Much Birch, which has ribboned its way along the road. Nearby is Little Birch and the distinction between these two 'places at the birch trees' is the Old English 'micel', meaning 'great', which has become 'much'. We briefly paused at Peterstow Post Office with tantalising glimpses of the Yew Tree Inn and soon reached Bridstow, a 'holy place of St Brigid' where a fine old church is dedicated to this Irish patron saint.

We passed once more over the Wye, the river having snaked its way here from Hereford by a slightly different route. From the midst of this dramatic scenery we suddenly came upon Ross-on-Wye. The town looked small and friendly from the bus, a collection of houses, municipal buildings and shops, running up and down from the river, topped with a tall church spire. Although this has long been a market town, as evidenced by the fine seventeenth century Market Hall, it received a real boost in the mid eighteenth century when people began to visit just because it was nice to look at. In other words, they came as tourists and were some of the first people in England to do this. The growth of Ross-on-Wye as a tourist attraction seems to be down in large part to two men. The first was Dr John Egerton, a rector in the town. In 1745 he began to take his fashionable visitors for boat trips along the river to allow them to enjoy the views. The second was Rev. William Gilpin who came to the area in 1770 in one of a series of summer excursions. During these excursions, Gilpin was making notes and sketches and defining what, for him, was truly 'picturesque', that is 'suitable for painting'. His *Observations on the River Wye* was finally published in 1782. Other writers followed suit and Ross and the Wye became a popular destination by the turn of the nineteenth century.

Ross-on-Wye still has a lot going for it. For a start you have the position by the river which provides a great setting for the town. Then you have the fact that the town has been spread over a hill. As a result you have changes in ground level, gradients and streets that slope. Again, this may not be fabulous if you have to push twins in a buggy or deliver a freezer, but to the unencumbered it makes for streetscapes of greater interest. On top of this, literally, add the architecture, which in Ross-on-Wye's case is pretty close to brilliant. There are timbered buildings amongst the dominant sandstone but all go together to create a gentle harmony.

Once out of town we passed through the rural countryside that many have grown to know and love. This is an amazing 'patchwork quilt' of worked fields and hedgerows which is such a recognised feature of our landscape. It's all romanticised and unreal, I know, but these pastoral scenes seem to be deep in our British psyche; well some of our British psyches at least. I know it's all pretend and it's not meant to look like this, because great big prairie fields are much more economically sound and you can use huge bits of farm machinery like they do in America, but I'd miss the hedgerows and the trees and the awkward shapes of the fields and those isolated copses of trees and everything else that makes this type of countryside so idiosyncratic and consequently so comforting to look at.

We passed through an increasingly wooded landscape taking in Weston under Penyard and Lea before eventually crossing the Severn and then over the Over Causeway and into Gloucester. Another Cathedral city, another Cathedral missed. I needed to make another decision. I could call it a day regarding onward progress, see a bit of Gloucester then make a fresh start tomorrow. Or I could push on a bit further and make more headway towards my southern and western goals. I went for the latter, picking Slimbridge as a destination from my trusty Tourist Map and from the available options at the bus station.

Slimbridge is famous for the Wildfowl and Wetlands Trust's Slimbridge Reserve where thousands of birds gather at various times of year to marvel at the thousands of humans who congregate there. I thought this might be a pleasant place for an overnight stop and had identified The Tudor Caravanning and Camping Park as a possible place to lay my weary head.

The bus was heading to Dursley but dropped me at the 'Slimbridge crossroads'. When the bus had disappeared I surveyed my surroundings and thought that they most resembled a scene from Hitchcock's film *North by Northwest*. I awaited the arrival of a low-flying crop spraying aircraft but nothing appeared and so I set off on the rather long walk to my destination. There was a distinct lack of half-timbered caravans, open sewers, street urchins, people wearing neck ruffs or indeed any other visible sign that the caravanning and camping that went on here was any more Tudor than anywhere else. Perhaps I had misunderstood. It wouldn't be the first time.

Actually I was glad I didn't have to undertake Tudor camping because I'm sure they didn't have carbon-fibre poles at their disposal nor lightweight water-repellent fabrics, and I bet it would have taken them more than 12 minutes to get their tents up. Yes, that's right, it only took me 12 minutes to have a perfectly adequate place to sleep. Adequate is a carefully chosen word here.

As I settled for the night I set an alarm for 7.00. This in itself was quite alarming but I had checked timetables at the bus stop and there was one bus due at 9.01. Again, the emphasis was on the *one* bus. There would be others eventually but after a delay that would threaten to ruin the day. It was quite a trek out to the bus stop and would be a long walk from there to civilisation, which anyway would not have been worth it. So, missing the bus was not an option, as I would potentially have had to endure hours of waiting in the desolation that was the Slimbridge crossroads. No, it was all too terrible to contemplate. I had to be up with my shelter packed away and on my back in plenty of time. I would endeavour to do my bit but would the B7 from Beaumont Travel arrive as promised?

Day 18

Back to the coast, eventually

22nd *August*

Another glorious morning helped me face the early start and deal with the business of tent-collapsing and bag-packing. I was at the crossroads in plenty of time. It was even more lonely and bleak than I remembered. Another problem faced me. There was more than one bus stop where the timetable indicated that the B7 would be calling. The timetables all showed the bus would go where I wanted it to go but they also indicated that it went in the opposite direction. I wasn't sure where to position myself. I could always ask the driver once I'd stopped the bus but how would I achieve this with the customary signal if I was in the wrong place? A lot was riding on the B7 and I hoped I would be too.

The absence of vegetation and the Roman-straightness of the roads meant I could see quite a long way down the roads. For a long while all I could see down the road was tarmac. Nothing moved. There was hardly a breath of wind and no birdsong. I was in an apocalyptic movie and the last man alive. Then at 8.53 a small blueish cuboid appeared in the distance and rapidly transformed itself into a minibus bearing B7 on a piece of A4 propped up on the dashboard. Panic over. It headed towards me and I managed to stop it. I boarded, bought a ticket for Thornbury and we set off—early.

What about people who might arrive later but still in time for the scheduled 9.01 departure? To be fair, you could see quite a long way in all directions and there wasn't anybody approaching on foot. Assuming that a reasonably fit adult can cover 1.2 metres per second, there was no-one in a three minute radius so our early departure was justifiable. I was able to adopt this rather phlegmatic attitude because I was on the bus and not standing by a bus stop at a windswept, desolate crossroads at 9.00, thinking I was in plenty of time for the 9.01.

My reason for choosing Thornbury as a staging post was that I reckoned this just might be the northern territorial limit of First buses, which operated in and around the Bristol area. If so, I could buy a day ticket to get into Bristol, out the other side and then on to I knew not where. Thornbury is a market town to the north of Bristol quite near the M5. When I arrived it looked pleasant enough from the vantage point of The Plain/ Rock Street area where I was deposited and from where I would continue. My 'Open Special' from First cost me a fiver. I felt quite good as I was on my way towards Bristol and it was only half past nine in the morning.

Our route took us to Almondsbury, a village in the Bristol–Bath greenbelt, sandwiched between the M4 and the M5 motorways or, if you are an estate agent, 'within easy access of the M4/M5 interchange'. Now, Almondsbury sounds similar in a number of respects to Thornbury. The latter was a 'fortified place where thorn trees grow' according to my Dictionary. I found it hard to believe that this was a fortified place where almond trees grew. The place-name dictionary revealed that the similar-sounding Almondbury in West Yorkshire was 'a stronghold of the whole community', from the rather wonderful Old Scandinavian 'almenn'. The South Gloucestershire version was apparently the stronghold of the rather more insular and exclusive Aethelmod. Aethelmod knew what he was doing when he chose his site because he would have had, as we did, good views across the Severn and to the Welsh Hills beyond.

Our resolute journey southwards along the Gloucester Road was interrupted by a short detour to the Cribbs Causeway shopping mall. What would Aethelmod make of this, I wonder? What did I make of it? You either like these places or you don't. You like shopping. You hate shopping. You like shopping and you want somewhere temperature-controlled and dry where you can shop all year round in a comfortable and relaxed atmosphere. You hate shopping so you do your utmost to avoid ever setting foot in such a place. Plenty of my fellow passengers were in the 'like shopping' group and left us. Cribbs was controversial in its time as a sure-fire way of destroying the retail heart of Bristol. The two now seem to co-exist quite happily, and the latter has had a recent face-lift; well, actually, serious reconstructive surgery.

Our visit was brief and we returned to the Gloucester Road and continued our long drive through Bristol's suburbs. And what a long drive it seemed as Bristol's suburbs went on and on. And on. Poor old suburbs, they have a hard time of it. Strictly speaking they're just the outlying districts of a city but they have managed to attract some less than flattering associations. We talk about things or people being rather 'suburban' when we mean they are provincial, narrow-minded, middle-class, mediocre and slightly dull. And, of course, some people, possibly me, talk about places being suburbs of somewhere when they deserve to be viewed as entities of their own. This might be true of Filton. Certainly it would have been true once, even at the beginning of the twentieth century when it was still a rural farming community. Such distinctions and boundaries were hard to spot on the ground when I passed through.

As we continued on our way the landscape became decidedly more 'urb' and less 'suburb' as the building density increased in line, no doubt, with an increasing value for the land. Down the length of Gloucester Road you could avail yourself of the services of innumerable hairdressers, feed from any number of take-aways and cafes, clothe yourself from second hand and charity shops, save pounds in a Poundsaver store, buy hardware, software and evening wear and even celebrate with a bottle of something from the offie. Gloucester Road mysteriously but briefly became Cheltenham Road before morphing into Stokes Croft and North Street from which we entered onto the roundabout that is St James Barton. A quick circuit of this and we terminated in the Bristol Bus Station, a fairly unsightly and unwelcoming shed. This is what I had come to expect of bus stations and Bristol's was no exception. Bristol is apparently one of the most-visited cities in Britain, and quite right too. It's a really 'happening', multi-cultural sort of place. It has great facilities, some wonderful and varied architecture, museums, theatres, music venues, parks, landscapes, a harbour and more besides. People arriving on the bus must wonder what they've let themselves in for. They should put up a sign that says something like "This building is not representative of Bristol as a whole. Please do not re-board your bus immediately. Trust us—the city itself is really nice."

And for the most part, it really is. Bristol is also a bit of a transport hub and all manner of opportunities for bus routes out of town presented themselves. I decided that I would strike out for the coast but rather than go there directly I elected to visit Wells in Somerset first. Why go straight to somewhere when there's a perfectly good long way round?

Having ploughed our way *in* through the suburbs, we now had to find our way out again, this time through Totterdown, Knowle, Hengrove and finally Whitchurch where we breached the built-up area and allowed the A37 to lead us on into an increasingly green landscape where we rose, to be presented with expansive rural views, or fell to be enveloped in pretty wooded valleys. Having spent much of the day so far in built-up areas, it was good to get out into the countryside again. One of the beauties of travelling in Britain is the speed with which you can leave behind the towns and cities, with all they have to offer, and find yourself in countryside where you can quickly forget that such large settlements exist. The place-names became altogether more fanciful and resolutely un-Scandinavian. We started off quite tamely with Pensford and Clutton, before moving on to the more esoteric offerings such as Temple Cloud, Farrington Gurney and Chewton Mendip whose associations range from the Knights Templar, the du Garnay family and the River Chew in the Mendip Hills. After this particularly pleasant piece of meandering, we came into Wells.

The 'bus station' is in Princes Road to the west of the city centre. I took in the array of shelters and bus bays and felt heartened that the connections to other parts of the area from here would be many and varied. I quickly checked on the chances of reaching Weston-super-Mare before visiting the city's most famous landmark.

The west façade of Wells Cathedral is a gorgeous edifice into which are carved 500 figures, 300 of which are medieval. It's impressive now but what must it have looked like when painted with deep-coloured hues and highlighted with gold leaf? The cathedral is currently set in an almost perfect position with the green in front and ancient streets to either side. Nearby is the Bishop's palace and through an archway (the Bishop's Eye) the Market Place.

The cathedral is as breathtaking inside as out. The columns rise to the point where any details are lost from view. Yet you somehow know that up there in the shadows are examples of the intricate and painstaking sculpting skills of stonemasons, every bit as good as the ones nearer the ground. Two attention-grabbing features in Wells Cathedral are an unusual scissor arch and a medieval clock. The arch turns out to be an ingenious emergency repair from about 1340, when it was implemented by master mason William Joy to avoid the impending collapse of the central tower. A solution that is a good deal more beautiful than a couple of RSJs. The wonderful medieval astronomical clock has a face showing a pre-Copernican universe with the Earth at its centre against a background of stars. The sun moves in a circle indicating the hour while a smaller star on an inner ring shows the minutes. A further inner circle represents the moon and a pointer indicates the age of the moon in its 30 day cycle. A particular treat is the set of jousting knights who appear on the quarter hour.

Out in the sunshine again I enjoyed some of the 'unspoilt heritage' in the little streets and alleys of the town that I took on my meander back to the bus station. On the bus we spent a leisurely hour and a quarter winding our way towards Weston-super-Mare, effectively following the boundary of the Mendips Area of Outstanding Natural Beauty. The surrounding country-side has long been cherished, in a similar way perhaps to the Wye Valley. It was certainly during the time that the Wye enjoyed its reputation as a tourist destination that at least one person down here was worried by the possible effects of the soon-to-arrive railways and the tourists they would bring:

*Must our unpretending valley, as yet unknown to tourists
and overturners of every kind, be ravaged by the invader
who has tapped the Lakes, disfigured the Rhine, and
pierced the heart of the Alps? Forbid it, heaven! Must we
have our quiet meads and rural lanes disfigured, the field
paths stopped by cuttings and embankments, the frisking
lambs disturbed in their sports, and placid cows in their
ruminations, and the feathered songsters of the grove scared
away by the engine's frightful squeal?*

*Baffle the threat, bright scene from Winscombe Hill; Plead
for thy peace, thou beautiful romance Of Nature!*

So wrote Theodore Compton, the author of *A Mendip Valley,
its inhabitants and surroundings* in 1892, looking back twenty-five years to the time when these fears had been expressed. That
was a time when 'the world to us was young' and 'the evil days
had not yet come when we should have no pleasure in coaching'.
Coaching, it seems, presented opportunities for 'the ever-varying
incidents of travel as we passed through country towns and villages and rural scenes' as opposed to the railway's 'hard new way,
with noisy machinery along flat, unbending rails, where all is
rigid and lifeless as iron, harsh and unfeeling as rock.'

We must have grown used to railways and you could argue
that, for a time at least, there was a certain love-affair. We
have certainly forgotten what a great upheaval they must have
caused and the alarm that was engendered by their arrival. The
extent of the schemes and the magnitude of the engineering
works involved is lost to us now. The proposed cuttings and
embankments which would have been so worrisome in 1850
have always been a part of *our* landscapes and for the most
part go unnoticed. Perhaps our modern day equivalent is the
widening motorways or the construction of bypasses. Frisking lambs and placid cows also soon got used to the engines
and their 'frightful squeals' and the doom-merchant's predictions of a ravaging of the countryside seem ill-founded. As
railways became an increasingly popular mode of transport
they were even promoted as a means of seeing beautiful parts
of the country, and it's still true today. The lines bought and

run by preservation societies have often been chosen for the scenic qualities of their surroundings and many walking and cycling trails follow old track beds, again giving access to great countryside. Bus travel, of course, has the benefit of wandering and wavering in a way that railways never could, revealing intimate glimpses of villages and hamlets that could only be viewed from a distance through the railway carriage window. I took the bus journey to be a modern equivalent of the 'coaching' referred to in 1892.

Whatever people might have felt, the railways came anyway. At one time there were three stations in Wells to service lines run by each of the Somerset and Dorset, East Somerset and Bristol and Exeter Railways. All these were in place by 1870 and the author who had noted the pre-railway concerns also expressed, from the vantage point of 1892, that Nature had managed to 'spread her mantle over Man's rude works'. Today, courtesy of Nature and Dr Beeching, you would hardly know that the railways had ever made their presence felt.

Draycott village displayed cosy-looking cottages, some small shops and St Peter's Church, designed by C. E. Giles and built in 1861. Just outside the village a sign advertised strawberries and cream for sale, reminding me of the need to keep up my pursuit of regional delicacies. This was timely as we were about to enter a village whose local delicacy has truly gone global.

Cheddar village is tucked in the shadows beneath towering limestone cliffs that rise up to form the sides of the famous and fabulous Cheddar Gorge. The land of the surrounding area is rich and this has made it prime dairy country, so it isn't surprising that cheese-making developed here. It is believed that the making of cheese through piling up and squeezing the fresh curds was developed as a way of making the commonly used curd cheese last much longer. The method was developed in Cheddar and there are references to Cheddar Cheese from 1170 so it has a long and distinguished pedigree. And pedigree is important. We all know you can buy 'cheddar' cheese almost anywhere in the same way you can buy Coca Cola, but the ubiquitous branding denies the true situation. You cannot really make Cheddar cheese in New Zealand, Ireland or

Canada or indeed anywhere else. To be proper Cheddar the cheese should be made here in the village that gave it its name. Originally, in order to qualify for the name, it had to be made from milk obtained from cows grazing within thirty miles of Wells Cathedral. For Daniel Defoe, Cheddar was without dispute, 'the best cheese that England affords, if not, that the whole world affords.' Fortunately, The Cheddar Gorge Cheese Company are busy keeping the production of this traditional cheese going.

The gorge itself is stunning, as you would expect from England's highest inland limestone cliffs which rise to over 100 metres. Hidden from view are the extensive caves which are an important part of the area's attraction for tourists. The idea that people would pay to visit these places is not new—cave explorers were busy exploiting just such possibilities in the late 1800s. Notable among these fellows is one Richard Gough, a former sea captain and tea trader, who moved to Cheddar in 1868. He spent long years and a good deal of money excavating Gough's Cave to reveal its wonders and in the process gave birth to Cheddar's tourist trade.

Onwards from Cheddar we encounter a series of delightful villages and small towns. Axbridge is a quiet and peaceful-looking place now but was a hive of Tudor industry with a burgeoning cloth trade and earlier still was part of the Wessex defence system against the Vikings. Winscombe was at one time a stop along the 'Strawberry Line' which ran from Wells to Yatton. The benevolent-sounding nickname came from the transportation of strawberries grown in and around Cheddar and is perhaps another indication of how local people's attitudes to the railway altered over time. We descended from the Mendips, passed through Locking and finally into Weston-super-Mare. Some would say that the use of the word 'super' in connection with this place is misplaced although the 'super' has nothing to do with the place being superior or superlative. What could have been Weston-on-Sea seems to have become Weston-super-Mare in the hands of an unknown medieval church clerk.

The town is a typical English 'seaside resort' in as much as it has street upon street of holiday accommodation offered by boarding houses, guest houses, bed and breakfast places and residential hotels. There are also places to buy tea, burgers, fish and chips, kebabs, pizzas, pies, candy floss, ice cream, toffee apples and large, garishly-coloured lollipops on sticks. You can buy postcards to send and mementos to keep as well as enjoying the thrill of watching your hard earned cash disappear into the machines inside the 'amusement' arcades.

What is there that might make Weston 'super'? What Weston has in spades is sand. The long, smooth, sandy beach, which is as ideal for building sand castles as it is for taking a donkey ride, is probably the resort's biggest draw. However, even this has a dark side since at low tide the sand gives way to reveal alluvial deposits which have earned the place its local nickname of Weston on Mud. According to my Tourist Map there are other attractions such as a helicopter museum, aquarium, pier, a sea front miniature railway, and even a Time Machine. I'm afraid I didn't see that. I didn't have time.

Calamine and galena, a lead ore, were mined locally until the nineteenth century and would have made an important contribution to the economy. During the same period Weston -super-Mare began to develop as a tourist destination with the rising popularity of 'taking the air' and 'taking the waters'. Where they took them isn't clear. Weston's first hotel opened in 1810 and there was a guide book by 1822. The Bristol and Exeter railway reached Weston in 1841 and a larger station was built in 1866 to cope with increasing traffic. A town like Weston needed a pier and Birnbeck Pier was duly provided. The pier was so good that many visitors didn't bother to spend much time in the town. If they came over on a steamer from Wales they may not have gone to the town at all. This was not great news for people who ran a land-based business. To address this, the seafront was improved and a promenade constructed in the 1880s. Once Weston became a stop on a railway through-route it was an obvious seaside destination for those from Bristol or Bath and places further afield, particularly the Midlands. The Grand Pier opened in 1904, and had an end-of-the-pier theatre where you could catch the top music hall stars of the day. The

sea front held the most attraction for me and I enjoyed a promenade on the promenade watching the happy holidaymakers on
the sands. I took the 102 heading for Burnham-on-Sea which,
in the hands of an unknown mediaeval church clerk, would
have been Burnham-super-Mare.

Breaching the edge of Weston-super-Mare we entered Uphill,
a small settlement of cottages, 1930s semi-detached houses
and the Parish Church of St Nicholas. On a hill above the
settlement are the ruins of a Norman church and a windmill.
Isambard Kingdom Brunel stayed in Weston while supervis-
ing work on the local railway and he also designed 'The Devil's
Bridge' which spans a deep cutting and carries the Bristol to
Exeter line between Uphill and nearby Bleadon. Brunel is said
to have exclaimed, when shown the next obstacle in his path,
'Bleadon Hill!'

The landscape again became more rural and there were good
views back to Weston, across the water and back over the Mendips. And also, stretching out in their white ranks of thousands,
were caravans. We passed through Brean with its funfairs, long
sandy beaches and holiday camp and on to Berrow a little further down the coast. More extensive sandy beaches—miles of
them in fact, backed by dunes and marshy areas with unkempt,
tousled grasses.

Approaching Burnham-on-Sea, the Bristol Channel looked
a little 'choppy', but it was quiet. At one time, and for a considerable time, these waters were extremely busy. Bristol was the
second busiest port in the country and most of the country's
transatlantic trade in the early eighteenth century came this
way. Regretfully, this success was largely bound up with the
slave trade. These days, as well as regretting the period of slav-
ery, we might wonder about the benefits of bringing in large
quantities of another commodity which formed part of the
'slave trade triangle'—tobacco. Trade was brisk in many other
less contentious commodities but, whatever the cargo, there
were several dangers facing all these vessels and so lighthouses
were built along this piece of coast in response. The Pillar
Lighthouse with its impressive 30 metre tower quickly became
a tourist attraction as it afforded fine views across to the coasts

of North Devon and South Wales. It was not astoundingly successful as a lighthouse because it was too low to account for the massive fall in water level at low tide and possibly because it was always full of ruddy tourists. To supplement it another lighthouse, this one on legs, was built in 1832.

If these were not enough for the lighthouse hunter, Burnham-on-Sea has yet another, the 'Round Tower', two storeys of which remain. The lighthouse apparently came about because of a fisherman's concerned wife and a candle in the window. The story goes that one stormy night, worried about the safe return of her husband, the woman who lived in a cottage near the church put a candle in the window. The light from this guided her husband safely home. Other sailors then paid her a small sum to keep a candle burning at all times to guide them home. The church sexton is then supposed to have given her five pounds for the right to place a candle in the taller, and therefore more efficacious, church tower. Later still, the sexton was given twenty pounds by the Rev. David Davies, curate of Burnham, who built the Round Tower.

People didn't simply build lighthouses, of course. Burnham became part of a set of resorts, together with Weston and Clevedon further north. The parts of Burnham displaying the gentility and elegance of Victorian architecture from this period are perhaps the most attractive feature of the town. I headed for the pleasantly uncluttered Esplanade where the central attraction was the Pavilion on Britain's shortest pier. This looks rather odd when you first see it and you wonder why they bothered. It's the end-of-the-pier without a pier to be at the end of. I suppose it avoided any tiresome walking. For all that, it's a marvellous, elegant Edwardian building and perhaps even enhanced by being a bit eccentric.

I picked up some information about buses from Burnham and then sat to consider the onward journey and refuelled with a hearty Cheddar cheese roll. I was enjoying my time by the coast and was hoping for a trip that would allow me to travel along it. My information seemed to suggest that this would not be possible beyond Bridgwater. From there I would have to head inland and then back out again.

The countryside was low-lying and sporadically quite heavily wooded and as we approached Bridgwater the higher ground of the distant Quantock Hills was coming into view. This busy market town was originally 'a place at the bridge held by a man called Walter'. The bridge would no doubt have been for crossing the River Parret on which the town is positioned. It has a long history of being a thriving port and was a centre for the export of woollen cloth from many parts of Somerset. The town opted for the royalists in the Civil War. The Parliamentarians flattened most of the domestic and commercial timber buildings during a three day bombardment in 1645. Afterwards they decided to destroy the castle as well. The town survived as a settlement but it suffered when the cloth trade moved north and as Bristol became increasingly important as a port. A brick and tile industry saw it through the nineteenth century but this declined in the twentieth, to be replaced by Cellophane, an industry that made its presence felt upon the air many miles away.

Bridgwater is also important for some because it is near Athelney. This is significant because legend has it that it was here that Alfred the Great went into hiding after the invasion of the Danes (them again) in 875 and it was during this very difficult stage in his life that he allegedly burnt the cakes. It's understandable in the circumstances, I think.

We caught glimpses here and there of the Bridgwater to Taunton canal, an inland link of some 14 miles. This was first opened in 1827 as part of a scheme to link the coast at Bridgwater with the south coast of Devon, thereby providing a route for shipping from Bristol that avoided the treacherous waters around Land's End. The grand plan never happened but the Bridgwater and Taunton Canal had a reasonably good run for about 40 years. It was sold to the Bristol and Exeter Railway Company with control eventually passing to the Great Western. Perhaps not surprisingly the railway companies did not do a great deal to keep this rival means of transport going. The route of the canal became a line of defence during the Second World War.

A little while later church towers and steeples reaching up

above the rooftops heralded our imminent arrival in Taunton, the County Town of Somerset. The Saxon village of Tone Tun had become a town by the tenth century with its own charter, mint and market. By the thirteenth century Taunton was busy fulling, weaving and exporting wool. The year 1111 was not a good one for Taunton. The town burnt down. But it picked itself up, dusted itself off and started all over again and by the mid-thirteenth century was boasting two fairs. The town had a rare old time of it during the Civil War. The town sided with the Parliamentarians in 1642. In June of 1643 the town meekly surrendered to a Royalist army so the castle changed hands. A year later in July it was captured by the Parliamentarians who held on to it, even through a siege in October until April 1645. The Royalists captured most of the town but were not able to take the castle to which the Parliamentarians had wisely relocated. The approach of Parliamentarian reinforcements saw off the Royalists but again much of the town was a smouldering ruin. Taunton picked itself up, dusted itself off and started all over again. Once reinstated, Charles II took away the town's charter as a bit of a slap on the wrists and he also thought it might be an idea to destroy the castle in case any more rebels decided to use it as a base.

One such rebel might have been the Duke of Monmouth. He led a rebellion against James II in 1685, which is usually referred to, helpfully, as 'The Monmouth Rebellion'. The people of Taunton, obviously not staunch royalists, or supporters of incumbent monarchs at least, backed the Duke and even proclaimed him king in The Parade. The Duke was finally defeated at the Battle of Sedgemoor and the Parade returned to being the place where you held a market rather than proclaimed a king.

Taunton continued on as a market town and centre of the wool industry until this began to decline at the end of the eighteenth century. The town responded by developing brewing and iron founding industries, and by the manufacture of shirt collars. I'm not sure why they didn't go the whole hog and make shirts but there you are. Perhaps they didn't have the skills base for the entire garment or perhaps different elements of shirts were required to be made in different locations by a long-lost royal decree. Making different elements of a shirt in separate locations must have given rise to the widespread agreement that it is important to check that the collar and cuffs match.

Taunton's small bus station is tucked away conveniently close to the city centre which allowed me a brief exploration. As well as shopping areas there are old architectural treasures including Gray's Almshouses on East Street and a surprising Municipal Hall. I don't know what you conjure in your mind at the thought of a 'municipal hall' but, unless you live in Taunton, I doubt it's a building from 1521–1522 which, with its towers, turrets and ivy-clad façade, looks a good contender for a location for a Harry Potter film. The building housed Taunton Grammar School from 1522 to 1870, which must be some kind of record.

Back at the bus station I boarded my last bus of the day. After about 20 minutes of rambling through beautiful Somerset countryside we arrived at the charming village of Bishop's Lydeard. Not only does the village have a lovely collection of red sandstone and brick buildings which make it worth a visit of itself, but it is also the southern terminus of the West Somerset Railway. This restored line offers the chance to experience a steam-hauled rail journey through the foothills of the Quantocks and along the coast to Minehead. I was heading in the same direction and our paths crossed at a number of places including Williton, Watchet, Washford and Dunster. Dunster is a treat if you like your villages quaint and medieval. The main street is dominated by The Yarn Market, a fabulous octagonal building dating from around the turn of the seventeenth century. It squats on sturdy pillars and the large, gabled roof almost looks as though it was at one time atop a much higher structure that has collapsed under the weight. It would have been built to shelter the traders during spells of inclement weather and is a clue to the historical importance of the cloth and yarn trades in the area. If you like listed buildings, Dunster is the place to come since you have about 200 to choose from. Another delight is the rather magnificent Dunster Castle, a fantastic concoction of towers and turrets which commands a prominent position on a hill above the village.

With the West Somerset Railway below us, and between us and the Bristol Channel, we approached Minehead, the bright white canopies of a holiday camp acting as a beacon. The bus driver kindly alerted me to the best stop for the youth hostel and I disembarked. Unfortunately the best stop was still a two mile walk up a fairly serious hill. The climb was hard but the prize was worth it—a charming house nestled in amongst the trees.

I sorted out my room and dumped my gear. As I pondered the possibility of a walk into town I was joined by a fellow hosteller. It was gratifying to meet someone else with a rucksack of similarly-ridiculous proportions. This feeling was short-lived when it transpired that he was carrying things that he would actually need rather than having surplus 'insurance items' like spare jumpers and extra underpants. He was also doing an alarming amount of strenuous activity each day, walking a National Trail across West Somerset. His rucksack contained not only suitable clothing and a small tent but also a small mobile kitchen, complete with stove, a set of three saucepans, cutlery, plates and drinking vessels. I didn't share the secrets of my rucksack but we did talk about our different journeys as we later made our way into town. On hearing of my bus-based exploits, my new acquaintance informed me that he had bus associations of his own. In fact he was an ex-bus driver and had worked for a time for London Transport. Rather a short time, it transpired, due to the unpleasant nature of many of his encounters with the travelling public. It was quite shocking and disturbing to hear about all the verbal abuse and threatening behaviour he experienced especially on the late night runs. I really wonder what's happened sometimes. When did that kind of thing start happening? I don't remember seeing notices saying "We will not tolerate physical or verbal abuse of our staff" on buses in my younger days. Now they are there and in railway stations and even hospitals! Was it always like that? Did I miss something?

Once in the town we surveyed Minehead's beaches which are a main attraction, naturally enough. There was a generous stretch of barefoot-friendly sand which turned more pebbly and harder to traverse towards the harbour. There were still one or two hardy souls enjoying the beach as the crowds slowly dispersed towards the end of the day. The town itself had attractions too, especially the thatched cottages of 'higher town' and the harbour, where what was once purely functional has now become an appealing feature. Walking the curved harbour walls provided for good views back along the beach and out across the waters while the wooded ground rising behind provided a sylvan backdrop. A soundtrack was provided by the lapping waters and the clinks and creaks from the small boats anchored in this little haven. It all went to create an extremely pleasant atmosphere and environment. We ambled around for a short while, enjoyed a pint, bought some food to cook back at the hostel and braced ourselves for the walk back up the hill.

At the end of what had been another brilliant day, I assessed the progress made. It certainly felt that I had come a long way and seen a good range of varying countryside since leaving the early morning quiet of the Tudor Caravan and Camping Park in Slimbridge. The buses had once again provided a great way of travelling, joining up for me in all the right places. I was still enjoying my own thrill at how it was working out.

Day 19

A zig-zag west

23rd *August*

My ex-bus-driving room-mate was up early, packing his bag with space-conscious efficiency. We exchanged a cheery farewell and he wished me luck with the rest of my journey before setting off to continue his perambulations across the wilds of Exmoor.

I had a more sluggish start but was making my way down the wooded hill with plenty of the morning left nonetheless. I was feeling quite positive because, having looked at my trusty Tourist Map, I realised that I had definitely turned a corner. I was firmly in that thin bit of England that pokes out towards the south west and into the Atlantic. I may still have been in Somerset but I was in the same 'leg' as Devon and Cornwall and that's where I needed to go. There was one small problem. There didn't seem to be any buses that went there from here. As far as I could make out I might have been able to make it along the coast a little further but then things seemed to dry up. Again I needed to travel in a completely different direction to the one in which I really wanted to go.

The day of bus journeys began with a trip courtesy of First who were prepared to convey me and my belongings to Tiverton for £3.20. We initially drove back to Dunster and then headed into the Exmoor National Park. This is officially recognised as an Area of Outstanding Natural Beauty and I'm not about to argue with that. The views were stunning and never monotonous. We passed along wooded lanes and gazed out over the agricultural landscape, tamed into fields bordered with fulsome hedgerows, towards the more distant, rugged moorland.

We passed through Timberscombe ('a valley where timber is obtained') which has, amongst other things, St Petroc's Church, a grade 1 listed building with a fifteenth century tower. Despite the fad in the 1970s for owning a Pet Rock, I don't think we can lay this at St Petroc's door. He was in fact a Celtic Christian who ministered to the Britons in this part of the world in the sixth century. 'Sancte Petroces stow' in Cornwall is now more familiar as Padstow.

We made our way through the rich agricultural landscape that borders the wilder moorland. Dunkery Hill, topped by Dunkery Beacon, the highest point on Exmoor, rose steadily to our right as we approached Wheddon Cross, a compact and charming village with cottages, post office and war memorial all neatly laid out around the roads. From here the views were simultaneously stunning and therapeutic while the pace of the bus suited the terrain by being de-stressing rather than distressing. It was lovely, uncomplicated and sparsely populated countryside, the patchwork slopes gently undulating away into the distance. Not great if you have a phobia of wide-open spaces, I'll grant you, but for those who don't it's a real treat.

Dulverton was a slightly larger settlement that provided a brief diversion before we continued our meanderings which eventually led us down into Tiverton, a small market town built near the confluence of two rivers, The Exe and The Lowman. These two rivers were both forded and gave the place the name Twyforde. With the addition of a 'tun' we've got 'the place by the two fords' which has become the Tiverton of today.

Tiverton has a number of attractions for the visitor who wants more than a pretty town in a lovely setting. Not far from the bus station was Tiverton Museum and there is also a rather romantic castle, the origins of which lie in the commands of Henry I in the 1100s and which was substantially rebuilt and enlarged in the thirteenth and fourteenth centuries. Tiverton is also a border town though not in the sense of Ludlow or Oswestry. There were no marauding hordes to keep at bay. The border in question was between the territories of two different bus operators.

With the routes on offer here, I still had to travel in a 'wrong' direction for the next stage. I was heading almost due south using the word 'due' to mean wayward or meandering. If you have to do wayward meandering this is the countryside to do it through. Largely given over to agriculture, here again is the typical 'patchwork' of English countryside punctuated only with a few small to medium-sized settlements along the way. Thus we passed through the 'woodland clearing on or near a pointed ridge' that is Bickleigh, the 'farmstead near the gully ford' of Silverton, the 'row of houses' at Rewe and the 'outlying settlement owned by the canons' of Stoke Canon. Finally we arrived in the 'Roman town on the River Exe' that is Exeter, a university town, bustling and busy with traffic on this Friday afternoon.

The impression I gained from walking down the High Street and surveying the nearby shopping centres (plural), made me wonder if all there was to do here was shop. To be fair, much of the historic heart of the city was lost during the terrible air raids of World War II and, less forgivably, through subsequent travesties of development. All that being said, Exeter is fairly compact and the more interesting areas are easily reached. There are plenty of reminders of a colourful history and the different roles the place has had. Dominating the sky-line was a prime example, Exeter Cathedral, which proclaims a long-standing significance for the town as an ecclesiastical centre. A major feature here is The Great East Window. It is called that because it is a window, it faces East and it is great. Elsewhere are traces of the Roman town and buildings from Tudor times as well as an engaging quay area. Find the right places to go and you can change your impression of a place.

Pondering my next move I called in the assistance of Traveline, an organisation whose aim is to assist people using public transport. In response to my vague answer, 'West', to the question, 'What is your destination?' the helpful, unperturbed person on the other end of the phone suggested that there might be a route to Truro and from there to Penzance.

I was considering this possibility in the bus station when my eye was caught by a poster advertising an 'AtoB' ticket from Exeter to Boscastle for £2.50.

To 'AtoB' or not to 'AtoB', that was the question.

£2.50 was a bargain. I would be heading almost due west. To cap it all I knew there was a youth hostel in Boscastle village.

To 'AtoB' was the answer.

Once clear of Exeter's built up area we were back into 'proper countryside', the tame variety at least. Once again we passed pocket-sized settlements dotted about the place. Tedburn St Mary, Cheriton Cross, Crockernwell and Whiddon Down led to South Zeal which was all thatched dwellings and flowers. There were also pubs, a hotel and the oldest working school bells in Devon. Apparently Charles Dickens stayed here in the Oxenham Arms while writing *The Pickwick Papers*. Another lovely village, Sticklepath, came and went, or rather stayed where it was while we came and went, and after that we were seeing more and more of the expansive stretches of Dartmoor which formed a dramatic backdrop to the gentler landscapes of the foreground.

We were soon at the considerably larger settlement of Okehampton, which seems to have begun life as 'a farmstead on the River Okement'. The wide Fore Street hinted at the importance of a market in the town while the fairly imposing St James' Chapel which overlooked this hinted at an equally important role for faith in the community. The Parish Church was just visible up a hill a little way out of the town centre as we climbed out and onwards.

With the grand tors of Dartmoor rising in the distance, we glimpsed Meldon Quarry as we made our way west. In 1874 the railway line for what was then the London and South Western Railway was being laid along the northern edge of Dartmoor. At Meldon they needed to forge a cutting through some tough rock before attempting to span the next obstacle, an impressive gorge over the River Okement. The cutting produced a hard hornfels rock. Almost twenty years after cutting the cutting, engineers recognised that this material would actually be quite useful for rail ballast and so the quarry was developed to increase extraction and to supply the material further afield. Within ten years 100,000 tons of material was being taken out every year. The quarry became a major employer and there were 170 men in employment immediately after the Second World War. By the 1950s annual production was up to 300,000 tons. With improvements in extraction technologies, twenty people can manage the whole affair today.

We were making good, steady progress and were treated to a glimpse of Lewdown and the lovely church of St Mary's which presided over the village centre, before continuing on our way, eventually crossing the Tamar and arriving at 'the gateway to Cornwall', that is Launceston (the 'estate near the church-site of St Stephen'). Recorded settlement of Launceston goes back to the Celts who knew a thing or two about the strategic advantages of hill-top locations. The town guarded what became the main northern route into Cornwall. The Normans obviously saw the benefits too, since they built a castle, the remains of which still overlooks the town. Launceston was Royalist in the Civil War with a major battle taking place on 23rd April 1643 at Beacon Hill. The Parliamentarian army was turned back and returned to Devon from whence it had come. The town has an interesting mix of Georgian buildings and medieval streets. The Parish Church of St Mary Magdalene was an exceptional building of carved Cornish granite.

We pressed on through Pipers Pool, whizzed within a whisker of a wind farm and hauled up to Hallworthy before climbing to Camelford which was the next sizeable settlement. Sadly the name has nothing do with riding a camel through a ford but rather derives from *cam* which means 'crooked', *alan* meaning 'beautiful' and *ford* meaning, well, 'ford'. 'Camalanford' slowly contracted to Camelford. Despite being able to ford the River Camel here, people must have become fed up with soggy trousers and by 1521 there was a useful bridge.

I was now in a part of the country that is rather obsessed with the figure of King Arthur, he of the knights, the round table, the chivalry and the magical sword of Excalibur. Camelford, for example, is one of a number of present-day locations put forward as a possible site of King Arthur's headquarters— Camelot. At nearby Tintagel is 'King Arthur's castle', or perhaps *was* King Arthur's castle is more appropriate. There are ruins there right enough, but these are of a castle built in the twelfth or thirteenth centuries. However, archaeologists have found evidence of a fifth century habitation on the site which ties in with the dates normally associated with King Arthur. Here also are King Arthur's Great Halls which sound very promising but were in fact built in the 1930s by somebody who made custard powder. Be that as it may, the building is said to be the only one in the world dedicated to the Arthurian legend and it is the base for the Fellowship of the Knights of the Round Table.

Around me there had been a subtle shift in the general demeanour of the countryside. Gone were the predominantly gentle and pastoral landscapes. As we approached the coast the sense of drama was heightened and everything looked decidedly more rugged. Since Exeter we have been travelling 'The Atlantic Highway' and we soon got the first glimpses of the ocean that ceaselessly beats against the coast here and gives the route its name. The road was high above the sea and my anticipation grew as we passed through Trethevy and Trevalga. Then at last it was time to drop down the precipitous valley slopes and into the marvellous village of Boscastle.

What a great spot this is. A settlement is enhanced by its surroundings and even places like Huddersfield or Bath would be diminished somehow if they were not set amongst their hills. Boscastle, too, benefits from being tucked into a landscape that plummets down towards the sea and encloses the settlement in a narrow valley. I stepped off the bus at a quarter to six, near a small bridge over the river that hurried towards the harbour. From here there was a good view downstream towards the harbour and the youth hostel.

I could simply have wandered down to enquire about the availability of a bed in the hostel. Sensing that it might well be full, I decided to ring from the nearby phone box, not wanting to have to show any disappointment in person.

I calmly enquired about bed availability. I calmly received the news that there was none. I was about to calmly offer my thanks and replace the receiver when I heard, "No, hang on. There's a cancellation. I *do* have a bed for tonight."

Calmness went out of the window, or the small opening in the phone box door. This is when I was really glad that I had phoned; if I had been there in person I would undoubtedly have given the hostel manager a grateful hug at this point, quite possibly jeopardising my chances of staying the night.

Trying to sound grown up and composed and not like a child who has just been given a new bike for Christmas, I said, "Oh, that's excellent. Excellent. I shall see you later."

I was suitably non-specific regarding my possible arrival time, not wanting to say that I could be there in about 5 minutes as I was in the phone box only a few hundred metres up the road. I took the opportunity to have a peaceful stroll around the village.

Boscastle is hidden away and yet to me felt cosy and self-contained rather than isolated and alone. It seems organic, having grown slowly and naturally as circumstances have demanded, rather than at the whim of some developer or planner. Settlement no doubt began and developed because of the natural harbour that offered some protection from the Atlantic. The sea can be pretty wild hereabouts before it is tamed into the Bristol Channel and finally meets the Severn Estuary. What sanctuary nature offered was later augmented by the man-made. There were a few small fishing boats bobbing on the water in the little harbour and an air of tranquillity made it difficult to imagine the place as the busy port it once was.

I organised myself at the hostel, and relieved myself of The Bag. With a considerably lighter step I set off to explore the headland above the harbour. The views up and down the coast were spectacular. The sea was calm and offered a perfect surface for reflecting the slowly setting sun. The sun's rays enhanced the effusion of golden browns and sappy greens of the vegetation clinging to the valley sides as these dropped towards the rocky outcrops and the sea. I meandered back upstream into the village and took some sustenance in the friendly and convivial atmosphere of The Wellington Hotel.

That night I took stock of the last couple of days. They had had their ups and downs. From the flatlands of Slimbridge, and through Bristol to the Mendip Hills and the memorable Cheddar Gorge. From the coastal plains of the Bristol Channel to the Quantocks and Minehead. Since Minehead I had encountered three moors and now I was perched on a high headland, gazing at a coast that could hardly be more different from the flat sands of Weston-super-Mare and Burnham-on-Sea. The rugged cliffs and headlands rose one beyond the other into the distance while below the ocean's subdued waves hinted at a wildness waiting to be unleashed. The distant sun was slowly sinking. I turned to watch the hues on the valley sides turn from green to gold, and as these slowly faded and the shadows deepened to purple and black I made my way back past the evening stillness of the harbour to the hostel and sleep.

Day 20

A Cornish Cruise

24th August

A certain William Camden (1551–1623) had done a good deal of travelling around Britain beginning in the late 1500s and subsequently published his amazing work *Britannia*, the first topographical survey of Britain. In this he described the south west peninsula as 'growing straiter still and narrower', and as something which 'shooteth out farthest into the West and has on the North side the Severne-Sea and on the South the British and on the West the Vergivian or Western ocean beating upon it'. At Minehead I felt that I had just begun my exploration of this part of the country. At Boscastle I felt I was considerably further along it but I knew I still had quite a way to go before I could see that Western Ocean actually doing a bit of beating where the land was shoothething out. To make progress in this direction I determined to catch the 125 service for Bodmin at 8.55.

This was one of the few mornings that had not started with bright sunshine. The mists restricted the views and added to a subdued atmosphere as we made our slow progress back up the steep valley sides, through Tintagel and Trevalga. At Delabole we were in sight of the country's first commercial wind farm where great turbines rose like giant ghostly sentinels guarding the nearby Gaia Energy Centre. What I couldn't see from the bus was the largest hole in Britain. This has not been dug by some lunatic attempting an entry in a *Guinness Book of Records* but slowly and steadily by slate miners who have been pursuing this task at Delabole since at least 1314. Slate from here was used during that year on Winchester Castle, and by Elizabethan times Delabole slate was being exported around the globe. The hole is apparently 425 feet (130 metres) deep and has a circumference of one and a half miles (2.4 km).

Bodmin Moor and Roughtor dominated the scenery to the south-east as we made our windy way to Camelford. Thanks to the atmospheric conditions the moor was looking particularly suitable as the setting for a dramatic novel. I dunno, perhaps the story could be about a group of ruthless men who wreck ships by running them aground before killing the crew, stealing the cargo and hiding out in an isolated inn with an exotic name, deep in the midst of the bleak and forbidding landscape. Something like 'Bermuda Inn' might work. It's just a thought.

The moor is a large chunk of granite upland with outcrops of this hard-wearing rock forming isolated high points or 'tors'. From these the landscape falls away to provide expanses of elemental, uncomplicated scenery that to some eyes borders on the bleak or desolate. It's fair to say that it looks slightly inhospitable, especially if you're thinking of taking up long-term residence. I would imagine scratching a livelihood from here would be extremely hard work but anyone here in their leisure time would find tremendous walking country.

Providing a place of retreat and comfort from the windswept landscapes of the moor was Wadebridge, a very charming town sitting calmly astride the River Camel. The sun had evaporated the last vestiges of mist and the town's attractive and historical features were clear. Wade is mentioned as having been granted a market and two fairs in 1313. The town was split by the River Camel and it didn't get a bridge until 1460. The construction of the bridge must have brought dramatic changes to life in the town as well as leading to a change in name. The town would have been an important trading centre for local sheep farmers and wool merchants and there was plenty of traffic along the river. The importance of the river slipped in 1834 when the Wadebridge to Bodmin railway line opened. Back in the day when they didn't have Big Brother to watch on the television, people had to find other forms of entertainment. On 13th April 1840 three excursion trains were run to carry people to Bodmin Gaol to witness the public execution of the Lightfoot Brothers who had been convicted of the brutal murder of a business-man, Neville Norway. The cheery onlookers at the execution finally numbered 25,000. Today we can recreate part of that happy experience by cycling some of the Camel Trail, which follows the route of the railway all the way to Bodmin. You can visit the gaol but you'd need to find an alternative amusement to watching a hanging.

On reaching Bodmin I found a bright and breezy town, or maybe that was the weather. No, the town did have a light and airy feel to it, mixed with a lightly held air of authority. This perhaps comes from the fact that for a long time Bodmin was the county town of Cornwall, before things civic moved to Truro. Bodmin has a long and distinguished history; its begin-nings associated with a monastery and good old St Petroc. The name Bodmin is thought to be based on an old Cornish word 'bodmeneghy' meaning 'dwelling of or by the sanctuary of monks'. It was the largest town in the county by the time of the Domesday Book and continued to be an important religious centre right up until the Reformation. Bodmin was equally an important focus for the tin trade. It also seems to have been a focal point for rebellions with significant such occurrences in 1493, 1497 and 1549. Of these, 1497 was a particularly good year. The first rebellion that year was led by a lawyer and a blacksmith who were protesting against taxes imposed by Henry VII. The second involved Perkin Warbeck who fancied his chances as king. Perkin was actually a young man claiming to be Richard of Shrewsbury, 1st Duke of York and the younger son of King Edward IV, one of the two 'Princes in the Tower'. He had travelled Europe seeking support for his claim and met with varying degrees of success. His march east towards Lon-don and the crown crossed Bodmin Moor, and the company of 120 men he started with had swelled to 6000 by the time he reached Exeter. Exeter didn't want them and quickly put up 'No Vacancies' signs in the window. So they moved on toward Taunton and that's when it all went pear-shaped. The antici-pated arrival of royal troops led Perkin to decide that running away was the best option. He made it to Beaulieu Abbey before surrendering. There was then a time of being detained at his majesty's pleasure during which Henry VII did his best to establish that Perkin was a Flemish boatman's son called Pierquin Wesbecque. Apparently he did 'confess' to this, although how much use was made of the fifteenth century equivalent of the CIA Interrogation Manual is unclear. Perkin's penalty was execution in 1499.

In 1549 the Cornish rebelled again, this time because they didn't want to lose their Latin mass following the imposition of the Book of Common Prayer, which was in English. After this, things quietened down in Bodmin for about 100 years until the Civil War. Even then there was no fighting in the town as such, although it did serve as a Royalist headquarters, the upkeep of which was expensive. A rather dilapidated Bodmin emerged from the war and began to pick itself up again. This was helped by improved communications, especially the upgrading of the Launceston road in the eighteenth century. In the nineteenth century it was railways, that is the Wadebridge to Bodmin line, rather than roads that made a difference. When links were made to the Great Western Railway this meant the town was joined to the rest of the country and there was no looking back. Although Bodmin officially became the County Town of Cornwall in 1836 its status was rather short-lived and it began to lose important functions to Truro and as a consequence fell rather into decline.

It has put that period firmly behind itself and today all looks fine and dandy. It was very pleasant to sit in Mount Folly Square surrounded by elegant civic buildings. This is urban open space as it should be. Well laid out and properly proportioned, providing an unpretentious setting for the impressive buildings on its periphery, such as the grand Shire Hall.

A tourist map showed that there was plenty to do in this compact town including visits to Beacon Nature Reserve just down Crinnicks Hill, Bodmin Gaol, St Petroc's Church, a military museum and The Bodmin and Wenford Railway.

I made my connection for Truro and was off again. Bodmin is close to the A30, the main arterial route into and through Cornwall. Having crossed this we ambled through neat fields and pastoral pleasantry and it wasn't until we reached the old town of Bugle that the scenery changed once more. And, boy, did it change.

China clay was used in China over a thousand years ago. They could make fine, pure white porcelain which was extremely desirable. A small number of deposits were found in Europe but nothing of note until one William Cookworthy discovered it at Tregonning Hill in 1746. Cookworthy's Plymouth Porcelain Factory was producing fine porcelain for the gentry by 1748 and the industry grew from there. The product was also being used to whiten paper and demand steadily rose to the point where, by 1910, over a million tons were being extracted annually. Getting out all that clay meant producing large amounts of spoil since for every ton of clay there was seven or eight tons of waste. The mountains of whiteish spoil have been dubbed 'The Cornish Alps' by some but this is a bleakly ironic soubriquet, given that the landscape produced is lunar and lifeless. The industry is celebrated in the nearby China Clay Country Park which is a bold move towards making something useful out of the devastation left by the industry. Another idea for 'what to do with an old china clay pit' can be found not far away in Bodelva, the site of the spectacular Eden Project.

After this brush with an industrial landscape it was back to the rolling fields, hedgerows and trees of agriculture for the remainder of the journey to Truro.

Truro is an historic town with roots going back to the twelfth century, when a castle was built by Richard Lucy, the Chief Justice of England. Those were the days, when a man could be called Lucy and still become Chief Justice of England. By the fourteenth century Truro was an important port and one of five stannary towns in the region. In a stannary town, copper and tin were tested for their quality, or 'assayed' if you like technical terms, and stamped before being shipped out from the port. The Black Death visited the town and killed a large part of the population and drove most of the rest out, leaving an almost empty shell of a settlement. Following a period of neglect and despair, the town received a charter from Elizabeth I in 1589 which indicates how important it had once again become. The town blossomed in the seventeenth and eighteenth centuries on the strength of the tin trade with mine-owners and tin-traders displaying their wealth in the construction of fine and fashionable town houses. The surviving private buildings from these times made for some gorgeous streetscapes for me to admire, augmented by solid civic buildings and banks. In addition there was a good river frontage and I could see why some have said that the river provides the best way into the city.

The impressive Cathedral, which is perhaps Truro's most striking building, was begun in 1880 and grew out of the older parish church of St Mary the Virgin. Elements of the original church are still in evidence. The cathedral was completed in 1910 and the first Bishop of Truro was Edward White Benson, obviously a man of considerable drive and energy. The establishment of the Truro Diocese and the building of the cathedral are credited in large measure to his efforts. The building of a cathedral in Truro gave Cornwall another 'capital'. The region has never had one obvious centre but several places have dominated different areas for different reasons. Penzance has been seen as the 'commercial capital' in the west, Redruth and Cambourne have been focal points for the mining industries, St Austell was the china clay capital while other places such as Bodmin have perhaps been more associated with agriculture. Truro, thanks to its cathedral, became a point of pilgrimage and a centre of faith. Although the Cathedral was a new building rising at the turn of the twentieth century, it represented the long-established faith of the Cornish people. These links between the faith, the building and the land were forged afresh here through the choice of building materials, which came from the very ground of Cornwall itself: granite, china-stone, polyphant stone and serpentine. In addition to creating a diocese and a cathedral, Bishop Benson also devised the 'Service of Nine Lessons and Carols' which has been used in the Cathedral ever since and taken and adapted by churches the world over.

Truro was quite captivating but an X18 bus lured me away. This is like an 18 bus only with an X—for 'express' rather than 'X-rated'. The timetable promised me arrival in Penzance only about an hour after leaving Truro. We called at Truro railway station to see if there were any takers for a change of transport.

Then we were off for a forty minute, almost non-stop, cross-country ride to Hayle on the north coast. Here the sight of the queues outside Philips Bakery Shop with its proper Cornish Pasties highlighted the popularity of the regional delicacy which I looked forward to sampling.

Hayle isn't just about pasty shops, though. For fine coastal features it offers a three mile beach and a river estuary the edge of which we were now navigating. The river was shimmering in the sunshine and its banks, an internationally-recognised bird-watching spot, were covered with hundreds of birds, being watched by about six bird watchers. I say there were six but of course there could have been hundreds of carefully concealed bird watchers in all manner of places and in all manner of clothing that made them almost invisible, not simply to the wading bird population but to the likes of me as well. An individual bird can be quite stunning to look at, especially with suitable binoculars. The beauty of their shining eyes and the delicacy of the plumage are quite remarkable. Here the sensation was more one of awe, caused by the sheer number present.

The railway also passes through here and a train added a sense of tranquillity by making a fairly leisurely progress across the viaduct on its way to Penzance. We were heading there too, all the way from the north coast of Cornwall to the south. Actually, because England is very thin at this point it doesn't take long to achieve that. As we made our way through a predominantly agricultural and definitely rural landscape we passed through St Erth which had a mostly fifteenth century church, an ancient bridge and the Star Inn, dating from 1686. The village is also the location of Battery Mill which was constructed in 1782 to roll copper. The copper artisans from the Midlands came down bringing their skills and their Methodism. The first Methodist chapel was built in 1796 and the present chapel followed in 1827. St Erth is also a bit of a transport hub, being close to the A30 and on the main Paddington–Penzance mainline railway and you can take the picturesque branch line to St Ives from here.

Once through the small village of Crowlas I sensed we were almost at the coast. Then, quite suddenly, or so it seemed, we came into the quaint town of Marazion basking on the edge of a gorgeous blue bay.

From here there were splendid views of the equally splendid St Michael's Mount. Now if anywhere looks like it should be associated with King Arthur, surely it's this romantic castle sitting majestically on top of an impossibly steep hill. The hill is surrounded by water at high tide and is effectively an island. A hilly island with a castle on top! What more could you want? But St Michael's Mount resolutely refuses to be associated with King Arthur, it being medieval, although it does have a fascinating history which includes an episode with our old friend Perkin Warbeck, the erstwhile Richard IV. He refortified the castle and left his wife there for safe-keeping as he set off on his ill-fated road to kingship.

St Michael's Mount is now operated by the National Trust and is a wonderful place to visit. The fun starts with a causeway to the 'island' which is only available at low tide. At high tide you reach the Mount by taking a ride in a small ferry. Once there you can explore the steep, winding cobbled lanes that lead up to the castle itself. From the top you can enjoy wonderful views across the water and inland to Penzance or simply look down on the exotic gardens that have somehow been created on the steep slopes of the grounds.

Back on the coast in Marazion were wonderful, gently sloping sandy beaches being washed rhythmically by the waters of Mount Bay which farther out were sparkling and blue, dotted with sailing boats, wind and kite surfers, and altogether looking lovely. Marazion's winding lanes entice you away from the beach for some 'historic town' explorations. It is one of the oldest chartered towns in Cornwall and was the major town in this part of Cornwall and an important port. The port here declined as improvements were made to the harbour at Penzance and that town rose in significance as a consequence.

Drifting along the coast we breezed gracefully into Penzance, transport hub and commercial centre for the Land's End peninsula and the 'Capital of West Cornwall'. I alighted at the bus station, which is right next to the train station and an easy walk from the town centre. I checked out buses further west before exploring some of the retail outlets. I needed a few items and I needed food.

Cornwall is a Celtic region, full of people with historical similarities to Welsh, Scots, Irish and Bretons. An enduring feature is the existence of a distinct language which again had similarities with Welsh and Gaelic. Although most people speak English, a handy book offered some useful Cornish words and phrases, just in case.

Regarding my immediate food needs I decided that "Hou, meur kig pasti, marpleg" meant "Hello, may I have a large meat pasty, please." It seemed as though I might have to proceed with caution because the use of 'pasti' is controversial since some see this as an English interloper. They prefer 'cophan'.

"Pinta moreg, marpleg" looked as though it might suffice for a request along the lines of "A pint of beer, please."

I never worked out how to ask "Can I please put my tent up here?" but I thought most people in Penzance and the surrounding area would speak English quite fluently and I didn't think there'd be a problem in obtaining essential things such as beer, pasties and a place to put up a tent.

Penzance is a tourist destination as well as a commercial centre and has a sizeable permanent population so there were plenty of retail and food outlets to satisfy people's needs for 'stuff' and for stuffing their faces. I perused the nearby shopping centre, which wasn't particularly exciting although was saved by being on a hill. I wandered up Market Jew Street and bought a small rucksack to use on local walks. Finally I sought out a purveyor of a pasty, pastie, pasti or cophan. At that point you could have called it what you liked as long as it was big enough to satisfy my hunger.

The Cornish Pasty is a traditionally hearty concoction of meat and vegetables tucked inside a pastry case. The pastry case means that the pasty is easily transportable and can be taken on a picnic, as fuel while walking or, in former times, as an ideal meal for the workers in mines, on farms or at sea. It has long associations with Cornish tin miners who were unable to return to the surface for food breaks. The large pasties were an easy way of taking a good meal down the mine and would apparently stay warm and even act as body warmers. The thick crusts on the edge acted like a handle with which to grasp the food. Since the hands that did the grasping were likely to be filthy, the part that had been held was often chucked away.

There are variations on the pasty recipe but they usually consist of pastry (made with plain flour, vegetable fat or lard or a mixture of both, salt and cold water) and filled with beef (chuck steak or skirt), potato, swede or turnip, onion, salt and pepper. Some people have 'issues' about the pastry. Should it be 'short crust' or 'puff'? Others insist that the ingredients should be diced while others are equally vociferous in the call for slicing. What most are agreed on is that any vegetables beyond those listed are an abomination. Any item with more exotic ingredients has no claim to the name 'Cornish Pasty'. You will be pleased to know that there is a Cornish Pasty Association which exists to 'protect the quality and reputation of the Cornish Pasty' and to ensure that you get a genuine Cornish Pasty if that's what you are offered. The association, backed by DEFRA, is taking its battle to the EU where it hopes to gain Protected Geographical Indication (PGI) status. If successful only a pasty made in Cornwall will be allowed to be identified as a 'Cornish Pasty'.

Even if a genuine Cornish Pasty should only be made in Cornwall, you can obviously eat one anywhere, anytime, hot or cold, accompanied or not. However, they are possibly best eaten out doors on a windy moor, or looking out over the sea from a clifftop path or perhaps on a sandy beach.

I ate mine while looking out over Mount Bay, watching the helicopter coming in from the Isles of Scilly. The pasty itself was still warm and the pastry left pale flakes on my fingers as I drew it carefully from its paper wrapping. A small, dark encrustation of drying juices surrounded the slit on the pasty's curved surface which was otherwise a deep golden brown. The aromas of cooked meat and vegetables mingled with those of the fresh-baked pastry. All of this looking and smelling was an important preparation for the ultimate experience of tasting. It was first rate as far as my admittedly untrained and inexpert senses could tell me. I don't know if judges of such things (and there *are* judges of such things) would agree but it seemed pretty near perfect for me.

Having savoured my authentic, made-in-Cornwall-to-a-traditional-recipe proper Cornish pasty, I took an authentic made-in-goodness-knows-where-to-a-traditional-design bus to St Just. And not just because it is the westernmost town in England, although that was a good enough reason. The 40 minute journey took me through the stunning, craggy countryside that makes this area so special. We climbed towards Madron to the north of Penzance, a small village with a good-looking pub, The King William IV, and good views back to Mount Bay. Also on the route is Botallack, which has numerous relics of human activity from more recent times. I was travelling through the centre of an area that was once devoted to and supported by the tin mining industry.

Mining, particularly producing tin, copper and arsenic, brought sustained growth and prosperity to Cornwall for hundreds of years. Although mining in the area of one form or another is thought to go back about 4000 years, the many relics visible today are left from the much more recent period which saw the tin mining industry in particular at its height. These are the engine houses and associated buildings at or near the mine shafts. The mineral extrusions which produce copper and tin are, to all intents and purposes, vertical, as opposed to the predominantly horizontal layers of material such as coal. As a consequence there are innumerable shafts dotted around the landscape and therefore many engine, winding, stamping and boiler houses and their associated chimneys. The boiler houses have survived quite well because they were sturdily built not only to withstand the worst of the weather but also in order to support the massive beam engines which were needed to pump water from the mines. The need to pump water came about because the shafts were below the water table and in many cases actually below the sea.

I have to admit to a fierce admiration for miners, who are able to work in conditions that I think I would find unbearable. Apart from the heat I imagine there to be in a mine, there is also the difficulty, physical strain and let's face it, downright danger associated with the work. Couple this with the thought that you are under millions of tons of rock, some of which may decide to fall on you. Additionally, in the case of these Cornish mines, you are perhaps beneath the sea bed, which may decide to crack, allowing thousands of gallons of water to flood in. All this would combine to produce my idea of some of the least attractive working conditions on the planet. So, it's hard hats off to the miners (but only when you are in a suitably safe area). There were thousands of these miners at the height of the industry and they dispersed to countries around the globe when things got bad. The mining relics stirred in me a strange mixture of admiration and poignancy. They were reminders of human determination, innovation and skill which allowed for the exploitation of resources that significantly affected the world. At the same time these old, abandoned buildings recalled the hardships endured and the losses suffered. They also proved that nothing lasts for ever.

St Just is a small town centred on the elegant Market Square. Nearby, beneath a modest but striking clock tower was the Plen-an-Gwary. This open area is an old amphitheatre which originally had six rows of seats cut into the sloping banks. When I arrived, preparations were underway for the presentation of the third part of something called 'The Ordinalia'. This, it transpired, is a cycle of Cornish Mystery Plays somewhat akin to the perhaps more familiar 'Mystery Cycles' of York and Chester. The play was being produced and performed by The Ordinalia Company, reviving a tradition of community performance that goes back hundreds of years.

I suddenly remembered the need to sample local delicacies. I had already eaten a proper pasty, but Cornwall also does 'The Cream Tea'.

I found tea rooms nearby offering this particular form of temptation and as I enjoyed applying large dollops of Cornish Clotted Cream and glistening strawberry jam to my large, light and crumbly scones I discussed my camping situation with the proprietor. He mentioned one or two camp sites but also enthused about the idea of 'wild camping'. I'm afraid he wasn't able to enthuse a certain comfort-seeking wanderer. He did manage to convince me that a visit to the North Inn at Pendeen might be worthwhile, and not just for the beer.

A cream tea is a pretty marvellous invention but its consumption can induce a twinge of guilt about over-indulgence and all those 'empty calories'. So it is always a good idea to get out and walk about a bit after consuming a cream tea, because you can pretend that this will somehow burn it all off. Although I knew I would realistically need to jog back to Penzance in order to achieve that, I pandered to my self-delusion and opted instead to take a stroll out to Cape Cornwall. This windswept headland pushes out defiantly into the Atlantic just down the road from St Just and for many years was thought to be the most westerly point on mainland Britain. I thought I'd visit it just in case they were right.

Like much of the countryside hereabouts the cape is wild and wonderful. The thrilling effect is achieved in part by the land suddenly deciding to come to an abrupt halt, dropping away in the form of dramatic, sheer cliffs plummeting down to the swirling waters far below. No easy slopes leading gently down through grassy, soft dunes to a smooth beach lapped by soothing ripples. Here below me was William Camden's 'Vergivien ocean' and it was doing a fair amount of 'beating' upon the coast. The air here felt particularly clean and fresh which shouldn't have been a surprise as it was coming straight off the Atlantic. The combination of keen air and a particular clarity and quality of light produced a heady natural tonic. Furthermore there was a sense of solitude. Although the car park behind me had contained a few vehicles the occupants must have dispersed and there were surprisingly few people here. One or two walkers passed on the coastal path but otherwise I was left with only the wind, the waves and the occasional sea bird.

Later, back in St Just, I presented my First Day Plus ticket for a ride along the fabulous coast, north to Pendeen, with views of the rugged cliffs and churning ocean, interspersed with wanderings to little hamlets slightly inland as the winding lanes worked their way through the undulating topography. At the North Inn a small area to the rear of the pub was given over to camping. Although it made for quite basic camping (no hook-ups, for example, which didn't bother me) sanitary provisions were available in the rear of the pub and were accessible throughout the night. Where people admit that facilities are 'basic' they often also make a very reasonable charge. Here was reasonably priced camping ten paces from a pub! I booked for two nights.

The bar of the North Inn was lively and a convivial atmosphere pervaded. This was hardly surprising given the holiday period and the presence of excellent beer. Gazing across the room I saw the bloke who used to service my car back at home.

We exchanged the sort of greetings you reserve for meeting people from times past and places distant in a random way. You know the sort of thing... "What are you doing here?"

We spent an evening discussing the issues of the day where I recall the ban on foxhunting took a prominent position. The conviviality in the pub seemed to mysteriously increase as did the beauty and allure of the girl behind the bar. I was warming to her but noticed she had a pentangle, a symbol associated with the occult, on a pendant round her neck. This unnerved me slightly and I limited my communications to requests for beer and salted peanuts. I've seen 'The Wicker Man' film and you can't be too careful.

Day 21

Way out West

25th August

The day broke bright and clear. I and the few other campers and overnighters made our gentle way back and forth to perform our ablutions and all greetings and subsequent chats were conducted softly in hushed voices.

I bought a 'First Day Plus' all day ticket on the 10A back into Penzance from where I could choose from buses going here, there and everywhere. My first 'there' was going to be St Ives and I enjoyed another bus-based peregrination of wonderful flexuosity. By that I mean we wandered all over the place including another visit to Hayle with its sea birds, sea bird watchers and sands. We also passed through Carbis Bay.

Carbis Bay doesn't actually shout 'Quaint Cornish Village', or indeed 'Fascinating heritage', but rather mumbles 'Place somewhat overrun with holiday-style accommodation'. You might not come here to admire the architecture but you would certainly make the effort for the absolutely stunning beach laid out beneath dramatic cliffs and enclosed by headlands. From here you can also pick up the coast path and the ancient pilgrimage trail 'St Michael's Way'. This actually begins at St Uny's church in Lelant but Carbis Bay is the point at which it cuts inland. From here the path follows lanes and crosses fields to reach Trencrom Hill about 6 miles away. Here are remains of an ancient hill fort and, not surprisingly, astounding views. This is the high point of the walk and the rest is downhill towards the ultimate destination of St Michael's Mount.

When we arrived at St Ives it was bustling and indeed nearly busting at the seams. This is what you have to expect of popular holiday destinations at the height of the holiday season. My visit took place in the middle of the summer holidays and also on a Bank Holiday Weekend so the world and his wife were down here. People were spilling off the pavements, causing progress down the quaint, narrow streets to be extremely slow. Where the town met the sea the crowds fanned out across the crowded beaches.

I like St Ives and so, obviously, do a lot of other people. I think part of its appeal comes from the charm of its buildings and quirkiness of its street plan, if 'plan' is an appropriate word to apply here. We like the look of 'quaint' fishermen's cottages. We enjoy the intimate feel of the little streets. We don't even mind too much when the streets are clogged with people. This is partly because we feel that we can escape onto a beach fairly easily from almost any part of the town. An additional attraction here is the variety of beach on offer. The town is formed on a small peninsula and so is almost surrounded by the sea. The different aspects provide different beach environments. If you fancy a walk on the wild side then Porthmeor Beach on the north edge of town is for you. This is the haunt of surfers both aspirational and inspirational. Accomplished surfers probably avoid the place during the busiest periods when tiresome people like me are getting in the way on our body boards. I joined the crowd here for a while, all of us enjoying the sun and sand and many enjoying the exhilaration offered by the rolling surf. Just behind me, providing an altogether more tranquil form of enjoyment, was the 'Tate St Ives' art gallery, an eye-catching addition to the townscape which houses works of art from 'the St Ives School'.

After a while I made my way back through the town to the eastern side where I found the more relaxed Porthminster Beach whose near-white sands sloped almost imperceptibly down into the sparkling blue waters of St Ives Bay. This was pretty much as good as a beach gets. Added to this was the excellent Porthminster Beach Café overlooking the picture-perfect stretch of sand. The café matched the beach for relaxation and had a gentle, friendly feel, despite its deserved popularity and consequent busyness. Suitably refreshed I sought out a way of exploring further afield.

I found the 'Malakoff', a sort of headland within the town which served as a gathering point for buses. The 15 service was billed as being 'one of the most scenic bus routes in Britain.' I'd been on some routes recently that would put up some fairly stiff competition for that title but I tried not to prejudge. There was a jolly atmosphere amongst the sizeable crowd waiting for the bus. It's not often you can say that. Normally, it's, "There was a ridiculously huge crowd by the time the bus arrived and everyone was really hacked off."

The good mood continued as we enjoyed the journey. It seemed that other people appreciated the fact that they weren't driving as much as I did. If we had been driving we would not have been able to enjoy the frequent glimpses of the sea and views along the coast or across the wild landscape inland. When we took off down winding, and at times ridiculously narrow, roads it was someone else's problem. When we met cars bumbling along it was quite fun watching them trying to squeeze between the stone posts of a farm entrance to allow us room to pass. When we met a fully loaded holiday coach it was with a sense of quiet admiration rather than anxiety or impatience that we watched the unfortunate driver of that vehicle as he skilfully reversed all 10 metres of it back up the lane to a point where we could manoeuvre and inch our way through the gap.

'Don't you just love Cornwall?' queried our driver.

This was indeed a great scenic route and you could hop off at any number of places like Zennor, Morvah, Pendeen and Botallack and always find something interesting to do or see. Sennen Cove offered the opportunity to explore a tight collection of buildings huddled together by the shore, and access to the path around the coast. I stayed on board because of an unwritten arbitrary rule that I'd made up which suggested I needed to actually arrive at the final destination of the route by bus. I could probably have done this yesterday but I'd decided to put it off to experience a touch of delayed gratification. What I was doing was waiting to arrive by bus at Land's End which was as far west as I could go on mainland Britain on a bus. In fact, pretty much as far west as you could go by any other means of motorised land transport. This done, I could legitimately tick off another stage in my quest but to actually set foot at the very edge I had to walk through a theme park. This sounds worse than it is. You might imagine the odd fast food outlet with a giant plastic pasty slowly rotating above the roof while a jolly pirate beckons you in, or perhaps you think that you have to endure a 'Land's End Cliff Experience' rather than simply looking at the real things. But it isn't really like that at all. In fact, you can almost ignore it. What's more, you don't have to pay to enter.

Sitting high up above the waters of the Atlantic, literally on the edge of England, did not fail to thrill. It is seriously dramatic scenery. Not on the scale of the Grand Canyon or Victoria Falls I grant you but in many situations, thankfully, size isn't everything. And there is still a tangible sense of danger since falling off here would, in all likelihood, be just about the last thing you did. I mean, there are no railings! Thank goodness there are no railings. Please, please, please never let the health and safety people put railings here, or anywhere along the South West Coast Path or any other coast path or anywhere else that's wild and free and high and steep and potentially a bit dangerous. Instead, make sure that people know how to behave sensibly and safely in these kinds of places.

I might have been able to tick off my westernmost point but didn't want to leave it at that. There was far too much to see in the way of coastal scenery and I soaked in a bit more of it along with the sunshine and Atlantic-fresh air while the sea provided an ever-changing and endlessly engaging backdrop. You can lose yourself in this type of setting and I happily did just that. A good while later I was off again, keen to use my day ticket to the full.

Back towards Penzance and not far from Madron is Lanyon Quoit, an ancient megalithic structure of three upright stones supporting a massive capstone. It is possibly an example of what would then have been 'modern art', being a large abstract installation of a table entitled 'All the meals I have ever eaten'. All the food has obviously been long lost to the elements since it has been there since about 2500BC. Actually, it isn't art but one of numerous burial chambers, monuments and settlement sites from this period which are all over this wonderful corner of the country. Such a feature prompts me to wonder what life was like for these people and what thoughts preoccupied them. Presumably a large part of the time was focussed on simply surviving, but they patently had 'bigger' thoughts about such things as life, death and what might happen after that.

In contrast to the wildness which is so prevalent in the area are the delights available in Trengwainton Garden. There can be something therapeutic about a garden, large or small. It is true that someone has envisioned and created it so therefore it is not strictly 'natural'. Even so, the garden designers are connecting to something else and are attempting to create something that helps whoever visits make the same sort of connection.

In Trengwaiton a winding path keeps bringing you back to a bubbling stream which runs through the middle of the property. At the top of the sloping site is a summer house, positioned to offer you wonderful views down the garden, over Mount's Bay and beyond to the sea. A more intimate setting is obtained through wandering in the planted woodland. As well as the settings, the plants themselves produce different effects. The familiarity of trees such as ash, oak and elm is contrasted by encounters with more exotic shrubs in the walled gardens and the specialist plants of the bog gardens. This is an altogether lovely spot.

I made my way back to Pendeen and had another good dose of coastal scenery. What we can enjoy about the sea from the safety of the land often means significant danger for those actually at sea. Dramatic cliffs are awe-inspiring. Waves crashing around isolated rocks or swelling and swirling over submerged rock formations are stirring. But cliffs, rocks and powerful movements of the water are dangerous if you're out there in a boat. The proliferation of lighthouses between Cape Cornwall and St Ives and beyond gives a clue to how dangerous this stretch of water can be.

As soon as people started seafaring they would have known that it was difficult and dangerous. The hazards of a coastline were increasingly understood but any kind of solution was a long time coming. The Seamarks Act of 1566 gave powers to an organisation which exists today as Trinity House to set up 'So many beacons, marks and signs for the sea ... whereby the dangers may be avoided and escaped and ships the better come into their ports without peril.'

The organisation built their first lighthouse at Lowestoft in 1609 and the one to which I was heading at Pendeen Watch in 1900. It's a bit of a trek from the village down to the lighthouse but it is pleasant enough out along the headland. The lighthouse was quiet, stoic and isolated. It somehow spoke of permanence and dependability and I thought how comforting it must be for those in peril on the sea to know that such places exist. There was a gentle evening breeze, distant sounds from the sea, and the surrounding colours softened and began to lose their intensity. It was very relaxing and good to watch the sun slowly sinking. It's funny how our perception of this event doesn't reflect the true situation. Rather than a sun slowly sinking we are spinning away from it in the midst of a manic 1000 mile-an-hour rotation while on a 67000 mile-an-hour orbit of a vast star.

Later on, after a couple of quiet hours in the bar, the tent did seem to be making some attempt at emulating all this spinning but I can't think why.

Day 22

Exploring southern extremities

26th August

Another glorious morning which required a rapid exit before the tent transformed itself from freezer compartment to sauna. It was also departure time and I wanted to make an early start. I think it must have been too early because, without thinking, I bought a single to Penzance rather than a Day Ticket. A minor point I know, but annoying nonetheless to a budget-conscious traveller, since it effectively almost doubled my travelling expenses on the first part of the journey.

The rugged landscapes of this most western end of Cornwall were left behind as we dropped down into Penzance. At the bus station I bought a Day Ticket and took a bus to Helston. After weaving through some of the eastern parts of Penzance we hugged the coast and came again to Marazion and St Michael's Mount which was completely surrounded by the sea at that point in the day, its causeway submerged by the waters of the high tide. The journey continued and took me through Goldsithney, an ancient-looking spot, gave me a brush with Praa Sands, probably one of the best beaches in the area, and finally displayed Porthleven. This last is set in what we like to call 'unspoilt' countryside. If there is 'unspoilt' countryside there is presumably countryside that has been 'spoilt' and we probably need to be on constant alert to ensure the balance between the two is preserved.

Places like Porthleven can boast of an 'unspoilt' beach because it isn't overrun with kiosks or amusement arcades nor dominated by a thrilling roller coaster. We have also been unable to spoil the very lovely little harbour village and for this we can only be grateful. Once again what we now see as quaint, quiet and picturesque has an altogether more purposeful and industrial past. The town grew from a fourteenth century hamlet of fishermen's cottages to be supplemented by homes for farmers and miners. By the early nineteenth century a harbour was being built and a shipbuilding industry established. It has also been a thriving port exporting tin, copper and china clay and bringing in coal, limestone and timber. Pilchards have also played an important role in making this place what it is today— and I don't mean it's smelly.

At Helston I disembarked in, and was immediately smitten with, Coinagehall Street. The name comes from the French word 'coin' meaning 'corner'. Tin from the local mines was brought here and a corner/'coin' was cut off to be tested for quality. This all happened in the 'coinage hall' so the street name makes sense. It also makes sense of why we have 'coins' as part of our currency since the purity of the corner 'coin' assured the purity of the 'coin of the realm'. It doesn't, however, explain why the French call a coin 'un piece'.

An imposing granite ashlar monument to one Humphry Millet Grylls stood at the bottom of the street. This looked rather like the offspring of a church building and castle, having abundant adornments, crenellations and pinnacles. Humphry is deserving of such a great monument because of his efforts in 1830 to keep the local Wheal Vor tin mine open which resulted in the saving of over 1000 jobs.

Jostling together up the street are Georgian and Victorian buildings housing independent shops and stores and also, in an older building, 'Cornwall's Oldest Pub' the Blue Anchor. This was originally a resting place for monks which became a tavern in the fifteenth century. That is not to say, of course, that the monks weren't brewing a spot of beer as well as resting, before that time. The brewing tradition continues today in the cellar with a local brew somewhat alarmingly called Spingo. To borrow and paraphrase a line from a successful and long-running ad campaign for a soft drink—you'll know when you've been Spingoed.

If you come to Helston on the 8th May you will find the place bedecked with bluebells, gorse and laurel leaves ready for Flora Day. This is not a time for celebrating the invention of a spreadable alternative to the more traditional butter, but an ancient rite which apparently has its beginnings in the tale of a struggle between St Michael and Satan. Satan was planning to drop a huge stone over the entrance to hell, presumably thinking that this would mean nobody else could be sent there. St. Michael spotted him and rushed to foil this diabolical plan. In the ensuing struggle Satan was forced to drop the stone and the spot where it landed was given the name Hell's Stone. On the spot today you will find the pleasant market town of Helston. The people were so pleased that the Entrance to Hell had not been blocked (some interesting logic there) that they began dancing and so began the Helston Furry Dance or Flora Dance.

An alternative take on this involves St George and a dragon with the former, on behalf of 'good', overcoming the latter, putting in an appearance on behalf of 'evil'. Good overcoming evil is always a good reason for a spot of singing and dancing. Whatever the origin, Helstonians do a grand job in maintaining one of our more inscrutable customs: the willingness of large numbers of people to put on outrageous costumes and perform unfashionable dance moves in public.

From Helston I made my way onto 'The Lizard'. Now, if I was responsible for assigning a name to a place of great beauty and to which I hoped to attract a large number of people, I don't think I would call it 'The Lizard'. This might be appropriate for a ride in a theme park although now it would probably be considered a little tame.

Let's face it, the designers of these theme park rides have become increasingly proficient at creating the impression that the ride you are experiencing will in fact constitute your last moments on Earth. Consequently the names have had to change to suit. And so you might find yourself staring into Oblivion or facing some form of Nemesis, as well as experiencing the rearrangement of your internal organs. It's all very strange but we start subjecting people to this at a very young age. Small children, for example, are taken to the top of a simple slide which starts with a virtually vertical drop before a smooth if abrupt curve leads to an almost horizontal end. When the child seems reluctant, a mystified parent might ask, "What's the matter, sweetheart, don't you want to go down the *death* slide?"

So 'The Lizard' isn't named after a scary fairground ride or a scaly reptile. The name actually originates in the Cornish language and either comes from the words 'lys' and 'ardh' meaning 'court on a height' or, 'lezou' meaning headland. People can't decide. By the time of the Domesday Book it is recorded as Lisart. The actual settlement called 'The Lizard' is a small town at the foot of The Lizard peninsula. Throughout the gentle journey down the length of this most attractive geographical feature I couldn't help but notice how much agricultural activity there seemed to be. All those involved are carrying on from a long line of practitioners. And I mean a long line. There is evidence that people were settling and creating established farms here, complete with enclosures and round houses mind you, as far back as the Middle Bronze Age. That's about 3500 years ago. Back then this would have been their world. The peninsula probably formed the boundaries within which they were born, lived and died. All the food they ate would have been locally produced and would have included wheat or barley to make chewy bread. They would have kept sheep and cattle too, and so may have indulged in the occasional barbeque. It sounds like a simple life but it would have been pretty hard. I wonder, however, if some of their simple aspirations, self-sufficiency and ability to live within fairly limited boundaries, permeate the area today. If a place like this has a relaxed, 'laid-back' feel, and visitors comment on a slower 'pace of life', where does that come from? Why is it so hard to take it away with you when you go home?

We passed through Cury, a small farming community with an appropriately-sized church dedicated to St Corentin who came here from Brittany. Just below, the sea has nibbled away at the cliffs to create Poldhu Cove with its lovely enclosed beach. This unassuming spot is where certain experiments were carried out that would change the world. I don't think I'm exaggerating.

Guglielmo Marconi was born near Bologna in Italy on 25th

April 1874. By 1894 he was busy experimenting with 'wireless telegraphy', assembling such things as an oscillator, a telegraph key and a 'coherer receiver', whatever they are. At first he was working indoors, seeing if he could request a cup of tea from the sitting room of someone in the kitchen near the kettle. In the summer of 1895 he moved his work out doors and attempted requesting refreshment from the potting shed. Soon, after rearranging and improving his equipment he was able to send a signal over a distance of about 1.5 kilometres. This had the obvious advantage of alerting people who were out that the tea was ready and it was time to come home.

Marconi realised that he needed more funding if he was to create a system that would allow people to contact others at a greater distance to inform them of their whereabouts and to give an estimated time of arrival back home and therefore a time at which it would be good to serve tea. He didn't find much interest in Italy but then they've never been big on tea over there. So he made his way to London. Here he gained the interest and support of William Preece, Chief Electrical Engineer of the British Post Office (as opposed to the Chief Engineer of the Demise of the British Post Office who came much later). Marconi was now making clever use of a carbon granular rectifier. I can't imagine how he ever thought he could make any progress at all without a carbon granular rectifier but perhaps I speak with the benefit of hindsight. Having rectified his carbon granules, Marconi managed to send signals over about 6 km across Salisbury Plain and finally sent the first ever wireless communication across open water. The signal crossed the Bristol Channel from Lavernock Point in South Wales to Flat Holm Island with the message 'Are you ready (for tea)?' although the bit in brackets was lost amongst unrectified carbon granules.

The equipment was immediately moved from Flat Holm to Brean Down, increasing the distance to 16km. A signal was sent from France across the English Channel in 1899 informing the recipient of the readiness of une tasse de thé et du gateau.

In 1901 Marconi set up a transmitter in County Wexford, Northern Ireland and a high-powered station at Poldhu. The signal transmitted on 12 December 1901 was received 3500 km away in Signal Hill, St John's, Newfoundland. The contents of the message are disputed but the response was apparently 'Do you know what the damn time is over here?' This remarkable event is commemorated at Poldhu in The Marconi Centre.

Marconi apparently wondered at one stage, 'Have I done the world good, or have I added a menace?' I'll ask the people in the 'quiet carriage' next time I'm on the train.

By comparison with Cury, Mullion is a heaving metropolis, having shops, pubs and at least one garage. Here also is the church of St Mellanus, a sixth century buddy and travelling companion of St Sampson. These two seem to have been regular commuters between Cornwall and Brittany, also taking in Ireland and Wales on their busy journeys preaching and baptising. All this sounds rather easy to our ears for surely Brittany is only a simple ferry ride away? Not in the sixth century. St Brendan, for example, is said to have constructed a leather curragh (a small, narrow keel-less craft) in which he and seventeen fellow monks would sail across the Atlantic in search of the Promised Land. You have to admire a monk who will jump into a boat made of cow-skin and sail in search of a place which may or may not exist across a stretch of water that disappears towards the visible end of the Earth. But they did that sort of thing then, so Mellanus and Sampson popping across the Channel would have seemed comparatively straightforward, the vagaries of the currents, violent storms, tower-block high waves and so on notwithstanding.

The church of St Mellanus, in the centre of the village, dates from the fifteenth century but has elements from earlier times, suggesting a previous church on the site. The wooden benches have ends carved to depict episodes from the Bible. St Mellanus, or at least the church dedicated to him, has given the village of Mullion its name. It has nothing to do with the vertical structural elements that separate individual glazed units in a window. So why are they called mullions, I wonder? The thatched Old Inn, which looks like a pub should, has been serving the local community since the sixteenth century but probably not always with Cajun chicken supreme or half pound cheeseburgers.

Finally reaching The Lizard, the bus dropped me in what would pass for a square or perhaps a village green. This was surrounded by shops and pubs and was not far from Ann's Famous Pasty Shop which demanded a visit. It had demanded a visit from several hundred other people, or so it seemed, and there was an impressive queue. I had seen a similar phenomenon by the pasty shop in Hayle and took this to be a good sign, like seeing Chinese people eating in a Chinese restaurant. The queue was impressive not only because of its length but also because of its orderly nature. We in the UK are renowned, and sometimes mocked, for our queuing but it seems to me a mark of civility and a chance to show manners and courtesy. We were all very mannered and courteous as we waited for the number of people before us to slowly diminish. There are times when standing in a long queue that you begin to worry about certain things that could happen. Will the place run out of whatever it is they are offering? Will they simply shut up shop? Will there be a seat left? Am I in the right queue? And so on. Given the weather conditions a few of us began to worry about other things such as dehydration and heat exhaustion, but I think we were getting carried away. All in all it has to be said that Ann was running a pretty tight ship and dealing with the masses very efficiently.

Having made my pasty purchase I searched for a decent place to enjoy it. A proper pasty is alleged to stay warm for up to an hour so I could have made it back to Helston or even further but that seemed a bit ridiculous. Ridiculous not least because I had come all this way and still not quite reached the most southerly point on mainland Britain. This was a fifteen minute walk away down the hill at The Lizard Point.

Here was another fine landscape of cliff tops and coves set against the backdrop of the sea. It is the perfect place to eat a Cornish pasty. After my meal I spent a happy time gently working off some of the pasty's calorific value by wandering the cliff path between Lizard Point and Bass Point. From The Lizard Point the view north takes in the coast towards Pentreath Beach and Kynance Cove and to the east an old lifeboat station in Polpeor Cove. The walk to Bass Point took in a couple more delightful coves and the whole experience was fantastic, bracing and uplifting.

The sea was remarkably calm but at Bass Point a lookout station acts as a reminder of how quickly a calm sea can change. Here also is further evidence of Signor Marconi's expanding wireless empire in the form of The Lizard Wireless Station.

Nearby is The Lizard Lighthouse which overlooks one of the busiest shipping lanes in the world. The peninsula is also fringed by a series of jagged and treacherous rock formations with ominous names like The Manacles and The Man of War Reef. Given this combination of ships and rocks, it is hardly surprising that the place has been known as 'the graveyard of ships' nor that there have been many attempts to minimise the appropriateness of this nickname.

One of those attempting to address the problem was Sir John Killigrew, a fine philanthropic gentleman, who applied to erect a beacon tower which was finally finished in time for Christmas 1619. He had to agree that his light would be extinguished if an enemy vessel were seen to be approaching. He also had to overcome a certain amount of local apathy and even hostility. It seems that some people considered that the goods from wrecked ships offered quite a lucrative sideline and giving the mariners something like a light to warn them of the dangerous rocks would have been detrimental to business. Nice attitude, local residents. As a result, few local labourers were willing to help in the venture. Nice attitude, local labourers. Sir John's troubles were not over once the tower was built. Despite its being of considerable benefit to passing mariners, the vessels' owners seemed rather reluctant to cough up a voluntary contribution towards the upkeep of the tower. This reluctance, combined with Sir John's stoic efforts in keeping the thing going, resulted in him becoming bankrupt. Nice attitude, greedy ship-owners. James I subsequently set a fee of one halfpenny a ton for goods passing safely by the light. Nice attitude, James I. This was greeted with outrage and uproar amongst the ship-owners and the patent for the beacon was withdrawn, the light extinguished and the tower demolished. Again, nice work greedy ship-owners (who are not, let's remember, actually *in* the ship as it passes through these treacherous waters). Other applications to build a similar warning beacon were made by mariners but they had to wait until 1748 for Trinity House to get behind the plan of one Thomas Fonnereau. His building was finished in 1751.

All in all then a fairly fascinating place and a fitting final destination in my quest to reach the four cardinal compass points of England on service buses. This was as far south as I could go in such a vehicle. I had done it. That was it. And yet I didn't feel as though things were coming to an end. There wasn't really a feeling of climax or resolution. This was due in no small measure to the fact that I had to get home and this was nearly 200 miles away. I decided to make a start.

Although it is virtually impossible to take more than ten paces on The Lizard peninsula without finding yourself in a gorgeous secluded picturesque village brimming with historic charm and cosy cottages, the Lizard also hosted a facility that could scarcely have been more 'present day'. This was the Goonhilly satellite station, the incongruous domes and dishes of which were visible in the distance as we returned towards Helston. Long after Marconi's first attempts at wireless tea requests, the station at Goonhilly became the largest satellite facility in the world, dealing with tens of millions of international phone calls and gazillions of bytes of internet traffic.

The bus pottered through a few more villages before calling at RNAS Culdrose one of the UK's two Naval Air Stations. In 1942, Admiralty surveyors arrived to assess the land which was originally planned as a wartime airfield with a life expectancy of about ten years. Five years later the station was commissioned as HMS Seahawk, but the War was over. I think it was much better for the war to finish early rather than to hang on for the completion of the airfield. With the war over, the base developed other roles, and you can even have a nose round once a year when there is an Air Day. As if dramatic coasts, quaint villages, acclaimed pasties, wireless heritage and satellite stations wouldn't be enough for most people, the Lizard also has Flambard's Theme Park. So there *is* a theme park after all but I don't think it has anything to do with lizards.

During the journey I had been chatting to an elderly lady who explained that she lived in Truro and regularly enjoyed the ride down to the Lizard. This was an easy and accessible way for her to enjoy a day out, and she felt it was almost like a sightseeing coach tour. On her day out she spent a short time poking about in The Lizard, had some light refreshments and then took another bus home again. I think you'd class her as a satisfied customer.

The interior of the Truronian bus that carried me away from Helston showed that the designers were doing their best to satisfy other customers, specifically those travelling with young children. In addition to the equivalent of a fitted child car seat, there was a baby's activity centre attached to the wall, all bright-coloured plastic with wheels and buttons and shiny beads. It looked really good fun but someone else was already using it. The rest of the bus showed that the operators cared about their other passengers too. The seats were comfortable and the whole vehicle was fresh and clean.

Cornwall had its less dramatic face on as we drove through the largely agricultural landscape. However, not far to the north lay the mining area around Gwennap, while to the south were the quarries of Rame and Longdowns. We called in briefly via some twisting lanes to the small village of Stithians, had a brief tour of an estate of housing and then left. Other points en route included Perranwell, where you can connect with the present day railway, and Devoran where you can connect with those of the past. This small town on the edge of the Fal estuary was once a busy port with extensive wharves through which locally mined ore went out and timber and coal came back. To connect the port with the mines, a railway was constructed by an entrepreneur by the name of John Taylor, who owned mines at St Day. His railway was under construction in 1823 and finished by 1825 and the 50,000 tons of ore that travelled its course in the first year were all carried in horse drawn wagons. Steam locomotives replaced the horses in the mid nineteenth century. After twenty odd years the horses must have been knackered. They probably were. The line itself lasted until 1915. The object of the railway was 'to facilitate the conveyance of the produce of the rich mineral district around Redruth for shipment' according to the relevant Act. Today it facilitates the conveyance of walkers, cyclists and horse riders and connects to the Coast to Coast Trail at Twelveheads. So we have to be very grateful to Mr Taylor and his fellow nineteenth century entrepreneurs for doggedly carving out such an accessible route.

The journey drew to a close as we drifted down through trees overarching the road with more views of fields and a wooded valley. As the city of Truro's boundary was breached the sun was catching the impressive spires of the cathedral in the distance. We negotiated the outer urban areas and I was finally deposited once again in the elegant Lemon Street. I had a friend who lived nearby with his family and I had been able to contact him thanks to the miracles of mobile wireless communication. So, despite the nuisance on trains and all that, let's hear it for Guglielmo Marconi, without whom I might have found myself sleeping in a Truro shop doorway. Big thanks for the bed to Chris and Kay.

Day 23

Devon delights

27th August

The sun seemed to set the cathedral spires alight as I made my way back to the bus station. It was a morning that made you feel glad to be alive. Aren't they just *so* much better than the mornings that make you wish you were dead?

I had been through my daily routine of perusing my trusty Tourist Map, getting to the bus station and perusing bus time-tables and then attempting to establish a correlation between bus services offered and places I wanted to go. Today I was heading eastward and my map and the bus services correlated around St Austell.

Truro is not a large city and so we were soon in an open countryside of fields, hedgerows and isolated woods. Cattle were grazing peacefully as we fairly zipped (by bus standards) along the A390. At Tresillian we needed to cross a river. This was once the lowest bridging point of the Truro River and also the highest navigable point. The spot is famous for its bridge, or at least what happened here one day in 1646 when the Royalist Army surrendered to the Parliamentarians. Another associated landmark is The Wheel Inn, which dates from the fifteenth century and was the local headquarters of the Parliamentarians. The pub has its own peculiarity—a spoked wheel of straw on the thatched roof. I caught a glimpse of Holy Trinity Church, its bells unusually visible in the bell tower. We passed through the small settlement of Probus where Georgian houses and old cottages lined the main street, overlooked by the impressive tower of St Probus and St Grace church.

Views became more panoramic as we approached

Grampound on the upper reaches of the River Fal. The Romans had built a great bridge across the river here. To the Normans this would have been a 'Grand Pont' which helps us see where the name comes from. This small but perfectly-formed village has a hard-working past that includes a thriving leather tanning industry, cattle markets, spinning, fulling and woollen mills as well as glove manufacture. A high point for the community came in 1332 when the town was granted its first charter by Earl John of Eltham. This allowed the cheery townsfolk 'the right to hang convicted thieves'.

We pulled up and out of the village in the direction of St Stephen-in-Brannel, and bussed on past fields and through woods, making our way towards Coombe. The views from the higher ground were suddenly gone as we trundled down through thick woodland, passing impressive nineteenth century viaducts whose arches carry the railway high above the valley. We avoided getting stuck in Sticker and at Trelowth we picked up some members of the older generation on their way to St Austell for a bit of shopping. They pointed out that it was a nice morning, which could not be denied. Their number was added to at Polgooth. There were greetings and a brief conversation that established that the new arrivals were also intending to visit some retail establishments in the nearest sizeable urban area. Someone mentioned the clemency of the current weather conditions. Everyone agreed that this was the prevailing situation. That business concluded, everyone settled down for the onward journey, admiring the scenery and enjoying a chat.

London Apprentice, a tiny hamlet, snuck up from nowhere and was gone almost as quickly, and it was in this way that we reached St Austell, named after Hoystill, founder of the first lodge offering young people budget accommodation, and a daughter of 'Brychan of Wales'.

An account of a visit to Cornwall by Henry VIII mentions St Austell as being a small village gathered around a church in which there was also a granite bridge. It doesn't sound like it was much of a place to write home about for that particular chronicler. The fortunes of the 'small village' were affected by the ubiquitous tin and copper mining which would have brought income and employment to supplement those derived from fishing and farming. But it was the discovery of the china clay deposits in the hills to the north of the town that really turned the world of St Austell and its surroundings upside down. In a book of 1910, the writer C. A. Dawson Scott observed heavy wagons rolling through the narrow streets in an endless procession carrying either uncovered lumps of clay or powdered clay in barrels. She noted that the clay was found in Hensbarrow, Bumgallow, St Stephen's and the Bodmin Moors and that it was exported from Par, Fowey and Charleston. According to Dawson, a certain Wedgwood leased a nearby mine in 1763 and at her time of writing about 60 000 tons of the material found its way to the Potteries and into Lancashire. Such insights really help to conjure up in your mind's eye what the place would have looked like here about a hundred years ago and it is a scene that could hardly be more different.

Today St Austell is a fairly busy little market town and also a focal point for a number of tourist attractions in the area. There is no sense of the toil and turmoil of the great clay industry that powered the economy for so long. In the pleasing town centre the buildings are gathered round the fifteenth century Parish Church of The Holy Trinity. The tall tower of local Pentewan stone is full of niches in which reside carvings of, amongst others, Christ, angels, bishops and saints. In the churchyard lies the mysterious Menagew Stone which is said to have once stood at the junction of three manors. Various traditions and superstitions seem to surround the stone. It may have been a place for declaring war and proclaiming peace, a place to display previously impounded cattle or even a place of execution. My stay in the town was brief, not even allowing for a look in at the St Austell Brewery Visitor Centre. I left on the 269 service, operated by DAC Coaches who agreed to carry me to Liskeard for three quid.

After a brief break from built up surroundings we came upon a rash of places whose names refer to St Blaise. Here and hereabouts are St Blazey Gate, St Blaise and St Blazey. St Blaise was martyred in 316 in a really unpleasant way which involved, amongst other things, iron combs. Consequently, he is the patron saint of wool combers, who need a patron saint as much as the next man, I suppose. We had truly left the clay-mining country behind us and were moving around the lowlands near the coast. We made a brief detour into environs that are more familiarly of the seaside, finding Par, a small coastal town next to the extensive beach of Par Sands. Out through Tywardreath we made the long climb up to Penpillick from where the glorious landscape of rolling fields parcelled by plump hedgerows was once more stretched out.

Lostwithiel, meaning 'tail end of the woodland' is billed as 'Cornwall's lost treasure' and it certainly put forward an alluring presentation as I passed through. The town is on the lowest bridging point of the River Fowey and is at the high tide mark of that stretch of water. It has plenty of romance and charm itself, helped by lovely surroundings.

We passed quite near Restormel Castle, now under the care of English Heritage. The ruins here are of a motte-and-bailey castle, built in 1100. Sweetshouse is a tiny hamlet in a lovely rural setting with small cottages made of gingerbread, chocolate fingers and Smarties. No, not really. They looked as though they would be tough on the teeth in a different way, built strong and sturdy, ready to hunker down in the face of harsh elements. The elements were once again anything but harsh and the cottages with their pretty gardens were basking in the sunshine. The delight and joy of seeing Sweetshouse could potentially have been lost as we approached Maudlin. Brushing my sentimental tears aside I noticed we had reached the National Trust property at Lanhydrock.

Lanhydrock is a vast house, largely Victorian, begun by Sir Richard Robartes, a wealthy local merchant, in 1620. He died in 1624 and his son continued the work. The house has had a bit of a tough time of it. The East wing was demolished during the 1780s, and what was left fell into disrepair. The place was revived and modernised in the mid-nineteenth century only for the south and west wings to be destroyed by fire in 1881. The North wing and Long Gallery survived and formed the basis for another major rebuild. If you have a couple of hours to spare there are forty-nine rooms to look through. We did not linger long and were soon once again in Bodmin. Our return here emphasises the importance of the town as a transport hub. This is due in part to the fact that the northern route taken through Cornwall by the A30 via Okehampton and Launceston meets the southern route of the A38 coming up through Plymouth and Liskeard.

The countryside of the onward journey was looking glorious in the sun and it was lovely just to sit back and enjoy it all. At Two Waters Foot, where the St Neot River meets the Fowey, we call into Trago Mills, a popular spot for those who need to exchange cash for stuff. Many such folk left the bus at this point. The shopping complex actually has the feel of a small village complete with parks, lakes and distinctive castle-like buildings. There are statues and sculptures here and there, many with an almost satirical edge, such as the large scales where 'Administrative Justice' is seen to be easily outweighing 'Natural Justice', the caption to which seems to be asking the then Attorney General Sir Michael Havers QC, "Why beholdest thou the mote that is in thy brother's eye, but considerest not the beam that is in thine own eye?" Other targets are local opponents of the founder of the business, Mike Robertson, who has since shuffled off his mortal coil while his statues, and his business, live on.

The woods became thicker as we made the upward approach to Doublebois, once the summit of the Cornwall Railway which ran from Plymouth to Falmouth. We pushed on through Dobwalls and into Liskeard, an old stannery town and a long-standing (as in 1240) market town, placed above the valley of the River Looe and stretched between two high points. The town was compact and comfortable and seemed to have a sense of purpose without succumbing to straightforward functionality. An array of historic buildings added plenty of architectural interest and a great deal of charm, enhanced by the number of Victorian shop fronts retained by many smaller independent establishments. Another benefit for the town in my view was that it wasn't level.

For me, the effects of uneven topography on a building's elevations add more interest. Steep Hill in Lincoln and Catherine Hill in Frome wouldn't be half so inviting or pleasing to the eye if they were laid out flat. They would also be erroneously named and that could cause all sorts of problems. Anyway, 'Level Street' and 'Flat Road' just sound rubbish. The terrain in these places has forced people to produce buildings that cope with being constructed on a slope and that usually means something a bit quirky or unusual is going on.

The Tourist Information Centre and Museum in Liskeard was a good example. The building expresses an element of respect for the existing landscape. Rather than come in with mighty earth-moving equipment to strip away the natural shape to produce a nice, flat piece of ground, the builders have worked with the contours, not ridden rough-shod over them. So we have a jolly set of buildings that offer a stone structure of three storeys, over an imposing set of arches guarding a stepped and covered area accessed off the steep street. And round the corner where the building disappears into the slope of the land, a small porch which would perhaps be just as much at home acting as the entrance to a humble cottage. There is something about a building that is so obviously moulded into the ground. It feels organic, it fits and it belongs. I liked Liskeard immediately and the feeling was boosted by the small, well-proportioned urban space created by The Parade. The impressive clock tower on the Guild Hall, built in 1859, is testament to earlier wealth and prosperity, not to mention architectural ability and stonemasons' skills. Another advantage of these smaller places for me was that I could dash round and get a sense of the place quite quickly before I had to catch my next bus.

I travelled from Liskeard Town Centre to Plymouth on a £3.00 ticket courtesy of Plymouth Citybus. It proclaimed itself as 'Your local bus company' and it meant this in more ways than one. The company shareholding is retained by Plymouth City Council, which presumably means it is funded by council tax and is run 'for the people, by the people'. This all sounded very exciting to me.

Merrymeet, a small village through which we passed, sounds like a good place for socialising or indeed a snappy name for a dating agency. Not long after this Menheniot appeared. A curious name, seemingly based on the Cornish for land (ma) and a person's name 'Hynyed'.

An important local was Dr John Moreman of Southold who was famous, according to the writings of Daniel Defoe, for being 'the first clergyman in England for venturing to teach his parishioners the Lord's Prayer, Creed and Ten Commandments in the English tongue and reading them so publickly in the parish church of Mayenhennet, in this county, of which he was vicar.' I wondered what was so special about teaching some Christian liturgy to Cornishmen in English. My first thought was that the need to translate services or liturgy at that time would arise because they were ordinarily only available in Latin. In this case, however, it seems that the issue was that the congregation at the time were not used to Latin but to Cornish. Dr Moreman was working at a time prior to decrees demanding that services be carried out in English; decrees that led to a bit of a Cornish rebellion. All this preaching and teaching presumably took place in the fabulous fourteenth century church of St Lalluwy and St Antoninus, which boasts a fine steeple.

The journey on south took us through stunning countryside, to the extent that a fellow-passenger was moved to comment, "'tis such a pretty ride." Approaching Saltash we were about to leave Cornwall and return to Devon, or as the Cornish would probably prefer, return to England. I reflected on my few days in this wonderful part of the country and wondered what it was that gave it such a distinctive feel.

Firstly, there were the great upland masses that provided the high rugged landscapes of Bodmin Moor and the coastal hinterlands of the far west. Then there are the glorious coasts of the north and west, combining dramatic cliffs and intimate coves which contrasted well with the fabulous sandy sweeps of the beaches in places like Carbis Bay and Marazion. The landscapes are so varied and offer everything from the bleakness of the northern moor to the sub-tropical gardens of the south. And there is such a feeling of space. There is no great huge, sprawling metropolis, with even Penzance hardly coming into that category. So, even the larger settlements are small and they are spaced well apart in great settings that are an important element of their attractiveness.

Musings over, I noticed we had left the higher ground of the hinterland far behind us and descended to the sea. The views were accordingly maritime and particularly so across the estuary of the River Tamar. The sight of the engineering wonder of Brunel's dramatic Albert Bridge from 1859 is impressive from our vantage point on the modern suspension bridge (toll free passage on the bus). We looked down on new waterside development and boating areas, and it all looked rather sophisticated and clean. For William Camden it was a place 'well replenished with merchants and endowed with many privileges'. Daniel Defoe, however, writing in the 1720s, found it to be 'the ruins of a larger place' and he saw many houses 'as it were falling down' and did not doubt that 'the mice and rats have abandoned many more'. He does note that there is a market in Saltash which attracts many customers in part by virtue of being cheaper than Plymouth. This, he thinks, 'is like to be a very great advantage to the town of Saltash, and may in time put a new face of wealth upon the place.' It seems he may have been right.

Where was Drake when he decided to finish his legendary game of bowls as the Spanish Armada approached? Where did the Pilgrim Fathers finally set off from to make their home in the New World? From whence did James Cook embark on his voyage of discovery aboard HMS Resolution? Where did Henry Winstanley build the first offshore lighthouse? The answer to all these questions is Plymouth.

Despite all these historical links, Plymouth doesn't have a very historical look. This, in a roundabout way, is partly due to its longstanding association with the sea. There have been naval dockyards at nearby Devonport for hundreds of years and those in existence in the Second World War became a target for the German Luftwaffe. Although ostensibly targeting the dockyards the German bombs made a pretty good job of destroying the city centre. What was left was taken care of by Sir Patrick Abercrombie, a town planning consultant, and Mr Paton Watson, the city engineer. These two were appointed to prepare a regeneration plan for the city and both decided that they would need to have a 'clean sheet' if they were going to be able to carry out any effective redevelopment. This would involve the removal of properties and wreckage from pockets of land in the central area which were then owned by all manner of people. They lobbied government to produce a new act which would allow for the 'compulsory purchase' of the land they needed. These machinations eventually found fulfilment in the Town and Country Planning Act of 1944.

As a result, Plymouth is, centrally at least, a 'new town' with occasional gems of history like the sixteenth century Merchant's House and the Elizabethan House scattered here and there. It wasn't alluring enough to keep me long from making further use of the First Day Plus ticket I'd bought in Truro which would take me onwards. We left town, passing the mud flats of the River Plym, which had a covering of white sea birds, groups of which would occasionally erupt skywards, startled by movement from the few people in attendance.

On the fringes of the larger town we passed through Plympton, which was another ancient market and stannary town. It had been an important port in its day with locally mined tin being the bulk of the export. Problems slowly crept towards the town in the form of silt, making navigation to this point on the River Plym increasingly difficult and eventually impossible. As a result the town's prominence was lost to Plymouth. Plympton has the ruins of a 1000 year old castle which is thought to be on the site of an even more ancient settlement whose earthworks would have acted as a defence against marauding Danes. They get everywhere, don't they?

The countryside had taken on an altogether more rural feel as we left the urbanisation that was Plymouth and Plympton behind. Ivybridge, from Ivebrugge out of ifig brycg (OE) meaning 'bridge covered with ivy' is a small settlement on the southern edge of the Dartmoor National Park. The village's name is hardly one of the most cryptic I had encountered: there is an 'Ivy Bridge' at the top of town. This was once part of a medieval packhorse route which crosses the River Erme and has been a choice of many a landscape artist including JMW Turner. In the past the town has also boasted a tin mill, an edge mill, a tool mill, a corn mill, a tucking mill and two paper mills. All quiet now but the town is a good spot for keen walkers, with The Two Moors Way National Trail starting from here heading north and the Erme Valley Trail wandering more sedately south. At Rattery I wondered briefly if this was a place to take your pet rat when you went on holiday but soon discovered that it is a place near a red tree or 'read treow' in Old English. Rattery also contained the fine-looking Church House Inn. We stopped briefly at the Cider Press Centre, a visitor centre of shops and eateries on the edge of the Dartington estate before continuing on, moving away from the moor and down towards the coast.

We pulled into Totnes, formerly the promontory of a man named Totta, an appealing little town with many old buildings and a lovely setting on the River Dart. Totnes was founded by the Saxon King Edward as part of the tenth century defences against, yep, the Danes. They were already making a nuisance of themselves over much of the more northern expanses of the country. There was a mint here in Anglo-Saxon times, which is an indication of its importance. By the time of the Norman conquest Totnes was second only to Exeter in size and wealth in all of Devon. The Norman baron Judhel built a castle which still presides over the town, albeit in a rather ruined state. By medieval times the town was growing increasingly prosperous from the woollen trade, itself driven by the sheep farming on Dartmoor. The town was by this time a busy port and had a 'sea mill', which made use of the power of the running tides in the river. The people of medieval times seem to have had a pretty good grasp of renewable energy resources, which makes you wonder why it seems so difficult for us today. Just as the remains of the castle overlook the city so an impressive sandstone tower belonging to St Mary's Church presides over the goings on in the High Street. It looked almost as lovely as Ludlow.

We continued our gradual descent until we reached the coast at Paignton where the landscape and scenery changed and I returned to an environment of seaside holiday resorts. The town sits on the edge of Torbay and offers long sandy beaches. The River Dart empties into the sea here and there are cruises from the town and an interesting harbour too. Another attraction is the Dart Valley Railway which steams away to Kingswear.

For a while the bus journey took me round the edge of an extensively built-up environment, crossing imperceptible boundaries. I could not tell when it was that we slipped from Paignton into Torquay but we did and after it happened I realised I was in the throbbing heart of The English Riviera. Actually, that makes it sound a little bit exciting and I wouldn't want to mislead you. Also, you might start to confuse it with a similar sounding destination slightly further away—the French Riviera. This latter, also known as the Cote d'Azur, became a popular resort area for sickly British types towards the end of the eighteenth century. By the mid-nineteenth century it was the playground of aristocracy and would have been on a television programme like 'Lifestyles of the rich and famous' if there had been televisions and people wanted to make that sort of programme. Anyway, where was I? Oh yes, the scintillating nature of the French Riviera, visited by everyone from Queen Victoria to Brigit Bardot and Pablo Picasso to Elton John. That area includes such places as Antibes, Cannes and St Tropez and enjoys 300 days of sunshine per year. And it is in France.

Torquay came out fighting for the English Riviera, which is in England. There were claims for the health benefits available from a visit to the town as early as the eighteenth century. One early visitor declared,

Instead of the poor uncomfortable village we had expected, how great was our surprise at seeing a pretty range of neat new buildings, fitted up for summer visitors, who may certainly here enjoy carriage rides, bathing, retirement and a most romantic situation. [*]

The railway arrived in Torquay at pretty much the same time as it did the French Riviera but it hadn't started from the

---

[*] Matson's Observations on the West of England 1794-6 (quoted in Torquay harbour conservation area character appraisal, www.torbay.gov.uk/torquay_harbour_conservation_area_appraisal.pdf.)

same place. It brought huge numbers of visitors who couldn't be bothered to schlep all the way to the Riviera in France. This was the period which saw the greatest expansion of the town and as a result it is handsome in a Victorian way.

The journey here from Liskeard had taken the best part of two hours. The sun shone and the sea glistened. The sun shone and I glistened too. Having reached a temperature close to overheating, I cooled down with a large ice cream. A traditional, local, Devon ice cream, naturally.

I set about partaking of some of the health-giving properties available courtesy of the sun, sea, fresh air, 'retirement and a most romantic situation'. The area around Torquay enjoys a mild climate which in turn allows for growing rather exotic plants that add to the Riviera feel. The waterfront enhances this deception even further with its flotilla of yachts and small craft bobbing about on the slight swell, with whatever it is that makes that mysterious clinking sound steadily making a mysterious clinking sound.

Complementing the Victorian hotels is the Princess Pier from the late 1800s and the Torquay Pavilion from 1912. This is a concoction of ornate ironwork, white-tiled exterior and copper domes which is frankly quite weird but at the same time wonderful. It was originally a 'Palace of Pleasure', which these days would be a dangerous thing to type into an internet search engine. Originally it was envisaged as a major entertainment venue which in its time hosted the Torquay Music Festivals and pulled in many top names. Those were the days. The council in the 1970s appreciated this architectural wonder and its many local associations so much that they wanted to knock it down. It was saved from this fate and now houses a shopping centre. If you've got to have a shopping centre why not have it in a jovial building which reflects some of the fun and enthusiasm people had for the seaside back in those lazy, hazy, crazy days of the early 1900s? From the outside it still looks as though it should be filled with flapper girls and be awash with aspidistras.

In fact, rather than aspidistras, the plant perhaps most often associated with the area is the 'Torbay Palm'. It is hard not to feel a little disappointment when you learn that this is in fact a cabbage tree, but perhaps that is a problem with our associations with cabbages as boiled-to-the-brink school-dinner vegetables. Anyway, the plants look more like palm trees than cabbages, which is fine. There was a profusion of flowers in the nearby sub-tropical gardens and the overall effect was almost enough to make me feel like I *was* on a holiday abroad. It was almost 5 o'clock in the afternoon when I handed over my £3.05 for the single to Teignmouth. It was just up the coast and this represented one of my most expensive single journeys per mile so far.

Also along the coast were Babbacombe and St Marychurch, two villages which perch on the red sandstone cliffs and keep watch over the beaches below. Babbacombe may be beaches, model villages and cliff railways to most but it just reminded me of John Babbacombe Lee. This association came courtesy of a Fairport Convention LP. (For anyone under 25, that's like a big black plastic version of a CD and it was these things that provided people in the olden days with a chance to listen to recorded music). The LP told the story of John 'Babbacombe' Lee.

He was accused of murdering his employer, a certain Emma Keyse, at her home in Babbacombe on 15th November 1884. Having been convicted on mostly circumstantial evidence he was sentenced to death. On February 3rd 1885 they tried to hang John Lee. The trap doors failed so they tried again. The trap doors failed again. They tried a third time and still the doors wouldn't open so they asked John if he'd mind stepping outside for a while as they were having a bit of trouble with their trap doors. John, being an amenable type and probably being bound hand and foot and surrounded by guards, could hardly refuse. In the meantime, the Home Secretary thought that experiencing near death three times was enough for any man and commuted the death sentence to life imprisonment. Lee had been protesting his innocence throughout his incarceration and his petitions finally resulted in his release in 1907. This allowed him to take up a lucrative career as an after-dinner speaker, 'The Man They Couldn't Hang'. He would not be the last person of questionable character to take up after-dinner speaking as a lucrative career.

As we crossed Ness headland we came upon Shaldon, resting quietly and rather sedately on the western side of the Teign estuary. Shaldon has quaint cottages, winding narrow lanes, pubs, eateries and gift shops. A regular and frequent foot ferry offered transport across the estuary to the heady delights of Teignmouth.

The eastern end of Teignmouth had a very relaxed feel and enjoyed a variety of public open spaces, shopping areas and quieter back streets. The sea front promenade was backed by 'The Den', a semi-formal park, and there was also a fine pier. As I was still on the English Riviera there were plenty of giant cabbages, sorry, 'Torbay palms', and masses of flowers. Like many other towns down this way, Teignmouth is a popular place for retirement and this part of town was full of retirees, walking about on the prom or sitting in cafes drinking tea as if there were no tomorrow. Or, at least as if this is precisely what they will be doing again tomorrow.

Further along the promenade the entrance to the pier offered the usual array of distractions, and further on again the town faced on to the estuary. The ferry boat to Shaldon plied its way back and forth, dodging the many yachts and pleasure craft, moored or moving, which frequented the waters. There were fishing boats and larger commercial vessels over at the town's still-functioning harbour. The port here has been in existence since the early 1300s when it mostly dealt with fish and salt. If only they'd had the missing ingredients of chips, vinegar and the Daily Mail they could have spearheaded a culinary revolution. However, it was not to be and they had to content themselves with salt and fish. The development of the Bovey Basin clay works in the eighteenth century introduced a new commodity to be shipped out. The town's fortunes received another boost in the nineteenth century with the arrival of the railway. Visitor numbers increased to the point where the town was the second most popular resort in Devon. Given that people were taking the waters here in the late 1700s, we can hardly call this an overnight sensation.

At one time there were several ship-building businesses on both sides of the estuary and other nautical connections from the past, with an emphasis on the 'nauti'. Yes, the locals have been known to indulge in a bit of privateering and smuggling. Cod fishing off Newfoundland was also big business, apparently. All in all there was still a real sense that the town has genuine, meaningful and current connections with the sea, which gave it a feeling of integrity. It wasn't pretending to be something it was not and I liked it all the more for that.

I reflected again on a day in which I felt I had covered a good distance in the day and called at some lovely places en route. Teignmouth was shaping up as a good place for a brief respite from the travelling.

Day 24

Teignmouth treats

28th August

Teignmouth *was* a good place for a stop over, partly because it helped you feel you could just hang about. It was relaxed and friendly and encouraged the dissipation of some of the momentum I had built up in my trek from the far-flung corners of Cornwall.

It would not have been so relaxing on the 26th July 1690 when boatloads of Frenchmen arrived and mounted an invasion. As part of their 'invasion' they burned down 116 houses and 'rifled and plundered' 173 more. Not content with this they set about two parish churches which were 'much ruined, plundered and defaced'. What were these frightful people thinking? Perhaps they wanted to change the future. All too aware of the future possibilities of this fabulous stretch of coastline, one day rivalling the charms of Nantes, Cannes and St Tropez on their own yet-to-be-invented French Riviera, they decided to trash it before any of that started. Well, they did make a good job of trashing the place but if they thought that would put an end to any plans for a future seaside resort they hadn't counted on the indomitable Teignmouth spirit or the 'we're-in-this-together' pluckiness of the Great British public. The raid was a devastating blow to the town but it also raised much public sympathy throughout the country. This in turn raised much public money with which the town was effectively rebuilt.

Anyway, all that was in the dim and distant past and must have been almost forgotten even 100 years later, for by that time people were coming here to bathe and to drink the sea water. That's right, drink it, not just sit in it. According to the

Teignmouth and Shaldon Museum a report in the Royal Magazine stated that 'cripples recovered the use of their limbs, hysterical ladies recovered their spirits and lepers were cleansed.' I had no idea that sea water was such powerful stuff—it's even able to calm hysterical women! Remarkable. Fanny Burney, who was a novelist and diarist and not a hysterical woman, visited in 1773. She records: "I was terribly frightened and really thought that I should never have been recovered from the plunge. The shock was beyond the expression great." A little while later she was back in the bathing machine and glowing, deciding that actually, "It was the finest feeling in the world."

Well, make your mind up, Fanny!

I was in the fortunate position of being able to embark on a languorous exploration of the town. The promenade provided for a bracing walk overlooking the beach with its distinctive dark sand, ground from the red sandstone cliffs that rise behind it. I followed a small road from the eastern end of the Den Promenade which rose from the seafront, passed the swimming pool and crossed the railway. This became a path that led to a cliff-top walk and Eastcliff Park, a lovely large open space from which there are some fantastic sea views and all is calm and peaceful.

Back in town there were plenty of little nooks and corners to discover down narrow streets and more pleasant time to spend watching the activity on the river. The foot ferry to Shaldon provided an interesting diversion and a chance to explore this little village a bit further. Some lovely Georgian street frontages and a village green make this a rather special place. A tunnel through the headland offered access to a secluded sandy beach, while the more strenuous route I opted for took me up onto Ness Headland itself with more fabulous views over the town, across the estuary and down along the coast. It was a lovely, lazy day spent wandering here and there, eating tea-time treats and enjoying a quiet drink in a friendly little pub.

Day 25

Homeward bound

29th August

My two days resting up in Teignmouth put me in fine fettle for the push home. In the town centre I coughed up the £3.70 for the first phase, a return visit to Exeter. We took the coast road and enjoyed some good sea views before dropping into Dawlish. Here is another town which, like Teignmouth, owes its foundations and early flourishing to salt and fish and probably salt-fish. The area was overrun by Romans and Anglicised by Anglo-Saxons but disregarded by the Danes in the 800s. This strikes me as odd, given the nature of bacon and the way in which it is so often salted. It's very unlike the Danes to pass up an opportunity to rape and pillage and get their hands on a ready supply of salt. One strand of thought is that they didn't fancy their chances of even getting here because of the shallow waters and marshy land on the shore.

Dawlish looked very charming as we passed through. Victorian and Edwardian architecture were much in evidence and suggested the popularity of the place as a resort during those periods. A significant figure in enhancing this popularity was Isambard Kingdom Brunel, whose railway is such a feature of this stretch of coast. Brunel's railway runs through Dawlish and as we climbed up and out of town the line could be seen snaking away, hugging the coast before disappearing into a tunnel.

Dawlish Warren was all holiday homes, chalets, touring and caravan parks, everything dribbling away to the edge of the River Exe. We turned inland and headed toward Cockwood about which my dictionary of place names was silent. It does suggest that similarly-named places would have been the haunt of a person named Cocca which is not as bad as it could have been for the gentleman in question. River names like 'Cocker', as in Cockermouth, suggest 'crooked' so perhaps we had here some woods near a crooked river. Another possibility could be that there were plenty of woodcock amongst the trees. There was no sign of woodcock and it was hard to see that 'crooked' was in any way an appropriate adjective for the Exe at this point, with the broad sweep of its estuary stretching across to Exmouth on the far bank. Of course, the place name could have come to us from an entirely different origin.

The road and the railway met and we ran parallel along The Strand, with the railway riding high along an embankment. A small harbour area revealed pleasure craft and rowing boats stranded by the low tide. At Starcross a station was dramatically perched on the estuary's edge and there was a ferry to Exmouth. Here too was a former pumping station from Isambard Kingdom Brunel's Atmospheric Railway, which now serves as a museum.

The Atmospheric Railway is a bit of an engineering curiosity. Certain engineers of the early 1800s were experimenting with the idea of using atmospheric pressure differentiation inside a tube to propel trains along a track. A piston would be suspended below the train and would run along the tube through a slot cut in the top. This slot was sealed by flexible leather covers. Pumping stations built at intervals alongside the tracks would draw air out of the tube in front of the piston while air would be allowed into the tube behind it. The greater pressure behind the piston would drive it forwards. Sounds crazy to me but a small number of such lines were built. The trouble for Brunel was that he tried the ideas out in this particular part of Devon where the continuous salt-spray shower from the proximate sea played havoc with the leather seals covering the pipe slot. In addition to this the leather was kept supple through an application of cod oil and soap which apparently proved to be an irresistible combination to the local Devonian rats, who ruined the seals. The trains were potentially capable of 70 miles an hour (which must have felt like the equivalent of a Japanese bullet train) although 40–45 miles an hour was more usual. In addition to this relatively high speed, another advantage would have been the lack of 'smut' or burning embers which were definite downsides of conventional steam locomotives. Furthermore the trains would have been able to get up gradients effortlessly and there would have been greater fuel efficiency than with conventional trains. It should all have been a great success. However, there were too many problems and the system was abandoned after only a year. Conventional track was laid and steam locomotives used. At least The Atmospheric Railway inn still survives.

Meanwhile, we arrived at Kenton which lies in the valley of the River Kenn and is a pretty Devon village with thatched cottages, pubs and a fourteenth century red sandstone church. It is close to Powderham Castle, home of the earl of Devon, which boasts six hundred years of history. Nearby Exminster is so named because here stood a monastery on the River Exe, which has played a part in the life of at least one saint and an Archbishop of Canterbury. The saint was Boniface, originally from Crediton, who entered the monastery here and trained as an apostle. The Archbishop of Canterbury was William Courtenay, born here in about 1341, the fourth son of the then Earl and Countess of Devon. He became head of the Church in 1381 in the midst of the Peasants' Revolt.

Incidentally, having elected William Courtenay on June 10, the rebels moved on to London where they found the hapless Archbishop Simon of Sudbury. They killed him along with Sir Robert Hales and other officials. The fact that 'the people' today do not rise up and show their displeasure in the same manner must be a source of great comfort for unpopular figures who might be seen to have let us down, perhaps by precipitating or overseeing the collapse of the financial markets and bringing entire economies almost to their knees. I can't think of any individuals immediately, of course. We passed under the new transport system in the form of the M5 and then crossed the older transport system in the form of the Exeter ship canal. The first canal to have pound locks, the Exeter ship canal opened for business in 1566! So we arrive at Exeter, or Isca Dumnoniorum, southern terminus of the Fosse Way Roman road. I'd been here before and so had Daniel Defoe. When he visited in the early 1700s he thought it famous for two things, being 'full of gentry and good company and yet full of trade and manufactures also.' He also encountered a river so widened and deepened that ships were able to come 'quite up to the city' and was impressed with the 'ancient beauty' of the cathedral church. It hadn't changed much since my last visit six days ago but I doubt if Defoe would recognise it.

An 'Explorer' ticket set me back £6.00 and the 11.35 was soon out of town and speeding me towards Taunton along the M5. Here was another mini-revelation about bus journeys. Before my exploits began I was only used to thinking about buses doing stuttering stop-start journeys between places, and yet here we were speeding along a motorway! We took the exit for Cullompton and made for Willand which belonged to Etmar in 1042 and to Taunton Priory in 1098. A delightful little village with a lovely church, dedicated to St Mary. There was a church here at least as far back as 1263 and the 'new' one is at least 500 years old. We took a brief tour of an estate of 'substantial', 'exclusive', and 'luxury' mock Georgian houses before being shown a bit more of Willand's older housing stock. Then we were back out for a ramble through open agricultural country towards Uffculme, 'an estate on the Culm river, held by a man called Uffa'. By the sixteenth century it was playing an important role in the West Country wool trade and there were a number of mills. Coldharbour Mill, built in 1799, is still producing wool but is now also a heritage museum.

We retraced our steps—or whatever the equivalent action is when undertaken on a bus—crossed over the river again and were fairly gobbling up the miles with the Quantocks providing a cloud-topped horizon. Suddenly we were in Wellington, a busy little town of shops, pubs and cafes, probably once the estate of a man named Weola. Wellington is famous for its duke and the duke is famous for his boots. A monument to this noble fellow stands above the town on the Blackdown Hills.

Near here, on 10th June 1607, Sir John Popham popped his clogs (Wellington boots having yet to be invented). Sir John had been Speaker of the House of Commons, Attorney General and Lord Chief Justice of England. He presided over the trials of Mary Queen of Scots at Fotheringhay Castle, Sir Walter Raleigh at Winchester and Guy Fawkes at Westminster Hall. None of these defendants fared particularly well at the hands of Popham and his colleagues. Possibly as a result of his behaviour at these trials, Popham was viewed by some as being something less than a thoroughly good egg. This in turn may have given rise to the local legend concerning his demise. He is said to have fallen from his horse in the deep dell of Popham's Pit where he died in suitable agony before being consigned to hell and more agony. He apparently gets New Year's Eve off to reappear in ghostly form.

Between Wellington and Taunton we passed through the sailors' paradise that is Rumwell. My dictionary of place names suggests that the similar-sounding Runwell in Essex has connections with councils near springs, or indeed a 'wishing well'. Well if you could wish for a well to be running with anything, I suppose you could pick something far worse than rum. From here it was a straightforward re-entry into the county town of Zummerzet.

It was good to be back in Taunton and to enjoy its relaxed and welcoming feel, but it was just a brief respite before I continued on my way.

Leaving Taunton we reacquainted ourselves with the A38 heading towards Bridgwater. We had second thoughts about this and turned off to Glastonbury. We crossed the Bridgwater and Taunton Canal, little changed since last seen and passed through West Lyng, which proclaimed that it 'welcomed careful drivers'. We passed the garrotted corpse of the last less-than-careful driver who passed this way and made on for East Lyng. That would have to be a good deterrent, wouldn't it? Imagine if, as well as villages proclaiming that they 'welcome careful drivers', they also said "Nether Bucket garrottes careless drivers". East Lyng village was once a Saxon burg and the name derives from the Old English hlinc, meaning 'baulk' or 'ridge'. It is thought that this was also the site of a second defensive fortress built by King Alfred. Traces of defensive bank and ditch have been found to the west of the village. As we passed through this ancient parish along the hline, towards Burrowbridge, the Somerset levels were laid out below. This area, once an ancient wetland, is now mostly drained and managed as agricultural land providing mainly pasture. Being largely green it is very calming. It looks gentle and benevolent, beautiful even, in the sunshine. All this belies the harsh realties of life on the ground, especially in the past. Being wetland it must have presented tremendous challenges to those of our ancient forebears who chose to make this area their home. However, they were obviously resilient types, able to make the most of any situation and adapt to seasonal changes of climate and weather. For example, it is probable that flooding during winter led to a retreat to higher ground. When the low-lying area became accessible during summer the people would return and this is thought to have given rise to the county name 'Somerset' from Sumorsaete—the land of the summer people. I think that should be on some tourist literature somewhere: 'Come to the land of the summer people!'

The few outcrops of higher ground would have been obvious locations for settlements but it seems that people were also building artificial islands. Also, amazingly, they were building causeways to link these settlements and the Sweet Track, an ancient timber walkway, is reckoned to be the oldest known engineered 'road' in the world, having been laid in 3807 or 3806 BC! The levels are also the place to come if you are running low on willow or teasels or indeed peat.

We passed through Pedwell, one of those tiny places that you only realise you have been through when you read the 'Thank you for driving carefully through our village' signs on the way out. We were still in an elevated area and had stunning views before arriving at Ashcott, which is a positive metropolis in comparison to Pedwell. The village takes its name from the 'cottages where the ash trees grow', an indication of the vegetation that was probably plentiful at the time. Ashcott is a handsome settlement with a number of elegant buildings from the sixteenth to nineteenth centuries and some, perhaps less elegant, from the twentieth. Being on a fairly important route— the Glastonbury to Bridgwater Road—Ashcott has had several inns in its time. These have included the Black Boy, The Castle, Piper's Inn, The Blue Bowl, The Golden Hart, The Queen's Arms, The Ring O' Bells and The Royal Oak. The Ring O' Bells at least seems to have survived.

We continued to make steady if rather sedate progress, our speed tempered by a tractor towing a trailer of cows. Walton, on the edge of Street, boasts the remains of a windmill, said to have been a temporary hiding place for the poor old Duke of Monmouth following his defeat at Sedgemoor. The windmill has no sails and is no longer a mill but a private house. Here, too, is the rather austere-looking Holy Trinity Church.

Street is a small town on the edge of the moor, famous for shoes and fossils, the two of which are strangely connected. Street's connection with shoes goes back to the establishment of a business by Cyrus and James Clark, two Quaker gentlemen who set up shop in 1825. Cyrus had opened a business tanning leather and producing sheepskins. Some time later when Brother James had joined the company, the latter was idling away amongst the sheepskins and leather off-cuts when he dreamt up a slipper which would become 'The Brown Petersberg'. This was so popular that by 1842 they were selling 1000 pairs a month. As Quakers, the Clark family were concerned to provide good working and living conditions for their employees. Many of the homes built for Clark's factory workers make up the urban fabric of Street. The building work for the brothers required material from a local quarry and the excavations revealed Ichthyosaur fossils. The Ichthyosaur is now part of the symbolism associated with the town although the town's name came about because a causeway was laid from this location to Glastonbury in the twelfth century. The Latin 'strata', meaning 'paved road', became the name of the settlement. Meanwhile, in the twenty-first century, we passed Clark's Shopping Village, a 'factory outlet' retail park based around the former Clark's factory. It is rather sad that shoes are no longer made here. We seem to be making less and less even though we manage to shop more and more.

We left Street and entered Glastonbury, but since the two are virtually contiguous it was difficult to know when this happened. Glastonbury is famous for its Tor, Abbey and legends. The legends have helped to make this a centre for weirdness and wonderment. For a start, Glastonbury sits on 'The Isle of Avalon'. This is the island of Arthurian legend where there must have been facilities for forging metal, since it was here that Arthur's sword Excalibur was made. The place must also have been good for 'healing' since Arthur came here to recover after the Battle of Camlann. It's not all good news though, because here too lived Morgan le Fay, a powerful sorceress.

In 1190 the Glastonbury monks discovered bones which they claimed were those of Arthur and his queen. Cynical people suggest that this was just a publicity stunt to raise cash for repairs to the abbey which had been badly burnt in 1184. Well, if the fête, the bring-and-buy and Brother Brendan's sponsored abseil down the tower hadn't raised enough cash they would have been quite desperate. Any repairs have not stood the test of time and the abbey is now a set of romantic ruins, steeped in history and mystery.

Here too is Glastonbury Tor, an unusual conical hill, which has associations with Gwyn ap Nudd, King of the Fairies and Lord of the Underworld. Holding those two positions must be quite a challenge. As Lord of the Underworld you would obviously need to be fairly assertive, if not downright frightening, and you can imagine that the role would command a good deal of respect. Being King of the Fairies sounds like an altogether different proposition. The Tor has seven symmetrical terraces surrounding it, which have caused plenty of speculation regarding their purpose. One point of view suggests that they were for growing crops or keeping cattle since much of the surrounding lands were useless in this regard. Another, far more sensible suggestion, is that they are the remains of a three-dimensional mystical labyrinth which leads to another world.

A rather more gruesome event was the hanging, drawing and quartering in 1539 of Richard Whiting, the last abbot of Glastonbury. It is not clear what he had done, but he had obviously upset Oliver Cromwell and it seems that was not a sensible thing to do. Whiting and two of his fellow monks were dragged up the Tor behind horses before their cruel despatch.

The Tor is also a place where 'ley lines' (the proposed mystical alignment of ancient sites, monuments and megaliths) converge in great numbers, with the result that many people who are into ley lines also converge here in great numbers.

Before long I was back at Wells bus station which is tucked unobtrusively round the back of the town near car parks and modern shops. You get little sense of the history of the place coming in from this side, passing by the sizeable properties of the edge-of-town industries. I walked into the old part of town to get another dose of wonder from the cathedral's West Front.

The next bus was my last of the trip and I experienced mixed feelings. It had been a good few weeks and I'd really enjoyed this whirlwind tour. I'd seen many wonderful and inspiring sites and visited plenty of fascinating and intriguing places, all offering their own particular brand of charm and interest. Soon it would all be over. Appropriately enough a steady drizzling rain began to fall as we made our quiet way through the gentle Somerset countryside.

Something began nagging away at the back of my mind. Where was this sense of incompleteness coming from? Why was there a tinge of dissatisfaction with my endeavours? It had all happened in Winchester when I made my decision to head for Andover. I wondered what would have happened if I'd opted for a bus to Petersfield instead. How could I redeem the situation? I hadn't really seen anything of the proper South East of England and that was a big chunk of country. As we drew near to my stop and I prepared to disembark, I knew I'd have to fix that.

Part 2

Day 1

Back to the old haunts

Off we go again: The South East Experience

At the end of my 2002 tour of 'England' I realised that I'd missed out the entire south-east region. And, let's be honest, that's a fairly sizeable and important wodge of the country. It would also have its distinct topographical features and bits of heritage and examples of architecture not available elsewhere. Anywhere East of Winchester and South of London had escaped my attention and I had not been able to rest easy with that situation. I hadn't actually had sleepless nights over it but it niggled. I put up with the niggling until 2007 when I finally got round to addressing the shortcomings of my earlier trip.

Another reason for taking on the trip was to see if the idea of travelling around on buses still worked five years on from my original tour. I was much more bus-journey-savvy by this stage and had also gone a bit soft. Unlike my first outing, this one was not going to include any camping and I did some preliminary research to check that I could still get to Winchester. I felt it was important to recreate my original journey to that place and to give it a second chance. At Winchester I would attempt to create an alternative history by enacting a 'what would have happened if?' scenario at the bus station. What would have happened if I hadn't waited two hours for a bus to Andover? What if I had gone to Petersfield, or indeed anywhere else for that matter? It would be a catharsis and might allow me a slightly more positive attitude towards Winchester bus station at least.

Beyond that, I didn't want to do too much more research because, as before, part of the fun for me was finding out where I would be going next only on the basis of what onward buses were available when I arrived at any given destination.

So again the plan was to have not much of a plan. I thought I'd get to Winchester, drop down to the South Coast somehow and head to the Far East, meaning Dover, meander up from there to the north coast and then back westward. I thought I could do that in a week.

25th September

My Wilts and Dorset Adult Explorer was £7.50 and took me to Salisbury on the familiar route through Heahthryth's stronghold and all. Salisbury was as lovely as ever and I enjoyed a wander around the town, checking out the busy market square, just up from the bus station. As I was only planning to be away for a week I had scaled down considerably on my luggage. Instead of The Great Big Bag which had accompanied me on the first tour, I had a small rucksack which made exploring much more enjoyable and less like a Duke of Edinburgh endurance test. While in Salisbury I paid another visit to the fabulous cathedral and enjoyed some quiet in its precincts.

I even went back to Romsey to recreate the trip from there to Winchester rather than taking a direct route.

First impressions in Winchester led to me paraphrasing the old song, as in "The old town looked the same as I stepped down from the bus." The bus station remained resolutely a rather unattractive space between two other buildings. It was simply somewhere to get off your bus and get out of. So I did.

The town itself, however, still managed to impress. I had not dawdled in Salisbury or Romsey and so I had more time to look round and particularly to give more attention to the cathedral than on my earlier visit. It really is a bit of a gem. A Christian church from the seventh century was 'overwritten' by a Norman cathedral church, begun in 1079. Winchester was at the heart of a large diocese and the bishops here often seem to have wielded considerable power and influence. The building reflects this almost as much as it does the glory of God.

The nave is a vast enclosed space and if you've got to enclose a space, vast or otherwise, this is the way to do it. Here are soaring columns and fan-vaulted ceilings, all illuminated with natural light pouring in through huge windows. The cathedral also revealed literary connections with Jane Austen and with Keats. Austen lived at Chawton, about 17 miles away, from 1809 until just before her death in Winchester in 1817. The cathedral contains her tomb and a commemorative stained glass window from 1900. Keats was in Winchester in 1819 and was apparently inspired to pen his 'season of mists and mellow fruitfulness' Ode to Autumn by daily walks through the cathedral precincts.

It was easy for me to find the mill that had been so elusive on my earlier visit and which had housed the Youth Hostel. What my measly pre-trip research had revealed was that this was no longer a hostel but I wanted to visit anyway. The City Mill, restored to working order by the National Trust, makes for a fascinating visit. The Trust do their best to help you picture the place when it was a working mill, which means from the time when it was first built, in about 1744 through a staggering number of years up to its closure at the turn of the twentieth century.

Because I could not bed down in a working mill I needed the assistance of the good people in the Tourist Information Centre to find budget accommodation. It transpired that Winchester was not big on this and could not boast a particularly extensive selection of establishments offering bed and breakfast either, unless you could make it a couple of miles out of town. Since I was restricted to walking to such a place or finding one on a bus route, my choices were fairly limited. However, following a bit of conversation and a few phone calls, the very helpful staff managed to locate and secure me a resting place for the night which was only about 15 minutes walk away.

Bags and keys sorted I journeyed out in search of more architectural delights, which I found in abundance in the quiet lanes and back alleys of the old town. I was particularly taken with the experiences available at the sixteenth century rectory of St Lawrence Church, which is also known as The Eclipse Inn.

Winchester proved again that it was a very pleasant place in which to spend an evening and I made my way happily back out of town to my B&B. Things were looking up for Winchester but the acid test would be in the morning at the bus station.

Day 2

I must go down to the sea again

26th September

All sorts of people offer bed and breakfast but I doubt I will ever encounter another multilingual, highly qualified South American female civil engineer offering me a big English breakfast. For most of us, on a normal day, a bowl of cereal or piece of toast is more than adequate for breakfast. Some people never have breakfast because they've left it too late or mistakenly believe that by missing out a meal they might lose weight. Anyway, whatever our normal morning eating habits, when on holiday or simply staying overnight somewhere we suddenly find ourselves capable of demolishing a large plate of bacon, sausages, eggs, mushrooms and tomatoes. This is after we have consumed a bowl of cereal and before we tackle the toast and marmalade. This massive calorie intake might be sensible if you are about to spend the day digging trenches or carrying bricks or indeed walking the South Downs Way. I wasn't going to be doing any of those things but I ate a big breakfast anyway. It would have been rude not to.

Having said goodbye to my bed and breakfast hosts I made my way back to the bus station. This was the moment of truth. I tried not to think about buses to Andover. I didn't even look at the bay where a bus to Andover may or may not appear. I concentrated instead on my proposed journey to the south coast and pondered a route to Havant via Petersfield. Then I did a very unmanly thing. I went to ask for some advice. The guys in what passed for an enquiries office were really very helpful. They indicated that my best bet, in their opinion, was the bus to Fareham and there was one of those every hour and one due to leave quite shortly. This was a good result and the cloud that had unfairly hung over the town and its bus station due to my own poor decision-making and the unfortunate Andover bus fiasco lifted. So it was with a fond gaze that I bade farewell to Winchester from a comfy seat on a punctual bus that was the proper size and had parked in the right bay at the bus station.

We called at St Cross Hospital. You don't really need to catch the bus to get here from town but if you've got a ticket you may as well. The 'hospital' is a fabulous complex of buildings centred round the Church of St Cross. Its origins date back to the twelfth century but there are also wonderful almshouses from the fifteenth. The enterprise was originally founded by Henri du Blois, the grandson of William the Conqueror, brother of King Stephen and sometime supporter of Empress Matilda, in 1132. The original intention was to provide for 'thirteen poor men, feeble and so reduced in strength that they can scarcely or not at all support themselves without other aid'. It's quite easy to find thirteen such men in any reasonably large town centre on an average Friday or Saturday night these days. They are temporarily 'poor', because they've spent most of their money during several Happy Hours. As a consequence they can 'scarcely or not at all' support themselves. I don't think these are the kind of people Henri had in mind. A man ahead of his time, I think he was envisaging a kind of retirement home. The notion of hospitality was later extended to encompass pilgrims on their way to Canterbury and beds were also offered to knights on their last day in England before setting off for Southampton and the crusades.

The calmness and serenity no doubt engendered in the St Cross community contrasts with the frantic nature of the modern world as evidenced by the traffic hurtling along the M3, which we were soon ducking under. From here we made our way up Cox's Hill to Twyford on the River Itchen, a village enhanced by the gentle surroundings of water meadows. We are near to the Twyford Waterworks which are Edwardian and apparently a Scheduled Ancient Monument. If engineering, steam-driven pumps and bore-holes get your juices flowing this is the place to come. There are many delights, not the least of which would be the rank of three Babcock and Wilcox WIF water tube boilers and the Hathorn Davey triple expansion engine from 1914. I know, I know—it's incredible but true. Actually, these places are not only quite fascinating, even if that sort of thing doesn't normally fascinate you; here they also speak about the value of good, solid design and construction. You see, as well as being an attraction on scheduled Open Days, the waterworks are still functioning and fully operational almost a hundred years after construction.

We passed on through fields of green and gold and arrived at Colden Common, a meerkat's throw from Marwell Zoo. Near Holy Trinity Church we left the main road, passing under trees which slapped and banged a percussive accompaniment against the roof.

Bishop's Waltham is a charming Georgian town where the onslaught of retail branding has been fairly successfully held at bay. From its beginnings as a Saxon settlement, Bishop's Waltham grew to become one of the largest villages in the county, despite attempts by the Danes to prevent this. Their tactic was the subtle one of burning the place to the ground. The 'walt' and 'ham' of the name mean 'wood' and 'enclosure' or 'settlement'. The 'Bishop's' bit stems from it being gifted to the Bishop of Winchester in 904. Henri de Blois, not content with founding the Cross Hospital, also built a palace in Waltham in 1136. The ruins were glimpsed from the bus as we turned by the large adjacent pond. This fine building being in ruins is in large measure thanks to Oliver Cromwell who decided that it needed to be destroyed because... well, it just did, all right! He must have had some Danish blood in him.

The long association with Winchester, a very important and powerful ecclesiastical centre, meant that other significant figures lived and died here. In the dying category is William of Wykeham, Bishop of Winchester, founder of Winchester College, Oxford and of Winchester School, who ended his days here in 1404. A temporary resident of the village was one Pierre-Charles-Jean-Baptiste-Silvestre de Villeneuve. This gentleman was the admiral in charge of the French and Spanish fleets at the Battle of Trafalgar. As we now know, he was on the wrong side and, following Nelson's victory he, along with other French sailors, was imprisoned in Bishop's Waltham. The Admiral apparently had to endure captivity in the Crown Inn. The fate of the ordinary sailors is not so clear. Perhaps they were made to wait outside with a bottle of pop and a bag of crisps.

Our next stop off was Swanmore, which has grown from a few huts around a swan pond. There is plenty of modern development here but some interesting features from a Victorian expansion of the village remain. St Barnabas Church and the Methodist Chapel date from this period as do cottages which were built to accommodate workers in the brick-making industry that blossomed here from the late nineteenth century to the 1930s. We were soon at the very picturesque village of Wickham, laid out around an ancient market square. This, in an earlier spelling, is the Wykeham of William of Wykeham, who became bishop of Winchester and who died in Bishop's Waltham. You remember. It is another good-looking village and retains plenty of charm. It's the sort of place that gives you a ray of hope regarding people and their attitude to their surroundings and environment. Here, as in other well-kept villages, it would appear that the sentiments behind old campaigns such as 'Keep Britain Tidy' have taken root in the local consciousness and are still being applied.

We were all enjoying the journey. My fellow passengers were predominantly older and probably of pensionable age. I was guessing that a lot of them would have been enjoying a free, or at least subsidised, ride with a bus pass. They looked like people who may well have owned a car and yet they had decided not to use it. Understandable if someone else is picking up the tab, you might say. What it indicated to me was that people would happily choose to go places by bus, if the incentive was right.

Turning my attention back to enjoying the journey, I noticed that the feel of open countryside was rapidly dissipating as we breached the M27 and entered the South Hampshire conurbation, or less kindly, 'urban sprawl'. At the centre of this we found Fareham, tucked away in a corner of Portsmouth harbour. Here is a predominantly modern town with extensive housing developments from the 1960s onwards, a good deal of light industrial land use, augmented with the ubiquitous shopping centre. The bus deposited me pretty centrally and it was an easy walk to the shops in the modern Market Quay. A little further on was the rather lovelier High Street, which had a number of fine Georgian buildings.

It seems as though the Romans had settlements in the area and it is easy to understand why. There is easy access to the sea for that early morning dip and also a supply of fresh water from the River Wallington for that early morning cuppa. Fareham was an established settlement by the tenth century and much of its history is understandably linked to the sea. It has had ship-building industries and a vibrant port as central features of its economy. The strategic position, natural harbour and useful topography have also made this a good area for another kind of property development. East of Fareham is Portchester Castle, a Roman 'Saxon shore' fort which is the sort of thing people built when no-one had come up with the idea of a shopping centre or multi-storey car park. The Roman fort became a Norman castle in the twelfth century and a palace at the end of the fourteenth. It would have been a good place to defend the coast but also proved popular as a point from which to plan and launch attacks. The people from history who have planned and launched attacks have tended to be royal, and Portchester Castle has seen a few members of that esteemed group. For example, it was a staging post during the Hundred Years War (1337–1453) and accommodated Edward III as he planned his campaign involving the Siege of Calais and ultimately the Battle of Crecy in 1346. Similarly, in 1415, Henry V enjoyed B&B here before journeying to Southampton and thence to Agincourt with his band of brothers for a fight with the French. As Portsmouth gradually gained the upper hand, Portchester fell into a bit of a decline. The castle had a rather less glamorous role as a place to keep prisoners of war. To maintain a sufficient supply of these we had wars with the Dutch in the seventeenth and eighteenth centuries, with Napoleon in the early nineteenth and with our special friends the US in the Anglo–American War of 1814–15.

From Fareham a short bus journey brought us to Portsmouth and we managed to enter with little trouble. William Camden records the town as well fortified at 'great cost and charge' to Queen Elizabeth so that it was a 'most strong and fensed place', with garrison soldiers keeping 'watch and ward both night and day at the gates'. It's all so much simpler now; you can just drive in. As with Fareham you can see why this spot would be a good choice for early settlers. The harbour made a perfect place not only for a port but also for launching naval operations. King John established the first permanent naval base here in 1200 while he had an invading eye on Normandy. As we know, a long line of monarchs kept up the tradition of invading Normandy. Well, they started it! The French showed their displeasure by attacking Portsmouth in 1338. They destroyed a good part of the town, and then had a go at a bad part, before returning to wreck another good part and so on until the whole place was pretty much ruined. They waited for the town to be rebuilt before sacking it again in 1369, 1377 and 1380. Being a significant port, the town has seen many useful things arrive including wool, wood, wax and wine. A less sensible import was The Black Death which is popularly thought to have arrived on these shores courtesy of infected rats or merchants or both. The port would also have seen goods out and a famous export from Portsmouth was the party that left on thirteenth May 1787 to establish the first European colony in Australia.

War doesn't seem to go away and Portsmouth was in fighting mood again in 1805 when Nelson left from here to engage with the Franco-Spanish fleet at Trafalgar. The town also saw troops leaving for the beaches of Normandy as part of the D-Day landings in the Second World War.

It was the seaward rim of the town that drew most of my attention, which is what it's meant to do. It's had a bit of a face-lift around Gunwharf Quay, and a new structure, the Spinnaker Tower, dominated the skyline with its graceful and intriguing sail-like shapes. The tower provides several viewing platforms for people who manage the ride up the outside of what appears to be a fairly skeletal construction in a glass lift. Not being great at external glass lifts I took a break in a fairly unexciting café nearby and partook of fairly unexciting refreshments.

The views over Portsmouth are exciting, however, and can be had from various places nearby that don't involve great heights and glass lifts. A major attraction is Nelson's flagship, HMS Victory, a truly impressive sight in the Historic Dockyard. The massive and yet somehow elegant HMS Warrior is another quite awe-inspiring craft. This vessel was the Navy's first iron-hulled and iron armour-plated warship and she was built in response to secret news that the French had a similar ship, La Gloire. In a splendid two-fingered gesture, the Warrior was built twice the size of La Gloire and outclassed that ship in just about every way. Portsmouth has much to offer the nautically-minded history seeker but I had other places to go and, who knows, people to meet. The 700 bus service lured me away with an offer to 'Cruise along the coast'. It was an offer I had no intention of refusing.

The next major stop on the coastal cruise was Havant, most of which looked modern and fairly uninspiring. Its ancient heart is evidenced by St Faith's Church and some seventeenth century cottages, now a pub—'The Old House at Home'. St Faith's is known to have existed since the twelfth century and was possibly around long before that. Havant has been famous throughout history for the wonderful things that have been made there. The town was the source of a fine parchment renowned for its purity and whiteness for about a thousand years. This is rumoured to have been so good that it was the parchment of choice for both the Magna Carta and The Treaty of Versailles. More recently the town gave birth to Scalextric cars and it is also here that kitchen appliance manufacturer Ken Wood made his first Turnover Toaster. Eventually he was able to toast his company's multi-million pound turnover.

I arrived at Chichester still feeling fresh and looking forward to exploring the town and its famous cathedral. Chichester is the Roman town of Noviomagus, which was originally developed by them as a military supply base. A reminder of the Romans' presence is available in the grid pattern of North, South, East and West Streets. Not very imaginative as street names go but you know what you're getting or at least where you're going. Something altogether more imaginative stands at the centre of these streets. This is the magnificent Market Cross, built at the turn of the sixteenth century to keep poor tradesmen and women out of the weather. It is an imposing structure, having eight buttressed sides, each having an arched entrance and all topped with a pile of pinnacles. In the centre is a column, at the base of which is a seat. Several clock faces allow you to read the time from a number of directions, well North, South, East and West at least.

The Market Cross would have been a very welcome improvement to the traders' position, standing about in the wind and rain bartering beetroots or swapping Swedes for suede or sweetmeats. However, trading space would have been at a premium here and so, after only three hundred years of lobbying, local traders saw the opening of a brand new expanded trading area in the form of the impressive Butter Market, just along North Street. Despite the name, you could buy all manner of things in the market apart from butter and still can today. The building was designed by John Nash with a fine array of signature Doric columns at the entrance.

I strolled along East Street, then down North Pallant past an art gallery in a lovely Queen Anne building with an 'award-winning' modern extension. The words 'modern' and 'extension' are undeniably applicable to the new additions and cannot be argued with. The 'award-winning' element is equally undeniable but I couldn't think what the award would be for. Another turn into West Pallant, and again along South Street, and I was back at the cathedral. The buildings of the various Pallants create lovely streets and the appeal of the area is its sense of intimacy and human scale.

Even the cathedral has a kind of modesty about it. Chichester isn't large by cathedral standards but nevertheless manages to grab your attention and then draws you in to explore the vast range of craftsmanship and attention to detail on display everywhere.

We have St Wilfred to thank for bringing Christianity to Sussex in 681 and for establishing a cathedral at Selsey. We have the bishops Stigand and Luffa to thank for overseeing the construction of the architectural delight we have today. They did this between 1075 and 1108. Fires proved to be a bit of a hazard and there were serious ones in 1114 and 1187. Having a positive outlook is important and so fires are not disasters but opportunities for extension, renovation and development. Realising, perhaps belatedly, that wood was not the best material to use extensively in such circumstances, the restoration saw the arrival of stone vaulting, shafts and the occasional flying buttress. People steadily developed the cathedral over the next few centuries including the addition of chapels in the thirteenth and cloisters in the fifteenth. Tastes change and people's attitudes alter. The benevolent folk of the Reformation thought the place needed 'a bit of a makeover' and set about removing brasses and defacing stone figures and carvings. In 1642 the Parliamentarian troops did their bit too, taking particular exception to the library. Nice work boys. For the last two hundred years or so, people have been restoring the cathedral to a former glory and it makes an obvious focal point for any visit to Chichester.

Boarding another 700 service bus I was carried effortlessly back to the coast proper and to a proper coastal resort. I was in fabled Bognor Regis. Originally Bucganora, the 'shore of a woman named Bucge', the town became simply Bognor and was later granted a 'Regis' by King George V after a visit in 1929. It was a small fishing village and would perhaps have stayed as one if not for the efforts of Richard Hotham, an entrepreneur of the late 1700s. He had done a little bit of this and a little bit of that having been a maker of hats, a magistrate, a member of parliament, a member of the East India Company and, most significantly for Bognor, a property developer. Mr Hotham had become Sir Hotham by his sixties, but wealth and recognition are no guardians against ill health. In the summer months Sir Richard took to visiting Bognor and enjoying the sea air. Realising that others might be convinced of the beneficial qualities of a good dose of this he set about developing a resort. I'm sure Mr Butlin, who first built a large 'Recreation Centre' here in 1932 and whose holiday camp is still a major feature, was suitably thankful for the foresight of this gentleman. Bognor looked clean and chipper under the blue-sky weather as we passed through.

Further along the coast we came upon the fairly unprepossessing town of Littlehampton. Let's be blunt. The name sounds like an embarrassing physiological condition that no man would wish for. An obvious strategy for such a place would be to go all big and brash and try to cover up any perceived deficiencies in the size department. Actually, Littlehampton hasn't bothered. It seemed content to be a pleasant little place sitting quietly on the coast. The parts I explored were clean and it all had a fresh feel to it. This freshness was no doubt assisted by the coastal location and associated on-shore sea breezes bringing in plenty of ozone-rich air. Perhaps these also help with the cleanliness, constantly blowing any litter further inland to be collected by the good people of Lyminster or Poling. Off-shore breezes might perform a similar function by blowing any remaining detritus into the ocean to be collected sometime later by the good people of the Caribbean. Although it was September the temperature was still warm enough for shorts and T-shirts and the sky a good blue with what I reassured myself were 'fair-weather clouds'.

I was standing at another point where my path crossed that of the Empress Matilda. I had first connected with Matilda in Oxford, where she had escaped through the snow in a white dress. Her influence had been felt again in Northallerton where there had been a major battle involving her uncle who was coming down to support her from Scotland. And now I was standing where, in the autumn of 1139, her fleet passed by on its way to Arundel. The turbulent times of Matilda's struggle for the throne were hard to imagine in this lovely, peaceful place.

I considered the YHA hostel, located in the midst of the harbour development on the River Arun, as a possibility for the night's stopover. The YHA hostel had other ideas, having closed following the end of the summer season. I sat on the nearby harbour walls to look at the flotilla of small craft moored on the waters. I discussed my options with a group of swans on the slipway. We decided that although the closed hostel had put a slight dampener on proceedings I could have a short stop here and then press on down the coast.

Once more a 700 service cruised me on, at one point taking

me through Worthing. This was originally a 'settlement of the family of a man called Weorth', which spent many contented, if hard, centuries as a small fishing village before, in Georgian times, blossoming into a fashionable seaside resort. There was a good deal of elegant seaside hotel architecture to admire as we called into Marine Parade, as well as good views of the sea and the Pavilion. We seemed to move seamlessly from here through resorts at Shoreham-by-Sea, Hove and then into the bustle that is Brighton.

The outskirts of Brighton presented a certain blandness, which provided a doubtless unintended contrast to some of the architectural eccentricity available in the centre. By the Madeira bar and restaurant were four large masts complete with a variety of sail-like canopies. These nautical nods to the tall sailing ships of the past were almost adjacent to Brighton Pier, formerly and more formally the 'Brighton Marine Palace and Pier'. This extravagant pier opened in 1899 complete with a theatre at the seaward end. A long walk out over the sea with the promise of a good show at the far end was not enough for the discerning Brighton visitor. At least the people responsible for the pier didn't seem to think so since in 1910 the structure was augmented by an impressive domed pavilion and some 'winter gardens'. Sadly, the theatre has disappeared from the end, allegedly awaiting restoration and reinstatement. The presumably temporary replacement is an arrangement of roller coasters and thrill rides. Even with modern accretions, the pier is still an evocative and stimulating building and is somehow even invigorating. Piers are just great big 'follies' in a way, all a bit over-the-top and slightly daft really. They make me smile and I think they're meant to.

Another Brighton building that should bring a smile to your face and may even produce an occasional chuckle is the Royal Pavilion. If it were a racehorse it would be described as being 'out of the Wizard of Oz by the Taj Mahal'. This exuberant and fanciful concoction comes to us courtesy of a wild and rebellious Prince Regent who would later become George IV. The whole thing began life as a farmhouse which was extended by a certain Henry Holland. Between 1815 and 1822 it was given its current treatment at the hands of John Nash at the Regent's instigation. Some people might say it is a rather eccentric affair while others would deny this, pointing out that it is obviously completely mad. The Pavilion exudes indulgence, opulence and a wonderful sense of fun and I think it's great. I also have a sneaking suspicion that it in some way expresses the Prince Regent's attitude to the more prudish and staid members of the establishment, which could possibly be summarised as, 'Up yours!'

You could, I suppose, dislike the whole thing intensely, precisely because it shouts wealth and frivolity and privilege and such. What should we do, pull it down and build some affordable housing for key sector workers?

Another area of Brighton town centre worth exploring is known as The Lanes. This is a collection of, well... er... lanes, but not just any old lanes. No, these are packed with quaint old buildings and cottages, now housing a wide range of independent shops and eateries. I enjoyed a wander before refuelling with a baguette and a coffee.

Before making more determined efforts to sort out some accommodation I cast my eye along the track of Volk's Electric Railway which is another arrow in Brighton's quiver of eccentricities. The line of this wonderful curiosity runs eastwards along the seafront and was the brainchild of Magnus Volk. Magnus was a bit of an electricity nerd by all accounts and probably because of this was the first person in Brighton to have electric light in his house.

I made the trek out to Patcham on the outskirts of town in the hope of tracking down a bed in the Youth Hostel. I found the hostel fairly quiet on my arrival. The manager was very helpful and she efficiently arranged keys and dispensed bedding and so on before informing me that the place was due to close at the end of the season. I was glad to have made it before that happened and not only because it meant that I had a bed for the night. Just as important for me was the chance to stay in a sixteenth century manor house—it doesn't happen often.

Having sorted out my bed I returned to the reception. I discussed local food options and was told of a good Italian restaurant some walk away and an Indian restaurant in very close proximity, almost visible from the hostel. I decided to work up a bit of an appetite by walking to the Italian restaurant and back to the Indian establishment. The latter was hidden inside an Elizabethan cottage. There was something 'circular' about eating food which was strongly flavoured with spices that were first discovered and brought back to this country by seafarers whose contemporaries built the house in which I was sitting.

My frustrating 2002 attempts at leaving Winchester had produced a woeful journey of about 28 miles and I had only made Newbury. Today I managed a slightly more respectable 76 or so and had managed to fit in several enjoyable stops along the way. Back in 2002 I could have walked from my point of departure in Bath to Newbury in two days. I would get nowhere near Brighton after two days of walking and I let that satisfying thought finally lay my troubles regarding Winchester to rest. Then I lay myself to rest in a comfy YHA bed.

Day 3

Dover breached

27th September

On the morning's first bus I was joined by an older gentleman who was keen to tell me about his love of the area and particularly how special he found this journey along the coast. We were both enjoying the stunning scenery from our elevated position on the top deck. Inland was gently rolling chalk downland while the route, taking us along the cliff tops, allowed for seaward views too. When we descended into the valleys we skirted the sea and passed through interesting settlements whose place names were in turn, a pleasant surprise (Rottingdean), lively (Peacehaven) and confusing (Newhaven—much *older* than Peacehaven).

My travelling companion explained that he currently had a home in Florida. At some point he had fallen slightly out of love with Brighton and the South Coast, or at least been wooed by the warmer climes of the southern United States. He went on to explain how things were, in his opinion, falling apart in America. He felt there was something wrong about the place; the infatuation was over and he was considering a return to the UK. He was planning to come home for good and this patch had been his former home. You could do a lot worse, I thought.

By following the coast and not straying inland, the bus was skirting the South Downs Area of Outstanding Natural Beauty which effectively runs from Winchester all the way to Eastbourne. This looked like it offered some grand possibilities for country walks and would have been in striking distance of the coast by bus at a number of places. As we moved east the high ground of the downs was slowly coming to meet us at the coast and for the last stage of the journey we were technically passing through the tail end of this fabulously scenic area. In Eastbourne I wandered through a pedestrian area, down Terminus Road to Grand Parade. This latter forms part of a sequence of parades that run the length of the extensive sea front and are named King Edward's, Grand, Royal and Marine. You get the sense that these names were not picked out of a hat or decided on quickly over a cup of tea and a biscuit. No, these names were chosen to underline the fact that Eastbourne is elegant, Eastbourne is opulent, and Eastbourne has royal connections. Oh, and Eastbourne is by the sea.

It was not always this way. Eastbourne has a long history as a settlement and spent much of its developing years as a thriving fishing centre and focal point for sheep farmers and traders. So then, a fairly typical and unremarkable state of affairs for a settlement by the sea. Back in 1555, Eastbourne was sold to three Sussex families. Those were the good old days when a few families could buy a small town. Cash down, no questions asked. By the mid 1800s there were two main landowners, William Cavendish and John Davies Gilbert. These two were keen to develop Eastbourne and had an eye on the opportunities for tourism which was becoming popular in Victorian times. But the town had not taken off as a resort, which was unusual given the growing belief, backed by eminent men, that consuming sea water might be good for you. It is even more bemusing given that Eastbourne had enjoyed a bit of Royal patronage as far back as 1780 when George III's children had a summer holiday here. The determination of Cavendish and Gilbert coincided quite nicely with the arrival of the railways in 1849. This changed everything since the grand plans the two developers had for hotels and promenades and, of course, a pier would now actually have a purpose. Henceforth, people would finally be arriving for a holiday in significant numbers. So it all came together for these foresighted gentlemen and it is obvious that elegance was the watch-word for the development of the town since this characteristic is evident in the handsome buildings and expansive tree-lined streets. And very pleasant it all is too.

I surveyed the scene from The Grand Parade. The outdoor seating area of a nearby eatery was deserted. So was the beach below. It was late September and not a day of bright sunshine. In fact, the sky was almost glowering, but it was hardly cold enough to drive the usually redoubtable British from the beach. Other visitors to Eastbourne may have been on the pier, and why not? Despite some modern overlays it still has plenty of Edwardian charm. Still other visitors may have been taking a look at 'The Wish Tower', a little along the coast. This is an unusual defensive structure which owes its existence to Britain's keenness on war with France. We were at it again in 1794. Some Corsican patriots had asked for British help in removing French revolutionaries from their island. As part of the offensive, the Royal Navy attacked a tower at Mortella Point, a strategic spot on the island. On different occasions the tower withstood hours and even days of almost constant bombardment before a lucky (depending on whether you were inside the tower or not) shot caused a fire. The British were impressed with the tower's defensive capabilities, thought they would like some of their own and stole the idea. The British versions were called Martello towers. This name-change was probably a simple case of the British not paying particular attention to the spelling of a foreign word. Whatever the reason the 'Martello Tower' idea was born and proposals were put forward to have a line of such structures along the south coast to defend against possible invasion. The towers were to reach from No.1 at Folkestone to No.74 at Seaford. The 'Wish Tower' is No.25 and is called the 'Wish' Tower because it was near the 'Wash' and is therefore probably another example of sloppy transcribing.

Eastbourne has other military connections, there being significant associations with events such as the Armada and the Battle of Beachy Head in 1690. Today we mostly enjoy gentler times and Eastbourne caters well for the tourist who is not so much seeking thrills as relaxation. However, I could not relax for long and was soon off along the coast again to the place that was forever 'on the map' after 1066 and all that. The Norman invasion from that year is remembered for the Battle of Hastings but this was more correctly the Battle of Battle a place a few miles to the north of Hastings. The problem perhaps arose because at that time there was no place called 'Battle' in which to have a battle, since Battle only developed as a town around a monastery which was founded by William in 1067 to commemorate the battle. I suppose 'The battle *near* Hastings' didn't sound quite punchy enough to pass into the annals of history and so it became the Battle *of* Hastings.

The Saxon settlement of Haesta's people, named Haesta ingas, had become a small market town called Hastinges by the time of the Domesday Book. From then it had grown and prospered thanks to a vibrant fishing industry and no doubt a certain amount of smuggling. Oh all right, a pretty massive amount of smuggling. The town has also seen the usual turmoil of attacks by Danes (1011), a decimation of population during three sixteenth century visitations of the plague, attacks by the French (1339 and 1377), severe floods (loads) and, in more recent history, attacks by the Germans (1940–1944). Things have calmed down a bit recently and Hastings has, to the best of my knowledge, suffered from no foreign invasion attempts and is making a pretty good fist of being a popular tourist destination.

When the journey along the coast had brought us to clifftops, the views had been pretty enthralling. After leaving Hastings we entered an altogether different landscape. We left the higher ground and descended to the low. We didn't seem to stop descending when we reached the point at which I would have deemed it sensible to do so. We were entering the area of Romney Marsh and so found ourselves at times below sea level. I know land reclamation has a long and distinguished history and the people round here undoubtedly know what they are doing. I know that sea defences and sturdy walls have been constructed to give the sea its boundaries and keep the dry land dry. I know all that in my head but still something nags away at my innards. The sea is often no respecter of boundaries and water always finds a level, and I was below the level it would find.

The idea that the Romney Marsh could be a suitable location to set up camp may first have occurred to the locals in about 8300BC and there is evidence that by 2300BC the barrier across from Fairlight to Hythe was sufficiently stabilised for people to be living on the barrier and in the marshes behind. A precarious and presumably rather damp lifestyle seems to have been possible through the Iron Age and Roman period, but it was the Saxons who carried out early reclamation between 410 and 1065. Having invaded, the Normans set about more reclamation and even established the Cinque Ports. The Medieval period saw more reclamation, port construction, violent storms, and port destruction, and it was during this period that the town of Old Winchelsea copped it. From descriptions of the storms in the 1250s, it sounds as though the bank on which the town was built was now being swept away and breaking up. There were strenuous efforts to strengthen sea defences but the sea was having none of that and Old Winchelsea disappeared into the sea and out of history. Despite these setbacks, reclamation continued in the area and the Tudors took it upon themselves to build the Dymchurch Wall. The seventeenth century saw more reclamation and sea wall construction which meant that by the eighteenth century the area was ripe for sheep-rearing, seafaring and, naturally enough, smuggling. The latter two declined in popularity during the nineteenth century as war with Napoleon focused everyone's attention. Even the sheep gave up in the twentieth century and the area was given over to arable farming and became increasingly significant in terms of conservation. The drainage techniques have continuously been improving, the shorelines stabilised and ever-stronger sea walls constructed. So they say.

What the flat terrain and sparse population produces is a feeling of expansiveness, calm and tranquillity. Even from the bus I had a sense of space and freedom as the flat fields stretched away in all directions, punctuated occasionally by an isolated cottage or church spire. The landscape also sits beneath a wide and generous sky bounded by horizons in the far distance. Not as dramatic as somewhere like the Lake District or Dartmoor perhaps, but nonetheless it had its own 'presence'. As I say, the area provides flat and level ground. If certain people are presented with flat and level ground they build things on it. They build things like airports, one of which can be found at Lydd, or nuclear power stations, two of which can be found at Dungeness. Only one of these is working and you'd think that when something like that stops working it would be taken down and cleared away. Obviously it's not that simple. Turn your gaze away from incidental trifles like nuclear power stations and altogether the area is pretty special. It must be, because it is designated not only as a Special Protection Area but also a Special Conservation Area.

Dotted around the largely empty, open landscape are the main settlements at New Romney, Hythe and Dymchurch. One of the original Cinque Ports, New Romney was originally a sea port on the River Rother estuary, adjacent to the coast. Things never stay the same with rivers, coasts and silt. The town always struggled with silt, which relentlessly clogged up the river, and even the coast is now a mile distant. Things went really pear-shaped in the thirteenth century when, not happy with merely silting up, the River diverted to Rye after some particularly nasty storms.

Emerging from this interesting and unusual scenery, my next port of call was Dover and here too was my next Youth Hostel. This was a walkable distance from the bus station along the High Street and London Road. The house and its surrounding area may once have been fairly grand but there was an air of melancholia and decay about the place. The reason for this in regard to the hostel soon became apparent when I was informed that this facility, like Brighton, was about to close. I had made it with a few days to spare.

I spent a happy evening with some old hostellers who were visiting as one would an old friend on their death bed. They reminisced about the early days of the Youth Hostel Association as they remembered it and the times they had spent at various locations. They had spent many a happy time at Dover and were sad and surprised to see it going. I think they recalled the rather rudimentary accommodation that was offered in the past and which was accordingly truly 'budget' priced. One older lady indicated that she had just seen a nearby bed and breakfast offering comparable prices. Despite being a fierce and long-term Youth Hosteller and therefore a bit of a fan, she confessed that she understood why many would opt for the comfort and 'luxury' of having their own room with tea and coffee-making facilities in a B&B. These stalwarts of the YHA seemed unsure of the changes they were witnessing, seeing it perhaps as pampering to the desires of people who liked too much pampering.

My dorm-mates were a rather excited father and son, due to be up very early the next day to catch a ferry to France and a coach to Paris for a rugby match. Precisely the kind of people who you think would keep an establishment like this going. They were hoping for an early night and promised to keep their morning departure as quiet as possible. Both the early night and the quiet getaway suited me fine.

Day 4

Canterbury tales

28th September

I was woken but not perturbed by the two rugby fans making their daybreak departure. Later I took a rather uninspiring stroll down the High Street to Market Square, a place where both meanings of the adjective 'pedestrian' could be applied. Nonetheless there were simple pleasures to be had—a good coffee in a clean and friendly cafe, a bout of people-watching, and a leisurely browse through a newspaper. A perfectly good way to start the day and a decent precursor to a wander down to the sea and a glance at the harbour.

From Dover, France is only 22 miles away, and it is even visible on a good day. I experienced that sense of excitement, anticipation and possibility that is available at almost any point of departure on any transport system. Here, much more so than in an airport, was the visible reality that out there lay the rest of the world and you could go there from here. You could look out over the water and see where the start of your journey would happen, where you would actually be travelling. Dover is at the point where we in England can feel closest, at least physically, to our European neighbours. And let's not forget, this separation is only a relatively recent phenomenon.

Geologists tell us that the gap between England and France is a rift valley caused by a section of the earth's crust collapsing along some fault lines. And only a mere 10,000 years ago people wandering back from the south of France (where they had been holidaying while the Ice Age made the north rather unbearable) found on their return a 'land bridge' to England. Since this was there, they duly walked across, pulling sleds of cheap wine and boxed camembert. At this time the ice sheets of the Ice Age were melting and retreating and there was much concern over 'global warming' possibly caused by too many inefficient wood-burning camp fires and mammoth gas emissions, some of these latter actually emanating from mammoths. The people's worst fears were realised and the levels of the seas and rivers rose until the land bridge was no more and the opportunity for ferry companies to take people on holiday to France was born.

Keeping a watchful eye over the town today was Dover Castle, a powerful-looking fortress on a commanding bluff of land above the White Cliffs. A pretty obvious place to put a castle, the site has evidence of an Iron Age hill fort and a Roman lighthouse. William the Conqueror built the first castle soon after 1066 and this was replaced by great stone structures in the twelfth and thirteenth centuries. Being on the south coast they had to be ready for anything. They were ready for the French under Napoleon but they never came. The tunnels beneath the castle, first dug in the middle ages as protected lines of communication were, however, in use again in World War Two. It was from here that amazing events such as the evacuation of Dunkirk were planned.

My cursory glance at Dover came to an end back at Pencester Road bus interchange where I had my own, admittedly slightly more limited, sense of excitement, anticipation and possibility. Here I stood at the gateway to the rest of East Kent, which I admit may not be quite as exciting for some as standing at Dover harbour and imagining it as gateway to the rest of the world. I was now faced with a case of Deal or No Deal or a choice of Sandwich, Plucks Gutter or Canterbury. A place called Plucks Gutter is crying out to be visited even if it's just to buy something like a hat or a walking stick. You could choose anything really, as long as the item would prompt people to ask the question 'Where did you get that from?' However, I let my head rule my heart and decided on Canterbury.

I was by no means the first to make such a journey and the fact that the Romans made their way from Portus Dubris to Durovernum Cantiacorum on their way to Londinium still causes a degree of wonder. Many others have trodden the path since then. For example, since the Romans had laid such a decent road on this route, it seemed churlish of William the Conqueror not to use it on his way inland after his successful time at Battle. It has been a trading route and pilgrim road for centuries.

And so to Canterbury which, thanks in part to its cathedral, St Augustine's Abbey and St Martin's Church, is a World Heritage Site. This knowledge bodes well for the traveller keen on Heritage that is World Class. It was the twenty-first century rather than the eleventh which was prominent when I disembarked at the bus station. The hub of the operation is a circular building, perhaps loosely modelled on an Iron Age roundhouse, while the bus turning and parking area is dotted with bays and plastic shelters and the whole area is shielded from the main road by a high steel barrier. Adjacent to this is an interesting collection of modern buildings with the ever popular 'clean lines', alongside a rather peculiar affair with gables and a tower, all of which are a concoction of concrete, glass, brick, steel and wood. The overall effect is that these are in some way not 'real', almost reminiscent of the front of a film set or the entrance to a theme park. They are in fact the entrance to a shopping precinct and so I suppose the bus station is sensibly located in that regard. Perhaps I shouldn't complain; it's clean, it's functional, it's better than Winchester.

In an incongruous piece of juxtaposition, overlooking the bus station are the city's ancient walls. The Romans built the first set between 270 and 290 AD and these were used almost as foundations for the walls built in the Middle Ages, which are still here today. Within the old walls the town still retains much of its medieval character—streets that aren't quite straight, houses and shops jostling together in narrow lanes, a nice feeling of steady growth over time rather than imposed planning. When Celia Fiennes visited in 1697 she found many small houses given over to weaving, and a number of paper mills. The main activity now seems to be retail sales and the shops are accompanied by financial institutions keen to lend you money or to make money by looking after yours. Wandering through the shopping area I found all the familiar stores which I could have found anywhere else, but there were numerous narrower side streets with smaller outlets, pubs and restaurants. I lost myself in these places for a time and enjoyed the mixture of vitality and intimacy. Celia Fiennes also noticed large numbers of French people in the city engaged in silk weaving and winding. The French people I noticed were teenagers, probably on a school trip.

From outside the city the cathedral dominates the skyline. In the warren of alleys and lanes within the city walls it occasionally disappears as the buildings crowd in. You know it is there and its towers reappear to provide a monumental contrast to the more humble constructions in places like the cobbled Butchery Lane. As I neared the cathedral, the streets opened out into the Buttermarket, a lovely little market square, edged with handsome half-timbered buildings. There is much to see and plenty of history hidden behind the shop fronts and facades. Sun Street, just off the market, contained the building that was The Sun Hotel where, apparently, Charles Dickens once stayed. Also off the Buttermarket is the gate to the cathedral flanked by a building that was once the Gate House Hotel. It should be noted that the gate to the cathedral is not simply a gate. It is a GATE. If I had a gate like this in front of my house I would have to dig up the road and demolish a few neighbouring houses. In fact, I'd move out of the house and live in the gate—there'd be more room.

I spent a long time entranced by this entrance. It is a wonderful display of the stonemasons' and stone carvers' craft and art. There is a fantastic array of carved heraldic shields and a row of winged angels holding more shields. Prominent is a striking figure of Christ. I pulled myself together and remembered that I shouldn't use up all my awe and wonder just on the gate, so I passed through the archway, having parted with a 'contribution to the funds'. A stunning building stopped me in my tracks. I took in the ornate porch and let my gaze scan slowly skywards to the towers. The cathedral was a magnificent sight and was perfectly set off by other splendid buildings arranged around the walled precinct. Internally the cathedral

272

had a wonderful set of exquisite spaces ranging from the grand to the intimate and I let my spirit soar with the great tall columns of the nave that rose to the high vaulted arches of the roof. Outside, I loved the fourteenth century chapter house and it was wonderful to walk through the covered walkway of the cloisters. These cloisters are intimately linked with the deed for which Canterbury Cathedral has a certain notoriety. Striding down here, one fateful day in 1170, came the last men to see Thomas Becket alive.

Thomas was the then Archbishop and he was obviously a bit of a thorn in the side of Henry II who is said to have asked, possibly rhetorically, "Who will rid me of this troublesome priest?" Several of Henry's headstrong knights decided that this question wasn't rhetorical and took it upon themselves to win the king's favour. They murdered Thomas on 29th December. This act and subsequent miraculous occurrences saw the beginning of Canterbury's identification as a pilgrim destination. Canterbury Cathedral was having a powerful enough effect on me and I'd simply come up on the bus from Dover.

Thomas was buried in a lavish tomb and even in death he appears to have been an unbearable reminder for kings that they were not the highest authority in the land. Why else would Henry VIII order the destruction of the tomb and make attempts to blot out the memory of this man? Whatever the reason, the tomb is gone and a single candle lights the spot where it once was. The cathedral has many other treasures though, including simply stunning medieval stained glass windows. These are just glorious works of art, alive and vibrant.

Leaving the cathedral sometime later I wandered around the city again, where I encountered an ornate mock-Tudor building in the High Street. This was the 'Beaney Institute' Public Library and Museum which, as it declared outside, was originally intended as a place 'for the education of working men'. It was built in 1899 with a bequest of £10,000 from a Dr Beaney, the son of a local labourer. How does the son of a local labourer find £10,000 to bequeath? Well, he had received a 'good education' and then decided to emigrate to Melbourne, Australia. As an early example of the brain drain, Dr Beaney had become successful and also wealthy by the time of his demise. The founding of the Institute was a way of paying back something he felt he owed. It also reflected some of the ideas of the schools being established by the National Society of the time; namely that education should not just be for the rich and privileged. The Institute housed a museum and library with exhibits including drawings, paintings old and new, ceramics and some Anglo-Saxon jewellery.

I went back to the bus station and decided on a trip to Whitstable out on the coast, which is a short run on the number 4. Minutes after leaving the city centre we stopped outside St Dunstan's Church. Dunstan was born about 909, had been an abbot at Glastonbury, a bishop of Worcester and of London, and also Archbishop of Canterbury, and in his day was one of England's most popular saints. Amongst other things he is the patron saint of goldsmiths, having been a bit of an artist and calligrapher himself. The church here was founded towards the end of the eleventh century and has a number of royal connections although these are not particularly savoury. The first royal was Henry II. After the business with Thomas Becket, Henry needed to carry out some form of public penitence. He made it to St Dunstan's in his everyday wear but stopped in the church to change into penitential garb of sackcloth and to remove his shoes. He then walked barefoot to Thomas' tomb in the cathedral.

The other royal was Henry VIII, who had his own bother with another churchman called Thomas, this one being Thomas More. More was unhappy with Henry's desire to be the head of the church and ultimately lost his own head for this apparent disloyalty. His daughter asked that her father's head might be brought to St Dunstan's to lie in the family tomb of her in-laws, the Ropers. I'm glad it wasn't my job to deliver it.

We slipped the none-too-harsh bonds of Canterbury and pushed up Blean Hill, which was carrying us up past the wonderful Blean Woods. I sensed we were near the village of Blean. The woods here are not just any old woods but are ancient and therefore quite special. In his book, *The History of the Countryside*, Oliver Rackham points out that they are mentioned in an Anglo-Saxon charter of 850. They are extensive as woods go today but would have been vast in those times. Today they are crossed by walking trails and contain an RSPB reserve. All the climbing eventually led us to Borstal Hill, a good place to find young offenders and also to get good views across the Thames Estuary to the Essex Coast beyond. A windmill, glimpsed down Millers Court, gave a clue as to the prevailing weather conditions and to some earlier industry. It was downhill all the way from here, topographically speaking.

In and around Whitstable (or Witenestaple, the 'white post' or 'post of the councillors') is evidence of settlement going back to the Palaeolithic period. What attracted these people to settle here? Was it just the oysters? We shall never know for sure. What we do know attracted people here in the 1700s was the possibility of partaking of the waters through the use of the new-fangled 'bathing machines', first advertised here in 1768. Having people want to visit is all well and good but they need to be able to reach you. To reach Whitstable people came from London by ship or along the toll road from Canterbury. The familiar tale of the benefits brought by the railways holds true here. The Canterbury and Whitstable Railway was doing good business by 1830. This is one of the lines that lays claim to being the first regular steam-hauled passenger services in the world.

Although it's a seaside resort of sorts, Whitstable still has a meaningful relationship with the sea and is also really very pretty. It's easy on the eye; it's small and friendly and rather quirky and individual. Additionally it has numerous pubs with suitably nautical names such as The Old Neptune and the Quayside, and plenty of eating places. All manner of delicacies are on offer including oysters, for which the town has long been famous. A good place to get these seemed to be Wheelers Oyster Bar. If they've been going since 1856 they must be doing something right.

From the Horsebridge Arts and Community Centre it was a short stroll to the beaches and I spent a very happy time exploring. The wide vistas over the sea are countered by the intimacy and close-knit feel of the town. The architecture mixes weatherboard and half-timbered houses with those of stone and render. It all comes together to make a charming little place.

Other features of note are the 'Favourite', an old oyster dredging vessel called a 'yawl' and, east of the harbour, 'The Street', a half-mile long shingle bank that runs out into the sea. A new and more controversial feature is the Kentish Flats Wind Farm whose 30 turbines turned lazily six miles off shore.

A bus ride west along the coast was Herne Bay, which somehow seemed far less 'organic' than Whitstable. The reason for this could be that it was predominantly the brainchild of a few London businessmen back in 1830. These guys had an envious eye on Margate, further along the coast. This was a popular bathing resort, receiving large numbers of visitors from London. The bright sparks sitting in Herne Bay, probably enjoying a pint or two of Shepherd Neame, had watched the many steamers loaded with passengers pass by. They thought that somehow these potential customers should be encouraged to stop at Herne. So they put up some hotels, built a few houses, constructed a pier and eventually people who may once have passed became paying guests. By 1870 the steamer traffic had ceased so they shortened the pier. Thirty years on and the steamers were back. Wishing that the steamers would make up their minds, the good people of Herne Bay nonetheless provided a longer pier to accommodate them.

The sea front had a long and wide promenade backed by some neat gardens which created a good open space between the sea and the impressive row of hotels. The sea front clock tower is a particularly striking feature, especially on the hour. From a colonnaded base a central tower rises up within four tall columns, which support yet another layer in which the clock itself is housed. Above these sits a small arched turret. And to top it all, as it were, is a weather vane. This little fancy was built using a donation from a Mrs Ann Thwaytes of London and I suppose if she had the odd £4000 lying about there would have been worse things she could have spent it on.

Wandering back to the bus depot, the town reflected the fact that it had rather fallen from the dizzying heights of a former popularity. It seemed to sag with out-of-season over-capacity and looked a bit frayed at the edges. Perhaps it was worn out after a busy summer.

The bus briefly toured some of the less enthralling parts of town and the suburbs of Beltinge and Broomfield before reaching Herne, the original village which gave the bay, and subsequently the larger town, its name. This village was for many years the centre of the local smuggling operations which made use of various landing points along the coast. The village has an aptly named Smuggler's Inn and the nearby churchyard is the burial site of one Sydenham Snow. Snow was a 'preventive man' who lost his life challenging a ferocious band of smugglers. Whatever imagination they had regarding smuggling, they lacked when it came to thinking up a name for themselves and the best they could come up with was The North Kent Gang. The name might be a bit disappointing but they had no trouble with the rest of the image and PR—everyone was terrified of them. Well, perhaps everyone except Sydenham Snow and his men. In the early hours of Easter Sunday morning in 1821 the gang members were unloading their contraband rather than attending church. Perhaps they thought everyone else would be in church, but what they obviously didn't think was that they would be disturbed by a patrol of Blockade men, under the leadership of Snow. Despite being seriously outnumbered, the Blockaders challenged the smugglers. The smugglers fought the law and the law, not being familiar with the 1950s song, lost. Snow was badly wounded from pistol shot and his fellow Blockaders were held at bay by the gang, who made good their escape. Snow was carried to the Ship Inn where vain attempts were made to save his life. On his death bed he was able to give sufficient information to allow for the arrest of several gang members. In a sorry end to the tale, these men somehow managed to get off. Once again, small 'insignificant' places can reveal fascinating snippets from history.

Crossing the open countryside of Herne Common, I passed something called 'Wildwood', a visitor attraction celebrating and conserving Britain's wildlife. It seems this is the place to come if you want to find out about the work of conserving endangered species such as the water vole and the Hazel dormouse, or if you simply want to get a good look at a European beaver. We came to Sturry, which takes its name from the

River Great Stour on which it sits. It's an ancient village, but that fact is quite well concealed behind buildings erected to replace those lost in bomb damage during air raids on Canterbury. One of the buildings to survive the bombs is the Norman Church of St Nicholas. This is a bit of a gem really, with a tower from the twelfth century and a wooden porch from the sixteenth. It is quite simple, by which I mean it is not 'grand'. It has just been sitting here quietly being a House of God for 900 years. The bus carried me on the short journey from Sturry back to Canterbury and the end of what had been an excellent little triangular tour.

I made use of the fact that the city walls are so close to the bus station and walked along them to Dane John Gardens, a pleasant area of municipal open space that includes a roman burial mound for good measure. Although not a massive city, Canterbury needs 'lungs' like any other built-up area. The Dane John Gardens provide a remarkably peaceful and calm environment considering that the hustle and bustle of the shopping centre and city life is so close. I wandered around the city a little longer, just to glimpse some of the other great buildings it contains. Along with the atmospheric ruins of St Augustine's Abbey and Canterbury Castle there was the tower of St George's Church, notable for surviving the bomb that destroyed the rest of the building and for marking the place where the Elizabethan playwright Christopher Marlowe was baptised. In a number of places there are enchanting views of urban waterways courtesy of The River Stour which splits and makes its divergent way through the city. Where the river passes beneath an ancient bridge and is edged by medieval buildings you could almost think you were in Venice.

Altogether, I was very taken with Canterbury and found again that there was so much to see and so little time in which to see it. I got my priorities right, however, and found a small pub, or rather chose a pub from the many available. Later, I made my way along the busy New Dover Road, via the budget supermarket and on towards the youth hostel, which I hoped wasn't facing imminent closure.

Day 5

West through England's Garden

29th September

My companions at breakfast were members of an extended American family enjoying an extensive tour of the United Kingdom, at the end of which they would probably have seen more of the country than most of its indigenous inhabitants. We are told that Americans can eat too much of the wrong kind of thing. So, to avoid any embarrassment on their behalf, I followed my bowl of cereal with slices of cold meat, hunks of cheese, a few croissants and assorted jams. In between mouthfuls we talked about our trips and what they and I made of the places we'd visited. What they'd seen so far, they loved. It was good to meet people who were enthusing about all the things that England has to offer. Seeing someone take pleasure in discovering something that you've grown used to makes you sit up and appreciate it afresh. Plenty of people want nothing but to escape to a foreign country for their holidays while people in distant lands are saving long and hard to come here. A growing band of people are discovering the wonders on their doorstep, available at the drop of a hat and much of it easily accessed, as I have discovered, by bus.

Having rather overdone my enthusiasm for the breakfast, I welcomed the walk into town and considered what lay ahead. I was in for a long haul today. I had previously arranged with a friend that we would hook up that night and spend a bit of time assessing the merits of a number of traditionally brewed beverages. This all seemed like a good idea at the time and still felt achievable to me as I boarded my first bus of the day and purchased another Adult Explorer. I unfolded my Tourist Map and had my first twinge of doubt. Great Bedwyn, on the edge of the Savernake Forest in Wiltshire, suddenly seemed a very long way away.

This was going to be the big push, a new standard in Extreme Bus Travel. I quickly picked out a route of sorts, going for major towns on what looked like a fairly direct path. This would not be a day for lingering and sightseeing, but I was sure that even with this slightly different and pressured agenda there would be plenty to see. Where the buses actually went would, of course, play a significant role in the success or failure of this venture.

Ashford seemed a sensible place to aim for as a start, it being a major transport interchange. It was a little over an hour away. On our way we passed through Chartham, a village with a proper village green and a number of beautiful houses and a paper mill. Whatever the reason, paper has played a big part in Chartham's life and there has been a mill there for over 300 years. We pressed on through the little village of Shalmsford Street, which is almost next door and then crossed the A28 and into Chilham. We pulled into Felborough Close on the edge of the village and stopped. A few people got on. We waited. There was no-one else waiting to get on and no-one wanted to get off. It all seemed rather peculiar, until the bus driver asked about somebody who was obviously a regular.

"Oh yes," offered one of the recent arrivals. "I spoke to Mary yesterday, and she said she was comin' in."

So the bus driver said, "Well, she's late and that's tough so she'll miss the bus and I don't care." No she didn't. She said, "Right then, we'll wait."

It transpired that we, that is the bus, would be waiting for Mary! I found this little episode very refreshing and even uplifting. The normal 'rules' were turned upside-down. Passengers usually wait for buses, not the other way round. Also, this seemed to me to be an example of a proper bus service; something that was being offered for the service of people like Mary. And it didn't matter that people like Mary were occasionally late because we knew they could be counted on to eventually turn up. And I got the sense that even if she didn't eventually turn up, rather than being cross, people would be worried because she had said she would be there and if she wasn't there where was she, and had something happened to her? Somehow, that elusive thing called 'community' was happening here and even the bus was playing its part by dipping in and out of the village regularly, eleven times a day. I was reminded of the stories that circulate about the old Somerset and Dorset Railway. Apparently, at the appropriate time of year, the trains would stop for a short while at a certain location between stations to allow people a few minutes to go and pick mushrooms! The same wonderful attitude and connection with real people and their needs seemed to be echoed in delaying our departure for Mary's sake. Mary appeared, somewhat flustered and apologetic.

"Not to worry, Mary," smiled the driver. Not only had the bus waited for Mary but the driver knew her name. This was almost too much. Going by appearances there seemed to be some form of real human relationship between the driver and one of her passengers. All this happened in The Close in which we had parked, having pulled off the main road. It was almost as though we had not just pulled off the main road away from the traffic but also removed ourselves from the 'rules' and rushed time-frame that seem to govern most of everyday life. It was all strangely comforting, as if this part of the bus timetable had been prepared by a scriptwriter for a James Stewart film like 'It's a Wonderful Life'.

We had been on the outskirts of the village. In its older heart buildings clustered around a market square. There was also the fifteenth century church dedicated to St Mary and a large and fine country house in the form of Chilham Castle. This was built for Sir Dudley Digges in 1616 and is the sort of place you could have if you were the son of Sir Thomas Digges MP, married the daughter of Sir Thomas Kemp of Olantigh, were an MP yourself and were also a successful investor in The Virginia Company of London which was then busy establishing colonial settlements in North America.

As we continued on our way the surrounding fields gave way here and there to bits and pieces of woodland which are probably remnants of woods that once stretched all the way here from Blean. Godmaere had a settlement at a place we now call Godmersham. There did not seem to be a great deal to attract the attention or interest here. It is a small settlement close to the River Stour, pleasant enough but nothing extraordinary. Mention such thoughts to a knowledgeable local bus passenger and they will patiently explain that the manor house away to the right is Godmersham Park and Mansion. When the fact that there is a manor house and park doesn't seem to be impressive enough, the same local will start talking about Jane Austen.

Jane Austen's third brother Edward was taken under the wing of, and eventually adopted by, Thomas Knight and his wife Elizabeth who resided at Godmersham Park. Edward inherited Godmersham Park and moved in with his wife and eleven children. Well, he needed a big house with all those offspring. Jane Austen spent time at Godmersham, may well have wandered the village and is thought to have used the house, its servants and the local people as inspiration for several of her novels. Also in the village, you will be politely informed, is a church which dates from the twelfth century. It has some Saxon bits but is mostly Victorian. It is dedicated to St Lawrence the Martyr. It just goes to prove that you can't assume that an inconsequential-looking little place has nothing of interest about it.

We soon veered off from the main road, as is the way with buses, and carried out a little circuit of the pretty village of Wye. This was yet another historic village and I was beginning to wonder if the good people of Kent weren't being a little on the greedy side when it came to picturesque villages filled with fascinating old buildings and beautiful ancient churches. The church in question here is dedicated to St Gregory and St Martin and was glimpsed over the road from the end of Church Street. Wye began as a ford across the River Stour, was the site of a Roman villa and became a Saxon manor and market town. The Stour Valley Walk passes through and the North Downs Way is at the top of the hill.

The bus pulled into Ashford where a large shopping centre showed the modern face of the town. People have been settling here near the 'ford near the ash trees' since about 900 and the place developed as a market town and also as a communications hub. That tradition lasted into the railway age and no less than five routes converged on the town. Since the 1990s Ashford has also been graced, if that is the right word, with Ashford International Railway Station, which serves the High Speed rail link to Europe via the Channel Tunnel.

At a busy street market near the shopping centre I bought fruit and cheese and a couple of rolls from a nearby bakery shop. Thus fed I wandered in the direction of the Tourist Information Centre. This was tucked in a tiny enclave of historicity away from the Park Mall and County Square shopping centres and all the other hustle and bustle of modern Ashford. In this little haven of peace and tranquillity you could almost forget that you were in the middle of a busy, growing, modern town. Here the Church of St Mary the Virgin sat in its small churchyard bounded by rows of old houses. The TIC and museum buildings dated from 1650. They were created by Sir Norton Knatchbull as a free Grammar school. The good Sir Knatchbull endowed the school and gave it to the town of Ashford, and the museum had photographs of old Ashford and displays about Ashford at War and local archaeological and geological discoveries. The present church is mostly fifteenth century with a small section from the thirteenth. The earliest church here is believed to have been in the eleventh century.

Back at the rather less tranquil bus station I boarded the 510 for Maidstone. Twenty minutes later we pulled up in Charing, an old village which has had a number of mills and a market. A good collection of red brick and half-timbered houses were mustered along our route. Probably the grandest building in town is a palace, built for an Archbishop in 1348. The village is on the old pilgrim route from London to Canterbury and this explains the situation of the palace in what today might seem a bit of a backwater. The palace provides another link to some fascinating history because apart from affording accommodation to Archbishops making their way between London and Canterbury, both Henry VII and Henry VIII have stayed here. Henry VIII visited in June 1520 on his way to France. You and I might go to France for a chance to grab a few bargains in a Calais hypermarket. Henry was meeting with King Francis I, following a treaty of 1518, in the hope of cementing cordial international relations. Such are the onerous tasks of heads of state.

At Lenham we pushed through an expanse of modern development to find at the centre of the village the remnant of another, well, you know, lovely Kent village. There was a pretty square and again half-timbered and wooden-clad houses. The square has probably played host to a market since a charter was received in 1206. There are plenty of attractive buildings here, with The Red Lion providing an impressive end-of-terrace of white-washed walls and red-tiled roofs. The pub dates from the fourteenth century and speaks of the days of coaching inns and turnpike roads. There are tea rooms and green-grocers and another good-looking, although probably younger, pub called The Dog and Bear. The village is also the spot where the River Len rises before making its way west towards Maidstone, filling the moat of nearby Leeds Castle on the way. We stopped briefly at the brick-built Roebuck Inn at Harrietsham, and via Hollingbourne we finally reached Maidstone.

The journey to this historic county town had helped me to see why the area is known as the 'Garden of Kent'. We have spent a happy hour or so meandering through predominantly open countryside which is largely under productive-looking agriculture. What farmers grow is constantly changing, but I have been travelling during the month in which traditionally the harvesting of the county's most famous, and at one time most profitable, crop—hops—takes place. Kent was the first area in the UK to begin farming hops and it has been the most successful. By 1655 one third of the UK hop crop was grown here. It must have been quite something when hundreds of workers descended on the area for the annual picking. It's all very different now. In a little under 100 years, from the early 1900s, the acreage under hops had been reduced by nine-tenths. Part of this decline is due to something called 'lager' which has taken a large part of the market for alcoholic drink from the more traditional beers. Lager apparently needs fewer hops. All in all it has a lot to answer for.

The hop industry has also produced a peculiar local architectural feature, examples of which are still about here and there. These are the oast houses in which hops were spread out to dry on a floor above a fire. The warm air dried them and was circulated with the assistance of cowls in the cone-shaped roof above this part of the building. After drying they were pressed into sacks ready for transportation. I was glad to see that many of these oast houses have been preserved by being converted for alternative uses.

In the Domesday Book Maidstone was 'Meddestane' and this was a derivation from the earlier 'Maegthan Stan'. The name means 'stone of the maidens' and there is a suggestion that the maidens gathered by the stones that were put out into the river to allow for the washing of clothes, the distance from the muddy banks providing cleaner water. Maidens still gather today but are more usually found in The Royal Star Arcade or the Mall Chequers shopping areas.

By the thirteenth century Maidstone was a prosperous town, receiving a royal charter in 1261. The success of the town was due mainly to its location on the navigable river which provided for transport of goods such as fruit and vegetables up to the hungry consumers of London. By the sixteenth century the woollen industry was also growing in importance and weavers from Holland settled here, as in other parts of Kent. This industry fell into decline in the seventeenth century but local entrepreneurs helped the town survive through developing thread making, brewing and paper-making industries. When Daniel Defoe visited in the 1700s he found the town 'populous' and its inhabitants 'generally wealthy' and he makes mention of the manufacture of linen thread. He also describes an incomparable market and declares that from this town and its surrounding areas, London is supplied with 'more particulars than from any single market town in England'. You may also be lucky enough to share Defoe's pleasant experiences of engaging with the local populous, for he found that at Maidstone 'you begin to converse with gentlemen, and persons of rank of both sexes, and some of quality'.

Tucked on a bend of the river here are the Archbishop's

Palace and All Saints Church. My town leaflet told me that these are part of a 'wonderful cluster of fourteenth century buildings' and that the latter has been described as 'the grandest perpendicular church in England'. Another major attraction for the town is the Maidstone Museum and Bentlif Art Gallery which benefits from a) being free and b) being housed in a magnificent Elizabethan manor house.

To continue on my eastward quest I plumped for the 7 service, which would take me to Tunbridge Wells. As we crossed the River Medway there was a glimpse of All Saints Church and I have to admit it looked very perpendicular. After that was the rather less inspiring Maidstone West railway station. The town slowly ebbed away to reveal the village of Barming on its western extremity. The spire of the twelfth century church of St Margaret of Antioch peered over the roof tops, which eventually gave way to more open countryside busy with the agricultural activity of these September days. The rural landscape was punctuated with settlements such as Teston, which was crying out for a neighbouring village called Testoff, and Wateringbury, which was apparently called Uuotryngebyri at the end of the 900s. Keeping up the watery connections, at the end of the village was Pizen Well, which is a name and not an instruction. At the more substantial Mereworth the handsome tower of St Laurence's Church kept a silent vigil over the village.

Nearby is Mereworth Castle which is not a castle but a country house in the style of Palladio and is indeed seen by some as the finest Palladian House in England. Fine or not, it has to be seen from a distance since it is not open to the public. The Honourable John Fane commissioned the building of Mereworth Castle. Here was a man who knew what he wanted and, it seems, got what he wanted. The original village church upset the symmetry of the house and you could see the village from the estate. How frightfully tiresome! Mr Fane decided it would be best to move everything—butcher, baker and candlestick maker—half a mile north west.

As we called into the square at Hadlow, an extremely large tower loomed above us. This was part of Hadlow Castle, a late

Victorian Gothic home. As is so often the case with Late Victorian Goths, a simple home was not enough and the owner, one Walter Barton May, added the tower or 'May's Folly' as it was known. With its lantern on top it stood at an impressive 170ft. The tower has fallen into a state of some disrepair but fear not, there is a Save Hadlow Tower Action Group working for its restoration.

There were very substantial oast houses dotted here and there, now most likely acting as superior private houses. About 15 minutes later we were in Tonbridge (once called Tunbridge). The origins of the name are unclear. It possibly means a bridge belonging to the manor (tun) or to a man named Tunna or to a fish called Tuna. It is also possibly a contraction of 'the town of bridges'. This would come from the need for many such constructions to cross the river which by this point had split into several streams. Tonbridge had always really been called Tunbridge but there was some confusion regarding Tunbridge (Wells). Even though Tonbridge is older than Tunbridge (Wells), and had been called Tunbridge before Tunbridge (Wells), it was decided in 1870 that Tunbridge (Wells) could stay as Tunbridge, while Tunbridge should become Tonbridge. It just doesn't seem right somehow. Apparently this was all down to the general post office and was their response to some confusion down at the sorting office.

Tonbridge stands where the Saxons built a bridge over the River Medway. In the eleventh century Robert Fitz Gilbert de Clare built a castle here and you can still see the motte but not so much the bailey. The town experienced various besiegings and even a burning. It and the castle were rebuilt in the thirteenth century and the gatehouse remains as fitting testimonial to the sturdy construction. Most of the rest of the sturdy construction was not sufficiently sturdy to survive the attentions of Parliamentarian demolition teams at the end of the Civil War.

A big commercial player in the area during the eighteenth century was The Medway Navigation Company, established by an Act of Parliament in 1740, which gave the company the go ahead to make the river navigable. This must have been a matter of priority because being called the Medway Navigation

Company when you can't engage in Navigation would be very frustrating, if not drawing the attention of people enforcing the Trade Descriptions Act. Although the river was strictly speaking navigable, there was no provision for a tow path. This meant that men rather than horses had to pull the barges. You'd need to think well ahead when ordering your pizza because an express delivery from Maidstone to Tonbridge, over a distance of about fourteen miles, would take approximately ten hours. Pizza didn't actually feature as a significant section of freight traffic; it was more heavy goods such as coal, timber and stone. Other cargo represented a proper miscellany: anything from sugar to soap, cement to cider, beer to barley. Controversially, they also conveyed gunpowder. The gunpowder was made in mills along the river and was transported in special barges which carried a red flag. This might have made other river traffic more inclined to give the powder barges a wide berth and passers by less inclined to carelessly flick their fag ends. However, a red flag was not deemed to be a sufficient safety measure by the people of Maidstone and gunpowder transportation ceased in 1874. The navigation company had a pretty good, clear run for almost a hundred years. Then, in 1842, the South East railway arrived and the stiff competition saw the Medway Navigation Company begin a slow decline which finally saw the company off in 1910. There are a few remnants of the company such as the warehouses by the old wharf and a number of locks on the river. Evidence of a certain prosperity in the town is shown by the Town Hall in the High Street, while other 'less significant' buildings, including some half-timbered constructions, help to provide a relaxed market town feel.

We crossed the river and the railway, passed by St Stephen's church and headed out into open countryside. Once again there were plenty of trees and wooded areas, possibly more survivors of the removal of a once-vast forest. We called at Southborough Common, an open area thought to have been used as seasonal pasture by farmers way back in the Dark Ages and useful also for playing cricket. Apparently cricket has been played here since 1794. I know some cricket matches take a long time but that must be some sort of record. Southborough has an industrial heritage which includes iron works, textile and gunpowder mills and brick-works. It also has a far more refined heritage, having been a popular spot for the great and the good including Charles II and Queen Catherine, who paid an extended visit in 1663. However, it was the Victorian era that really saw the town expand. The local High Brooms Brick and Tile Company had to work at full pelt to keep up with demand and red brick is a dominant feature of much of the local architecture. It is the genteel side, rather than the heavy industry, that is evident from the bus.

We pulled into Tunbridge Wells, a town which is home to 'disgusted of Tunbridge Wells', an archetypal writer of complaining letters to newspapers, and which has a reputation for being rather unexciting. Some might say dull, even. But I wondered as I wandered here, is there anything wrong with being a not very exciting town? Too often excitement is confused with brashness. Too often places that are said to 'lack vitality' are assumed to be 'dead'. Surely there is a place for a quiet enjoyment that is provided by genteel and subdued surroundings? And I'm sure it's possible to show 'vital signs' of life without being all festivals and fireworks, noise and night clubs.

I arrived a year after the town celebrated the 400th anniversary of the discovery, by Dudley Lord North, of the nearby Chalybeate Springs. The fancy name just means that the spring waters contained iron. Lord North had drunk some of these waters and felt himself to be healed of an illness. Not slow to realise the commercial potential of such a thing, his Lordship returned to London and spread the news. It was time for the property developers to move in, although they were rather sluggish. Wells were dug to tap the springs in 1608 but no buildings arose until 1636. Lots of wrangling over the PFI contracts, no doubt, as well as plenty of consultants to consult. The first two buildings developed into early versions of Starbucks inasmuch as they were coffee houses. The buildings were complemented by a tree-lined walkway along which traders began to set up market stalls. It seems that there wasn't anything you could reasonably call the beginnings of a town until almost the end of that century. Following this, according to a Heritage

Trail leaflet, the town developed a reputation for being a 'pleasant place to live, work and visit.' 'Pleasant', you will notice, not 'exciting'.

Famous amongst those who promoted the town in the eighteenth century was Beau Nash, dedicated follower—and leader—of fashion. He spent part of his time in Tunbridge Wells as a self-appointed master of ceremonies and part of his time in the same role at rival Bath. As well as sharing a master of ceremonies, the two towns share gorgeous Georgian architecture. Possibly the best place to see some of this in Tunbridge Wells, and to obtain a sense of eighteenth century life, is the Pantiles. Here you find a colonnaded walkway, now full of boutiques and small shops, where the rich gentry would once have walked, taken coffee and people-watched. Today even the hoi polloi can happily engage in walking, taking coffee and people watching, and so I did. I decided that Tunbridge Wells did indeed seem a very pleasant place to visit.

I chose Crawley as my next destination because, well, why not? It was certainly in the right direction although I wasn't sure what I would find. I just thought it was close to Gatwick Airport and that would mean lots of noise and traffic. There are also associations with the nightmares of having to get there for a check-in at 4.30 in the morning. I was about thirty miles from London but still had the feeling that I would somehow be simply travelling through featureless, dull suburbs from here on. My ignorance and lack of experience of a part of my own country was once again about to be laid bare. The journey on the 291 Metrobus was lovely. We passed through the Tunbridge suburbs but these were not endless, treeless, uniform suburbs. These were 'leafy' and had advertisements for such things as a 'miniature horse and foal weekend' which spoke of countryside connections even in the built up area. Once out of the suburbs we were still in the Weald and traversing stunning countryside, fruitful fields, and coming across charming settlements.

We called at Groombridge, a picture-postcard place set in stunning countryside. The Crown Inn and a Victorian church overlooked a proper village green. The Crown Inn dated from the sixteenth century and formed the end of a row of pretty brick cottages. The church of St Thomas the Apostle dates from 1884 and was designed by Norman Shaw, the architect responsible for New Scotland Yard and The Piccadilly Hotel in London. This should be enough to attract people here, but the ace card for tourism is probably the nearby Groombridge Place Gardens. These are a series of formal gardens, laid out in 1674 as a series of outdoor 'rooms' for the owners of the house, which had been built by one Philip Packer in 1662.

A surprising history hides behind the quiet, calm and picturesque village of Groombridge and its large house. The house has murky links to the even murkier Groombridge Gang, notorious smugglers from the eighteenth century under the leadership of Robert Moreton and John Bowra who struggled with their gang name as much as The North Kent Gang. Surely these names must have been a bit of a giveaway for the authorities?

PC Dimwitty: The Groombridge Gang have struck again, sarge.

Sergeant: Right. Have we got any further with working out where they might be based?

The gang members did, however, manage a bit better with their aliases. 'Cat', Thomas 'Stick-in-the-mud' Gurr, Collison, Pizon, Isaac 'Towser' Pope, John 'Flushing Jack' Kitchen, Thomas 'Bulverhythe Tom' Ward and William Weston worked alongside the chilling 'Old Joll', 'The Miller', 'Yorkshire George' and 'Nasty Face'. The gang would use pack ponies to bring smuggled goods here which were landed on the beaches between Hastings and Pevensey. They are reputed to have hidden their ill-gotten gains in secret tunnels connecting Groomsbridge House to the Crown Inn, which they used as their headquarters. These were tough times and the smugglers faced severe penalties. In 1745 you would be in trouble if you were found loitering within six miles of the coast. The Smuggling Act also established the death penalty for running contraband, assembling to 'run' goods or even harbouring smugglers. A smuggler convicted of killing an excise officer would be gibbeted. The gangs were involved in serious organised crime and by all accounts were a bunch of appallingly violent and cruel men.

The Groombridge Gang were in trouble when some members were caught and pioneered 'plea bargaining'. A certain Jerome Knapp was captured in 1749. To get himself off, he revealed the names of those who had, by his reckoning, landed three thousand pounds of a certain product in 1745.

It is perhaps hard to believe that the product in question, the cause of much of this illegal trade, treachery, violence and death, was tea. A clue to what made this inoffensive beverage the eighteenth century equivalent of crack cocaine is found in the relationship between consumption and duty. According to the Tea Council, tea was immensely popular by the beginning of the eighteenth century. However, the East India Company had a monopoly and kept prices artificially high. On top of this, the government imposed massive duties, usually to help pay for a war. The high demand for cheaper tea was seen as a golden opportunity by people who were not overly concerned with keeping the law. Tea smuggling became more lucrative than the illicit trade in gin or brandy. Even though the link between price, demand and smuggling was understood, the government raised duty to fund a war with Spain. In 1711 a pound of tea leaves cost five shillings. This works out to be about £28.87 at 2008 prices. When this is seen as a comparison with average earnings the price jumps to £413.

In 1733, one Gabriel Tomkins had given information to an official inquiry into corruption in the Customs Services. He claimed to have sold between fifteen and twenty thousand pounds of tea and coffee to London dealers in a year. One estimate for the trade in the 1780s is that between 4 and 7 million pounds of tea was smuggled in on a yearly basis, a trade worth hundreds of millions in today's money. In 1784, William Pitt the Younger, who had become Prime Minister only a year before at the age of 24, introduced an Act which slashed the duty on tea from 112 percent to 12½ percent. Smuggling tea was now a mugs game and ceased almost overnight. The government switched its revenue-gathering to The Window Tax and the smugglers returned to gin and brandy.

Another pretty little village, with the emphasis on little, is Withyham. It has the required old pub (the fifteenth century

Dorset Arms) and church (fourteenth century St Michael's and All Angels). There were good views across enclosed fields towards Blackham and I was beginning to understand why so many people think this is a very special area and why I could never afford a house here.

The tally of pretty villages with ancient pubs and churches kept clicking up. At Hartfield was the eye-catching Gallipot Inn, formed by bringing together what were originally three Tudor cottages. A gallipot, I have discovered, is a small ceramic pot, used for medicine and such things. These were produced in one of the original cottages. At Colemans Hatch was the fifteenth century Hatch Inn, and in Forest Row the fifteenth century Chequers Inn and the Brambletye Hotel. The views from Ashurst Wood were fabulous and reminded me that I was still in the heart of some great countryside, despite approaching East Grinstead, which again I had mistakenly associated with Gatwick Airport rather than with the High Weald Area of Outstanding Natural Beauty. Once through the more modern accretions on the edge we arrived at the historic heart of this market town. Grenestede is mentioned in the Domesday Book and means 'a green place', and so was probably a clearing in the extensive woodland of the area. It had become a borough by the thirteenth century and by Elizabethan times was obviously a thriving and functioning community with a forge, a slaughter house and a windmill as well as a weekly market. The place has a fine character which is helped in no small measure by the existence of a row of fabulous fourteenth century timber framed buildings on the high street. Here and there are equally attractive buildings from the eighteenth and nineteenth century, all of which makes for a very handsome urban scene. This town and the almost contiguous Felbridge were, in the seventeenth and eighteenth centuries, at the halfway point on what was a two day journey to the coast. This position contributed greatly to their wealth and development. You don't need to stop here on your way to the coast these days but I would recommend you do.

We next stopped by the village green in Crawley Down or 'the hill near the clearing where the crows gather'. This small settlement dates from the end of the nineteenth century and grew as a result of extensive land enclosures, the development of a brick-making industry and the arrival of the railway. We pressed on to 'the coppiced thorns' of Copthorne and the last hint of leafy countryside before entering the urbanity that is Crawley and the end of the journey from Tunbridge, which had taken the best part of an hour and a half.

Crawley may have been a long-established, as in 1202, market town, but it was also a New Town, designated in 1947. The 1940s and subsequent decades were more obvious than any from the thirteenth century as we made our way in. The important thing for me was that it had a bus station and I was happy not to be particularly tempted by a prolonged tour of the town. I perused timetables and possible routes onwards. The 15.40 service 24 would get me to Horsham in about half-an-hour.

Horsham had an attractive town centre with a pedestrianised open area called Carfax, which was an odd choice of name given that there were no cars. From here 'The Causeway', a lovely street of medieval houses, provided a link to the wonderful Norman church of St Mary or was it the Mary church of St Norman? No, I think I was right first time. Horsham struck me as another example of a town facing the task of balancing the maintenance of character with an increasing popularity as a place of residence. People find a lovely, charming place with plenty of 'character'. Ideally it is also a commutable distance away from a town providing employment opportunities. London, for example. These people want to move to this pretty place to live. More houses, infrastructure and facilities have to be provided to cope with this influx. And so the process goes on. The danger lies with the expansion swamping any of the character that attracted people in the first place. When that happens all people are left with is a commute to work. It looked like expansion and development had been the recent experience of Horsham.

I took the 63 for Guildford and was again shown how my ideas about this area were just plain wrong. The journey was through predominantly rural landscapes where I had been anticipating a far more extensively urban experience. About 25 minutes into the journey we call at Slinfold, a small village with a few shops and a pub and a little later arrive at Rudgwick. Now, you would definitely get off here and have a good look around if you were not on some madcap escapade to see if you can get to a distant Wiltshire village. Rudgwick is where you will find The Kings Head, and if you were looking in the clay pits of the brickworks you might even find the remains of Polacanthus rudgwickensis, a heavily armoured, four-metre long herbivorous dinosaur. Someone did and that would have been something to write in the diary or talk about in the pub.

"You won't believe what old Jonesey found in the clay pit today."

"What did he find?"

"Only a polacanthus rudgwickensis!"

"A polacanthus rudgwickensis! I don't believe it!"

More meanderings through stunning countryside brought us to Ellen's Green where Ellen had allowed the construction of a very handsome bus shelter and an equally handsome Wheatsheaf pub. Cranleigh, the next stop, is claimed to be the largest village in England and presented a real mixture of old and new. There was a large supermarket, but apart from this Cranleigh appeared to be closed for the day. Perhaps I should not have been surprised since it was, rather alarmingly, a quarter to six. Shamley Green, our next port of call, wore its village credentials (a fine green and a duck pond overlooked by half-timbered houses) with pride. Wonersh and Bramley were two more pretty little villages with the now familiar half-timbered houses and a lovely old church apiece. The first recorded Women's Cricket Match held in England took place in 1745 between Bramley and Hambledon and was played on Godsden Common. According to the Reading Mercury of 26th July 1745, the eleven maids of each team 'bowled, batted, ran and catched as well as most men could do in that game'. No mention of the girls' ability to throw, I notice. I bet they threw like girls. At close of play the Bramley girls had 119 notches and the Hambledon girls 127.

Pulling into Guildford at six fifteen, I realised that it was a little over nine and a half hours since I left Canterbury and I was starting to feel rather weary and beginning to wonder if I hadn't set my sights too high. I asked some guys in the bus station about the possibilities for my onward journeys. I wondered about getting to Basingstoke, since this seemed to me to offer a good chance of a route to Newbury. They sucked breath in through slightly pursed lips and over closed teeth. They made slow and deliberate shaking movements with their heads. They employed numerous other movements and postures to convey a message which I think meant "Basingstoke—this time on a Saturday night—from Guildford? You're havin' a laugh aren't yer?"

Words were then used to underline the message: "Basingstoke—this time on a Saturday night—from Guildford? You're havin' a laugh aren't yer?"

Indeed, as it transpired, there were no buses actually going to Basingstoke from Guildford. There followed a brief period of conferring among the chaps, undertaken with low and sombre voices. One member of the group indicated that he thought buses ran from Camberley to Basingstoke.

There was a general agreement about this.

"Oh well, now *Camberley* to Basingstoke is an altogether different proposition. I won't argue about the possibilities of a bus from *Camberley* to Basingstoke."

My hopes were slightly raised. The hope-raising was checked by another interlocutor who thought that they stopped quite early in the evening.

"That's as may be, my friend. The existence of buses travelling from *Camberley* to Basingstoke is not in dispute. The issue, however, for our erstwhile traveller here, is whether the bus is still running at the time of night at which he requires it. For, let us not forget, we are not *in* Camberley. We are in *Guildford*. And our friend here must get to Camberley before the last bus for Basingstoke leaves." He checked his watch and, looking me steadily in the face, said, "You'll be lucky."

I decided to be optimistic. I decided to see if I would be lucky. They pointed me in the direction of the appropriate bus and the appropriate bay. So I made my way out through the Saturday afternoon in September that was fast approaching the time of twilight, and the vast tract of highly developed land known as Westfield, Woking, Knaphill and Bagshot embrowned itself moment by moment. The built up areas blurred and I arrived imperceptibly in Camberley. I was near a big hotel. I was by a main road. I was not far from the station. I checked out the nearby bus timetables. The man was right; there was a bus to Basingstoke! The other man was right too. The last one had gone.

So there I was, looking at a big hotel and a main road and a night in Camberley. I felt the first chill of the evening and surveyed my ever-darkening surroundings once more. This didn't look to be the sort of place where you could pitch a tent. I didn't have one anyway. I would have to find a bed and break-fast or a hotel. Again, this looked more Premier Inn country than cosy B&B and, bottom line, I didn't want to spend money on a hotel, or a B&B for that matter. I checked the timetable again. Definitely no more buses going my way tonight. Further scrutiny revealed that there were none on Sundays either. Sud-denly I was looking at a night in Camberley, followed by a day in Camberley and then another night.

I had been travelling for over ten hours and I was physi-cally tired and psychologically drained. I hadn't been lucky. I couldn't see a way out that didn't involve buses towards Lon-don and somehow out again, and that would all take time and I would need new tickets and it wouldn't work anyway. It was all suddenly too much. That's not much of an excuse, I know, and I'm not proud of what happened next.

I caught a train.

Having parted with enough cash to pretty much pay for two adult day explorer tickets I settled down to watch the dark-ness through the carriage window. I changed trains at Ascot for the 20.43 to Reading. A group of amazingly drunk women, who I think had been at a race meeting, provided some enter-tainment for a few stops. We arrived at Reading at about 9.15. I was still feeling a bit despondent about swapping my mode of transportation but I need not have worried. A notice that brought groans and sighs from fellow passengers on the con-course brought a smile to my lips and caused my heart to skip a beat. The train service to Great Bedwyn had been cancelled and a replacement bus service was in operation.

And so it came about that I was actually on a bus when I finally met up with a point on the circuitous tour of the country that I had undertaken in 2002. At Newbury in 2002 I had pitched my tent and at Newbury in 2007 I decided that this would be a good cut off point for the current trip, a place for 'closure'. I had seen the bit of England that I had missed when I faced the 'Winchester dilemma' and chosen to go north. I felt that this last excursion had brought some sort of completeness to my tour. I reflected on both the trips and felt my understanding of where places actually were in the country, albeit still woefully broad and uninformed, and my sense of the country I lived in and, hey, loved, was somehow more complete.

I'd seen market towns and mill towns, castles and cathedrals, ancestral halls and humble cottages. I had glimpsed the glories of the Dales, the Peaks, the Moors and Wealds. For the most part I had liked what I'd seen and I had a new sense of belonging to a place, being part of a larger whole, disparate and wonderfully varied though that might be.

I could have felt that something was ending as we drove through the dark Berkshire countryside and slipped into Wiltshire. I didn't feel that at all, because the more I had seen, the more I realised how little I knew. I had merely scratched the surface of all these places and there would be plenty more to discover. All of them had something to say about people or the past, of our people and our past. They were all part of our heritage and our 'narrative'. I didn't feel that I had 'done' England by any means. I could visit all these same places again and find a whole new set of things that I hadn't seen before. And although I had been round the whole country I had only been to a fraction of the places possible. The choice of destination was immense and the combinations limitless.

This wasn't sad, it was exciting. This wasn't the end. It was the beginning.

Afterword

What's it all about?

Why the book? What else is there?

I need to make a couple of things clear. Firstly, I am not a bus enthusiast, although I am quite enthusiastic about buses. There is a difference and for me it is quite an important one. A proper bus enthusiast will be able to tell you about buses. I mean properly tell you, providing you with details of all sorts of stuff. He, or indeed she, would be able to tell you how Devon General made use of their AEC Regal III with its classic Duple "A" style body in the 1950s. He or she would be able to point out a bus and tell you who had made it, how long the body is, what sort of a chassis it has, what alterations have been made to it and when, the different bus companies it might have served and the colours it was painted during each period. I can't tell you any of those things. I'm only really interested in a bus in terms of where it's going, whether it's punctual, clean and comfortable. And that doesn't make you a bus enthusiast.

Secondly, I have no connection with any bus operators although I am making a case for greater use of buses. I almost hesitate to engage in promoting bus travel because I sometimes feel in a bit of a 'cleft stick'. The problems arise because of a nagging fear that since the buses were 'deregulated' under Margaret Thatcher in the 1980s, they are operated by profit-driven private companies who are only really interested in making money, not providing a 'service'. The worry is then that in using buses am I not just helping to make a few rich people even richer, filling the greedy shareholders' trough, powdering the ugly face of capitalism? Deregulation was intended to see a growth in the number of bus companies and a consequent intensification of competition which would drive down fares. It seems at first glance now that a few major players have slowly carved up much of the country between them, usually swallowing smaller rivals along the way. This, as an A level economics student could probably have told the government of the time, was bound to happen. The trouble people have with this is that the 'big guns' effectively seem to run a monopoly in the regions over which they operate. There seems to be little or no serious competition and they can seemingly put prices up or down as they please. OK, they can seemingly put prices up as they please. If that's the situation and it's unlikely to change, what can you do? If you have no choice you have to stump up the bus fare no matter what. So why encourage people to use the buses more?

For a start, while it is true that there are just a few very major players, there are also numerous small operators, often family firms who are just running a small business, like any other. Do you refuse to have milk on your cereal because the milk market is dominated by a few large dairies?

Also, while we are suspicious of the focus on profit in bus company operations, we simultaneously have a sense that the bus system *is* a part of a public transport system and that buses *do* provide a service to the community. Indeed, local public transport is actually the responsibility of your local authority. The bus companies simply provide the means whereby the local authority can fulfil its obligations. And even if we don't like buses ourselves we have a sense that for many people, because of age, means, or other circumstances, buses are the only transport option. A sense of civic duty makes us think that, even if not for ourselves, bus services need to be sustained and supported. And when we read 'this service supported by (insert name of local authority)' on the back of a bus it is obvious who is doing the supporting. Furthermore, the route they are supporting is probably one of the less profitable routes which, without that support, could be cut. So bus transport seems to involve profit-motivated private companies who are engaged in providing vital public services. How do we hold these two notions in tension? How do we balance contributing to the profits of the bus companies and continuing to use a public service in order to maintain its viability?

I think I'm of the opinion that bus fares rise not only because of increases in operating costs (wage rises, fuel costs, etc.) but also due to a decline in passenger numbers. If fewer people use the buses, they each have to pay more for the privilege, if the company's profits are to be maintained. So, applying that logic in reverse, if more people use the buses, the fares could come down and the company would still maintain its profits. Your response might be, 'Flying non-ruminant omnivorous bristly mammal at one o'clock, Captain.' But you never know and we won't know unless we try.

A second reason for promoting bus travel is that it is touted as being 'green' or at least 'greener' than cars. This somehow makes sense: having fifty, twenty or even ten people riding around in one vehicle must be better than the equivalent number of cars needed to move the same number of people. Given that the vast majority of cars seem to have one person in them most of the time, this would be like taking fifty, twenty or ten cars off the road. More people on buses would lead to less congested roads, surely? Healthier bus use figures may encourage more research into ever-greener buses. Already there are super-low emission vehicles. What might the future hold?

The 'green' issues are becoming increasingly important with the gloomiest predictions giving us about 40 years before we're all stuffed. Everybody from the government down is supposedly making efforts to cut their carbon footprint, reduce emissions of greenhouse gases and avert the disaster that is climate change. So, if we've reached 'peak oil', the ice caps are melting and we're all doomed, it's time to take transport issues seriously. If you buy into that you can see taking the bus as doing your bit. Not everybody does buy the climate change notion, or at least the aspect of human culpability. But even for these people there is the argument that well-used buses make good use of scarce resources.

This book is also about inspiring people to make the most of the amazing and beautiful countryside, varied and exciting towns and cities and abundance of history, heritage and architecture we have available to enjoy in the UK. I do tend to extol the virtues of the country and not dwell on any negatives. This is not because I am blind to the fact that there are things wrong and that there are some very ugly places, buildings, features, failures and so on. However, this is not a 'state of the nation' polemic. I want you to get a taste of what it might be like to go out by bus. The journeys recorded here reflect a bit of a whirl-wind tour. Well, as much of a whirlwind tour as you can have on service buses. I hope I've conveyed the sense of fun and adventure from my trips and that you can see the potential for having some of this for yourself.

There have been major moves to get people onto the buses but these have mostly involved people over 60. What if, like me, you are not quite there yet? I hope the book has shown you that there are plenty of good-value 'rover' ticket options available from many operators and that in many cases a long-distance journey is not necessarily going to cost the multiple of your local journey into town. Of course, the 'rover' tickets with the widest range and therefore the best value come from the bus companies whose presence dominates a larger area. No-one said it was a perfect world.

I'm not suggesting that the bus is the best choice in all cir-cumstances. If you need to pick up a few lengths of 2.4 metre timber for a DIY project, I wouldn't recommend the bus. If you're about to give birth, don't take the bus to the hospital. Let's not be silly about this. All I'm saying is that every now and again, people could consider leaving the car at home and going out on the bus. I hope that recording my exploits inspires you to get out there and get on the bus and that you will also want to enthuse other people to do the same.

Over to you

If the end of my journeys wasn't actually the end but the begin-ning, what was it the beginning of? What happens now? How can we spread the message that bus travel is good, bus travel is easy, bus travel is fun?

The bulk of this book records events from 2002, with the South East experience being in 2007, both of which are a while ago now. Does this mean that all the information is irrelevant? Actually, no. Some attractions will no doubt have closed. Between my two journeys Boscastle was flooded and then recovered. More recently the pier at Weston-Super-Mare suffered a massive fire and is soon to be re-opened. So, things may come and things may go but, to a large extent, bus timetables and routes go on forever. Seriously, they seem to be pretty 'robust', even when the routes are taken over by different operators. I was recently in the area where I went to secondary school about 35 years ago. The same number bus still covers the same route! That said, some services *do* disappear (usually from lack of passenger numbers) so I can't say that everything in the book is still current. What I do know is that I didn't go on every bus in the country. I don't suppose I ever will. This is where you come in.

A new web site *www.lifeinthebuslane.org.uk* is being created to act as a depository. That's a depository, not a suppository. And what, you may ask, will be deposited?

The hope is that people will go on a great bus journey (a day out, a weekend away, a bus—walk—bus combination) and then go on the website to tell other people about their experiences. Once it is on there, others can browse through the routes described as they explore the possibilities of a day out for themselves. The idea is that as more and more people contribute to the web site, an ever-expanding bank of suggestions will appear. So, should you be considering an excursion, you can find out how someone else got on with it, which buses they used and some of the highlights of the trip. If you want to go on a walk and not have to make it circular, you can find out if anyone else has managed this by making use of buses. If no-one else has done the route you want, you can do it anyway and then add your information to the site, thus helping out all those who come along behind you.

Some bus operators also offer suggestions for days out. It would be good to know if anyone has tried these and how they found the experience. This will provide valuable feedback to the bus companies and let them know that we're interested and have things to say. And that might help to keep the bus companies on their toes.

I hope the website grows to be a useful resource and a place where people can share ideas and experiences and contribute to an increase in bus travel as a 'green' alternative to the car and perhaps also lead to greater 'passenger power' in relation to company practices and government policies. Who knows? Let's see what happens.

If you're not a web user you can find travel information from different sources. Your local bus operators will have phone contacts and there's usually plenty of information at bus stations. There are some other ideas in the Appendix (*p.*305).

To spread the word without the web you could form a local group and encourage people around you to use the buses and even organise group outings.

I've found all my excursions to be great fun. I hope you do too.

Pat Lunt
May 2010

Appendix

Finding out about public transport possibilities

My pre-journey planning was brief and sketchy. If you want to do some proper planning before you set off and you can access the Internet then a fairly new site, funded by English, Scottish and Welsh governments, will work out possible routes between two places. This is at www.transportdirect.info.

Another useful contact is Traveline, a partnership of public transport operators and local authorities whose aim is to provide comprehensive information about public transport. The national number for Traveline is 0871 200 22 33 and they are on the web at www.traveline.org.uk.

Further reading

Inspiration to write about the journey came in part from reading accounts of journeys undertaken in days gone by. Well known examples include H.V. Morton's *In Search of England* and J.B Priestley's *English Journey*. Going even further back it was fascinating to read about the travels of individuals such as Daniel Defoe, Willam Camden and Celia Fiennes. Their accounts, along with many other items of interest can be viewed at a fabulous website, www.visionofbritain.org.uk.

The writings can also be found in book form in various editions and manifestations.

For amazing insights into the natural history of Britain, read Oliver Rackham, *The History of the Countryside*, The classic history of Britain's landscape, flora and fauna (J.M. Dent, London 1986).

Resources

The Oxford Illustrated History of Britain, edited by K.O.Morgan (OUP 1984). Still good after twenty-five years.

When you're on the move you have to make good use of tourist maps and guides, church information sheets, booklets in tourist information centres, heritage trails and all that kind of thing. I've also looked at a lot of web sites while writing the book. Some of them were actually relevant, too. I am indebted to those who create and maintain them:

www.cityofwinchester.co.uk/index.html

'Medieval Oxford', in *A History of the County of Oxford: Volume 4: The City of Oxford* (1979), *pp.* 3-73. URL: www.british-history.ac.uk/report.aspx?compid=22803

'The city of Cambridge: Medieval history', in *A History of the County of Cambridge and the Isle of Ely: Volume 3: The City and University of Cambridge* (1959), *pp.* 2-15. URL: www.british-history.ac.uk/report. aspx?compid=66604

www.jesus.cam.ac.uk/college/history/womenexhib1.html

www.cl.cam.ac.uk/~ckh11/cam.html

en.wikipedia.org/wiki/Anglo-Dutch_Wars

www.cruquiusmuseum.nl/englishsite/english.html

www.derwentvalleymills.org/index.htm

www.nationalparks.gov.uk/learningabout/ whatisanationalpark/history.htm

www.derbyshireuk.net/ashford.html

www.huddersfield1.co.uk/huddersfield/huddsguide.htm

www.historyofyork.org.uk/timeline/victorian/rowntree-co-chocolate-manufacturers

www.hows.org.uk/personal/hillfigs/kilb/kilburn.htm

www.aycliffeangels.org.uk

www.battlefieldstrust.com/resource-centre

www.coldstream-scotland.co.uk/guards.html

www.kendal.mintcake.co.uk/about.htm

chesterwalls.info/chesterintro.html

www.rossett.org.uk/ron_about.php
www.delaboleslate.co.uk
www.channel4.com/history/microsites/H/history/n-s/
  perkin.html
www.cornish-language.org/English/Default.asp
www.twyfordwaterworks.co.uk
www.theheritagetrail.co.uk
www.volkselectricrailway.co.uk
www.martello-towers.co.uk/index.html
www.liv.ac.uk/geography/RomneyMarsh/RM Timeline/
  Timeline.htm
www.tonbridgehistory.org.uk/index.htm
www.smuggling.co.uk/index.html
www.historic-kent.co.uk/smugg13.html

Acknowledgements

Thanks are due to friends and family for all their encouragement and support throughout. A special thanks to those who offered accommodation on the original trips and to those who read early versions of the manuscript and offered helpful comments.

Thanks also to Martyn at Mushroom Publishing for his knowledgeable insights, editing help and input, and to Dave at soda-pop for design assistance and web mastery.